Money's No Object

Lorna Galbraith-Ryan, on whose work *Money's No Object* is based, is only available for financial consultation by personal recommendation. However, her company, Galbraith Ryan Associates, can offer the services of a fully-trained financial consultant for individual financial analysis and consultation. Contact Galbraith Ryan Associates at 146 Camden High Street, London NW1 0NE (Tel: 071 482 5229). Galbraith Ryan Associates is an appointed representative of the London & Manchester Group.

Lorna Galbraith-Ryan herself is available for business consultancy, including financial planning and budgetary control, staff recruitment, training and motivation, interpersonal skills and executive counselling. She can also be contacted at the above address.

Lois Graessle is a partner in Planning Together Associates, which provides consultancy and training to senior management teams in the public and voluntary sectors. She is co-author, with George Gawlinski, of *Planning Together: the Art of Effective Teamwork* (Bedford Square Press, 1988), with Pat McQuade, of *Making Sense of Work Experience* (Cambridge University Press, 1990) and *The Staff Development Manual: Vol. 2 – Staff Development in Action* (Framework Press, 1986), and with Su Kingsley, *Measuring Change, Making Changes: A Framework for Evaluation* (London Community Health Resource 1985).

Lois Graessle also offers executive counselling and designs training and evaluation for organizations. Any organization which would like to train their staff in using *Money's No Object* as part of their work can contact her c/o Planning Together Associates, The Croft, Milldale, Alstonefield, Ashbourne, Derbyshire DE6 2GB (Tel: 081 995 0244).

Money's No Object

FIVE STEPS TO CASH CONFIDENCE

Lorna Galbraith-Ryan
& Lois Graessle

With love —
and better 'luck' in
practising it all than g·ve
had !

Lois

Mandarin

A Mandarin Paperback
MONEY'S NO OBJECT

First published in Great Britain 1991
by Mandarin Paperbacks
Michelin House, 81 Fulham Road, London SW3 6RB

Mandarin is an imprint of the Octopus Publishing Group,
a division of Reed International Books Limited

Copyright © 1991 by Lorna Galbraith-Ryan and Lois Graessle
The authors have asserted their moral rights.

A CIP catalogue record for this title
is available from the British Library
ISBN 0 7493 0594 0

Note While every effort has been made to supply accurate
information, this book is intended for general guidance only,
and readers with specific financial problems should
consult a specialist adviser.

Typeset by Falcon Typographic Art Ltd,
Edinburgh & London
Printed and bound in Great Britain by
Cox & Wyman Ltd, Reading, Berkshire

Contents

Preface and Acknowledgements

Money's No Object is the product of a partnership between a financial consultant and one of her clients.

Lorna Galbraith-Ryan started her own financial consultancy in 1981 and has, over the years, developed the approach described in this book through her work with several thousand clients. Lois Graessle is a team management consultant and writer who came to Lorna when she recognized that she needed to gain control over her own finances.

She found that Lorna's method of dealing with money matters corresponded very closely to the one she used in her own work. Both felt that others should have an opportunity of understanding and benefiting from this way of dealing with money, which takes account of both the practical and the psychological sides of finance, something which is very unusual in the financial world.

In the process of translating our experiences as financial consultant and client into a book, we have had encouragement from many friends and clients. The examples we use throughout are drawn from actual experiences; the details are correct but all names have been altered.

We would like to thank specifically the people who have read and commented on our drafts from their own diverse experience and expertise: Dina Glouberman, Roger Hogan, Ludi Horbacki Kipping, Alan Kipping, Ruth Lesirge, Tommy Ryan, Josephine Seccombe, Jean Simpson, and Ramona Sterling.

The publishers whom we initially approached had difficulty in accepting a book which bridged two of their usual classifications, finance and self-help. Our appreciation, therefore, to Claire Ford, who believed in the importance of the book, and who, when she reluctantly had to turn us down, encouraged us to keep looking; and to Jane Carr, who took up the challenge and whose unswerving and enthusiastic support has seen us through.

Our special thanks to Angela Lavender, Lorna's business partner for ten years, for the balance and clarity which she has contributed to our work; and to Eric Bourne for the precision and humour with which he tackled our drafts.

This book is dedicated, with love and thanks, to our partners, Tommy Ryan and Eric Bourne, and to Lorna's daughter, Casey Ryan.

Lorna Galbraith-Ryan
Lois Graessle

Introduction

Money is as essential to us as the air we breathe. Whatever we do, and whatever we wish for, has something to do with money – even when we try to pretend that it does not.

Yet, the way we tend to think about money is out-of-date and limited – and often simply wrong. We are accustomed to seeing money simply as an object – what matters to us is how much or how little of it we have. *Money's No Object* will help you to see that this is only a part of the story. The other part is your attitude towards money – and whether you take your feelings into consideration when making financial decisions. Only when you can deal with both parts can you effectively sort out your money and your life, and make the choices which are best for you.

What's it about?

The message of *Money's No Object* is that it is possible to live for today and plan for tomorrow. You don't have to choose between living it up today and putting your future at risk. Nor between planning ahead for a secure future and short-changing your life today. Instead, no matter how little or how much money you have, you can both live for today and plan for tomorrow. The promise isn't that this will be easy to achieve but that it is possible, provided you are willing to deal with both the figures and your feelings.

How can you achieve this?

The practical way to go about this is a common sense approach – 5 logical steps which will give you control over your financial life, whatever issues you may be facing.

The 5 Steps

1 Acknowledge where you are – and what you want
2 Know the facts – your figures *and* your feelings
3 Consider the *real* options
4 Make choices – live for today *and* plan for tomorrow
5 Do it – and review it

The first two steps give you the information you need and the next two help you to decide what, if any, changes you may wish to make. Finally, Step 5 encourages you to do whatever you have in mind – and to review your progress regularly to see how things are working out.

Who is it for?

Money's No Object isn't a book about money problems. It's about managing your finances – how to check if you are doing this effectively, what to do if you aren't – and how to stay in control.

If you feel that you are having trouble with money, the book will not only help you to resolve difficulties but will also help you to decide whether you wish to move in a different direction.

If you feel okay about the way you manage your money, it will assist you to review your financial arrangements and to do any 'fine tuning' that may be necessary.

Where do *you* need to start? People who want to start dealing with money in a different way usually have a specific problem;

'I want to retire early. How do I sort out my pension?'
'I work for myself and I need help with the basics of book-keeping.'

Or they may be saying,

'My finances are in a mess, as usual, and I just want to sort them out once and for all.'
'Other people have managed my money all my life, and I want to do it for myself now, but I don't have a clue where to start.'

From wherever you start, *Money's No Object* is likely to be of use to you.

How can you use the book?

It all depends on what you want. Whatever your relationship to money, there will be something here for you. And as your relationship to money changes, so will the book.

You may find that all you want to do initially is to read through the book and get an idea of some of the issues – and that's fine. Next time you may want to read it from a different angle. You may need to do the practical work in one of the *Workbook* chapters. Or, before you see a financial professional, you may want to turn to *The Practical Guides* to do some homework of your own. [And after you have met her or him, you may want to come back and refer to the Glossary to make sure that you've understood what was said!]

The book has three functions:

Read it! The first section of the book invites you to *Consider the Issues* which money raises in our lives. Money is still a taboo subject in many quarters. Yet the first step to taking control of it is to find a way of thinking about money which takes account of both your figures and your feelings. At the end of each chapter there are some questions you may want to ask yourself about the way you are dealing with things at present.

Use it! Money is not likely to work for you if you just sit and think about it. *The 5 Steps Workbook* provides you with practical steps to take in order to work through a number of concerns about money. Each of the *Workbook* chapters takes you through the 5 Steps as they relate to a particular issue, and offers checklists and other material to help you reach the result you would like.

Refer to it! The final section, *What's What – and How To*, gives you information which you will need in order to conduct basic financial business, and translate financial jargon into ordinary English.

Money management isn't just a one-off exercise; it is something we need to do throughout our lives. So leave the book where you can reach it easily. It can help you to gain, and to keep, control of your financial life.

Will it make you rich – or what?

The first question that springs to most people's minds when they pick up a book about money is, 'Will it make me rich?'

Introduction

The answer is, 'Yes but . . .'. And here's the catch. If you are willing to be honest with yourself, *Money's No Object* can promise you a richer life in which you get the most out of your money, however little or much you have. And it can also help you to make more, if that's what you want.

What it *can* promise to bring you, every time, is results.

Each time you work through the 5 Steps, there will be a result, though it may not always be the one you had expected. The more you apply this approach to your financial life, the easier it will become – and you will always make progress.

What's the secret? The secret is that the 5 Steps help you to pull together all the separate bits of information you need – both practical and emotional – in order to sort out your money. If you work through them honestly, you will change your life.

What it can't offer you are right answers. When it comes to money, there aren't any. What it will do is to give you greater confidence to find answers that are right for you in your particular situation.

And what about the things that really aren't your fault? How, you may be wondering, can this approach work, when logic tells you that the blame for many financial difficulties lies elsewhere and beyond your control. It is, after all, not you who puts up the mortgage rates; you don't set the oil prices, and most people don't choose to be laid off. Besides, the economic system is unjust anyway. Right?

Well . . . yes and no. All these factors are real, and most of them are beyond your personal control, but they are only the stage settings. The main character in your financial drama is you, and it is your attitude that affects what happens. You may not have control over the circumstances of life; you do have a choice about the way you respond to them.

Summary

The responsibility for your financial life is ultimately yours, and yours alone. The buck stops with you. The aim of *Money's No Object* is to help you to develop the confidence to handle that responsibility well.

Introducing the 5 Steps
to Cash Confidence

The 5 Steps are the practical core of the approach in *Money's No Object*. They will enable you to take control of your finances and, as a result, achieve what you want out of life.

The 5 Steps are a systematic process. Only by taking them one at a time and in sequence can you arrive at the most satisfactory outcome. If you make choices without knowing the facts, then the result is unlikely to be realistic. If you don't know what you want, the figures will be meaningless and choices impossible.

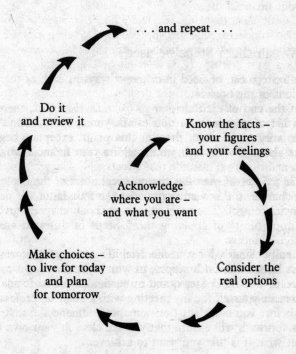

. . . and repeat . . .

Do it
and review it

Know the facts –
your figures
and your feelings

Acknowledge
where you are –
and what you want

Make choices –
to live for today
and plan
for tomorrow

Consider the
real options

But with the basic information from Steps 1, 2 and 3 – figures, feelings and goals, you can work out what your real choices are – then act on them. Each time you reach the end of the 5 steps you start again, but you don't go around in circles.

How can the 5 Steps help you?

As you read through this introduction, don't be surprised if it all sounds rather like common sense. For instance, 'if you are spending more than you are earning, you're not living within your income.' That *is* common sense. But most of us have areas in which, when it comes down to money, we ignore our common sense. By working through the 5 Steps whenever you face a money matter, you will come to recognize which step or steps you find particularly difficult. Don't skip that step, just take the extra time you need to get to grips with your difficulty. You need to work through each step in sequence to be in control of your financial life.

How can the 5 Steps be used?

The 5 Steps can be used in different ways in each of the three sections of the book.

At the end of each chapter in *Consider the Issues*, there will be a list of questions for you to ask yourself. You don't have to do very much about them at this point, except to begin to think about the way you are managing your financial affairs at present.

The 5 Steps Workbook is the practical heart of the book. The first chapter in this section provides the foundation for general financial control. The subsequent workbook chapters give you the opportunity of applying the 5 Steps in different areas of financial concern.

Finally, *What's What – and How To* gives you information about basic financial business, to which you may want to turn for help. Use the 5 Steps, and in particular the basic analysis, to prepare yourself for any meeting with a financial professional and before you make any decision about a financial transaction. This approach will ensure that you are clear in your own mind about what it is that you want to achieve.

INTRODUCING THE 5 STEPS

The relevance of each of the 5 Steps is explained below.

1 Acknowledge where you are – and what you want

Money is a tool which can help you to live better. Before you can use it effectively, you need to face the facts of your life today realistically and have some idea of how you would like matters to develop. Those two sets of information are the foundations. And that is why it is important for you to be honest, both about your present-day realities and your hopes for the future.

When you take stock of the circumstances of your life right now, you may want to look at your monetary situation, the state of your finances and also your physical health. You also need to acknowledge what feels positive to you at present and what bothers you. Don't judge yourself or conclude that your circumstances are either 'bad' or 'good': just note the information, honestly.

Then look to the future – this year, in 10 years' time, and beyond that. Do you feel that a fancy car and £500 in your pocket each month is for you? Would you like to be out of debt and able to afford some new clothes and a holiday for you and the children? Do you want to work less, or maybe go into business for yourself?

You may only be able make a sketch of the future at this point. That's fine – you don't need to fill in the details yet.

2 Know the facts – your figures *and* your feelings

There are two sorts of facts that you need to know about your money – your figures and your feelings. And they are of equal importance.

Some of us can handle figures quite easily but feel less comfortable when dealing with our reactions to them. Others draw a blank when faced with figures but are quite comfortable with the emotional issues involved.

In Step 2, the first thing you need to know are your figures. And you need to know them precisely. If you don't, you have no starting point for assessing realistically which options are open to you.

When you have sorted out your figures, reflect on your

feelings. Do you feel encouraged? Or depressed? Do your feelings tell you that something isn't quite right? Examine your feelings so that the next step you take can begin the process of matching your figures with the various options open to you.

A command of the figures together with an awareness of your feelings will provide the total information you need to meet your goals.

3 Consider the *real* options

The information gained from the first two steps will have given you a picture of your present situation, your hopes for the future, and the way you feel about all this. The next step is trickier. If you want to move forward you will have to make some choices and there will always be more than one way forward.

It is important to look at as many options as come to mind before you make a decision. This gives you a chance to look objectively at your future, rather than to apply old habits to new situations.

There are two stages in this process. The first is to think about as many ways as you can in order to reach a certain goal. For instance, if you want to gain more satisfaction from your job, you could choose to work part-time, to change jobs entirely, to go to work for yourself, to improve your own working skills — or to get rid of your boss.

The next stage is to consider which of the many options you have are actually *realistic*. If an option seems to make good financial sense but you don't feel comfortable with it, then it's not a *realistic* option for you. Remove it from your list, so that you finish up with options you feel you can handle. It might have done you good to imagine getting rid of your boss, you might have even considered the financial benefits if you got his or her job, but emotionally you just don't have what it takes to give your boss the push.

4 Make choices – live for today *and* plan for tomorrow

The message of this book is that it is possible to live for today and plan for tomorrow. Having sorted through your options, you now need to make some decisions about what you want to do – in the short term, the medium term and the long term. Where will you put your energy – and your money – first? Is your priority clearing any debts, taking a holiday or buying a house?

Before making final choices, you need to cost each of the options in terms of money and time. This will help you to decide how to balance your everyday outgoings against the time you need to reach your goals – spend a lot today and it will take you longer to reach your long-term goals; reduce your outgoings and you will get there sooner.

Remember not to put all your money into plans for tomorrow. You still have to live for today. And don't put all your money into today, because you may still be alive tomorrow. Whatever you decide, leave yourself some money for treats – those rewards, big or small, which help you to keep going and which give you pleasure right now.

5 Do it – and review it

If you have worked through the first four steps honestly and accurately, you will now be clear about what action you need to take. And because of the practical and emotional thoroughness with which you have done the planning, you are more likely to achieve the result you want.

However, you can't just leave it there. Circumstances over which you have no control may change. Mortgage rates could go up, or down, there could be an unexpected redundancy or promotion, marriage or divorce, birth or bereavement. Any of these will affect your financial situation and your options. And because you are now in control of your money, you will be more able to manage the changes.

To stay in control of your financial life, just remember to take stock of your situation and decide what, if any, changes you need and want to make in your goals, or in the amount of time and money you need to achieve them.

And finally, give yourself some credit. Whatever the outcome, you deserve it for recognizing that you are responsible for your financial life and for doing something positive about it.

Learning to use the 5 steps

Using the 5 Steps should, after a time, begin to feel like a routine part of your life. Whenever an issue or anxiety about money arises, learn to run through the 5 Steps checklist in your head:

Step		Mental tick
1	Acknowledge where you are – and what you want	☐
2	Know the facts – your figures *and* your feelings	☐
3	Consider the *real* options	☐
4	Make choices – live for today *and* plan for tomorrow	☐
5	Do it – and review it	☐

This will help you to see what's going on and give you a clue about where and how to start putting things back on course.

Summary

The 5 Step process can't guarantee that all your plans will succeed, nor can it prevent the unexpected. But by using the approach, you will be in control of your finances and better prepared for whatever life brings.

THE 5 STEPS

1 Acknowledge where you are – and what you want

What is life like right now? – financially, at work, within your relationships, and in other areas?

Do you know what you expect to get out of life? – in the short term, the medium term, the long term?

2 Know the facts – your figures *and* your feelings

Do you know your regular outgoings, how much you spend each week, your overall cost of living?

What is your reaction to the idea of gathering this information together?

3 Consider the *real* options

What courses of action seem to you realistic, both financially and emotionally, so that you can move your life in the direction in which you wish it to go?

4 Make choices – live for today *and* plan for tomorrow

If you are thinking of making changes in your life, which ones do you want to make first?

How will you take care of yourself today while actively working towards your future goals?

5 Do it – and review it

What steps do you need to take to implement the changes which you wish to make?

How will you reward yourself for persevering, and for coping with setbacks?

When and how will you make time to review your progress?

Further information

The 5 Steps Workbook W1: The basic 5 steps analysis

Read it!

Consider
the Issues

I Money and Work

Your money – your responsibility

Introduction

If you have an income, whether it is earned or unearned, then you are responsible for it. Although you may get help and advice from your firm or your union, the ultimate responsibility for your finances is yours and yours alone. Unless you accept that fact, you cannot get maximum value out of your work, your retirement – or your money.

There are two sides to your earning life:

- getting the best deal for yourself from your work;
- managing the expected and unexpected changes which, at times, you are likely to encounter.

The first two chapters consider both these aspects if you are *Working for Someone Else* or *Working for Yourself. Managing Changes in Your Earning Life* looks at how you can handle changes in your work and earnings, whether this involves a career change or a job loss or receiving unearned income through inheritance or government benefits.

Most of us end our working lives in retirement. *Planning a Quality Retirement* discusses what you need to do to assure yourself of the lifestyle you want.

Although this section is for people who are working for an income, it may also provide a helpful review for anyone who is not at present earning but intends to do so in the future, or who lives with someone who does.

1. Working for Someone Else

A fixed income – but not fixed options

Many people believe that as an employee they do not have to pay close attention to their employment details including salary, pension and benefits. They expect their employer to deal fairly with these on their behalf. Do you, for instance, believe that your employer will take care of you in return for your loyalty? Or that the accounts department is always accurate in its dealings with you? And that your job is safe?

In fact, nothing, including your job, is guaranteed. You owe your employer commitment, if you want to get the best out of your job in terms of satisfaction and material reward. But your primary commitment has to be to yourself.

In order to ensure that you are getting the best deal for yourself at work, you need to take responsibility both for the details of your pay and benefits, and for the progress of your career. Most employees also have to face clear-cut financial facts. Your income is fixed, therefore you have to contain your spending within it. If you choose not to do so, you must either increase your income, or fall into debt.

Taking responsibility for your income at work

Times have changed and you can no longer be sure of a job or even of a trade for life. Loyalty and commitment are important, both for your job satisfaction and for your promotion prospects. But they do not have to be to the same firm for life.

Checking your attitudes. Old attitudes, such as 'the firm will take care of me', die hard. Even employees who don't subscribe to this attitude often feel that if they just get on with the job, their interests will be protected. It is quite easy to assume that employers will take care of things. Or to feel gratitude for the job and the opportunities it has brought you. Or to be angry if you feel you are being exploited, especially if you don't see any option but to stay in the job. None of these attitudes is wrong. But because of them, employees often do not take responsibility for their financial situation within an organization.

Checking your salary and benefits. Getting the best deal at work includes making sure that your pay slip is accurate, that you are getting all the benefits to which you are entitled and that you are on the appropriate salary scale. *Workbook Chapter W2: Working for someoone else* gives you practical information about dealing with this. It is easier to check these details each month, so that mistakes can quickly be put right. It can be more difficult, and certainly more time consuming, to sort things out once a lot of time has elapsed.

> *When he was working out the details of a promotion, Colin D. discovered that he had been paid on the wrong salary scale for the previous 3 years. 'I agonized a lot about bringing this to the notice of my bosses when I'd just been given quite a rise. Finally I sorted it out, but was surprised at my own attitude. It was, after all, money to which I was entitled.'*

It is easy to advise you to check on these kinds of details. Getting hold of the information may be more difficult, and not only because of your own attitude. Whether you are employed in a large or small organization, you may encounter resistance or hostility to your enquiries. And even when you have some answers, you may not know if what you have been told is correct. Small organizations, in particular, may simply not be up-to-date themselves. Be aware that, whatever the answers and information you get, the decisions are still yours. You are the one who will suffer any long term financial consequences if you do not accept this responsibility.

Taking care of your future. Your employer is responsible for paying you an agreed salary. Although in some organizations, a superannuation or pension plan will be part of the available benefits, it is not your employer's responsibility to make sure that their scheme is the best one for you, and that it will provide you with sufficient income to sustain the kind of lifestyle which you would like to have once you retire.

There are many ways of arranging your pension, in addition to paying into your own company's scheme. *Chapter 4, Planning for a Quality Retirement*, and *The Practical Guide to Arranging a Pension*, will help you to check whether, as an employee, you are planning adequately for the kind of future which you want.

Spending your income

If you are an employee you receive a fixed amount of income. Does your lifestyle fit this or not? Your answer needs to be a straightforward yes or no. If you hedged your answer with 'sometimes' then your real answer is 'no'. Spending more than your income is a precise issue: either you do or you don't.

If you are spending more than you are earning, it is up to you to decide what to do about this. Sometimes people who are employees feel that they have no control over their money. Your income may be fixed, but you *do* have the control over whether you continue to overspend and build up debts, or cut down on expenditure, or find a way to earn more.

Cutting down on expenditure. Your genuine bills are your rent or mortgage, what it costs to heat and light your home, local taxes and insurance, and – to a lesser extent – the cost of food, transport to get you to work, and the telephone.

You have no choice over the fixed bills if you want to keep a roof over your head. After allowing for these, everything else is spending, and spending is your choice and within your power to change. The food you eat is your choice, the places to which you go, the method of transport you use, the clothes you buy and the holidays you take are all choices which you make. You do not *have* to take a taxi, you do not *have* to go to Bermuda on holiday, you do not *have* to eat out in expensive – or inexpensive – restaurants on a regular basis. Your shopping bills do not *have* to be huge. And you do not *have* to make so many phone calls.

Of course you have to eat, but you can choose what you eat, where you eat, and the type of food you buy. And there may be times when you need to take a taxi. Look honestly at those occasions when you choose the expensive option, to make sure that it is really necessary. You may have got into the habit of eating out because you are working long and stressful hours at work. That is a choice you are making and there may be cheaper options, like buying ready-cooked meals from supermarkets. Or you may have got into the habit of taking taxis because you don't leave enough time to get to your appointments on time if you travel by public transport. That is your fault and within your control. It is quite a different matter if you take taxis in order to avoid a dark route when you are returning home late at night. But you still need to investigate whether there are other options – or make sure that you include the costs of such journeys in your basic outgoings.

It is not 'wrong' to eat out or take taxis or have special holidays. The point is simply that *you* control your own money and *you* choose how you spend it. There are enough things, such as interest rates or the cost of your season ticket, which are beyond your control and about which you can moan. When the choice is yours, you cannot blame someone else.

Cutting down on expenditure may require you to look at the reasons for your spending habits.

> Sarah H. used to buy the coffees for her office. Her colleagues would offer to pay and she would say, 'It's okay, I'll get it from you later.' But she never did. Eventually she realized that she was spending as much a week on coffees as she was spending on travel to and from work. Given the fact that she had got into debt, she started to ask for, and accept, payment for the coffees. When she found that this did not affect her relationships with her colleagues, which is what she had feared would happen, she began asking others to get the coffees sometimes.

Changes that seem clear-cut financially are not always easy to come to terms with on an emotional level. But if you choose not to change your behaviour, make sure that you can afford to carry on as before – or accept the consequence of remaining in debt.

Seeking a promotion or a rise or a change of job. Check out your feelings about your work as well as your financial situation.

Consider whether you want to try to negotiate a rise or a promotion in your present job or whether you feel that you are ready to change jobs.

If you decide that you would prefer to stay with your present employer, how you go about negotiating for a rise or promotion depends on knowing the type of company for which you are working. If your job negotiations are conducted through a union, you may need to make the case that you have extra responsibilities which deserve recognition and entitle you to a higher salary. If you work in a firm where salaries are individually negotiated, you will have to make a persuasive case and perhaps get some help in the skills of selling yourself. Some people look for offers outside their own firms as a means for getting the rise or promotion they want. If their efforts fail, then they have another job to go to.

When you start to research the opportunities within your company or in your field of work, you may discover that prospects are limited, at least at present. In many public service jobs, such as teaching and the civil service, the normal route to increased income has been to apply for new jobs – in another school or department. When times are tight, these options for movement and promotion get squeezed. If this is the case – or if you have simply reached what you feel to be a plateau in your working life – then you may need to consider other options for increasing your income.

In many employment situations, women still face additional hurdles – both from employers and from themselves. If you know that you are doing a good job and if you see people around you earning more for less work, ask yorself why? In a recent experiment the same job was advertised in two papers at salaries which differed by thousands of pounds. The vast majority of those who applied for the lower paid job were women, whereas men applied for the higher paid job. All applicants had roughly the same qualifications and experience.

It is a fact that employers are seldom likely to value you more highly than you value yourself. If you know that you are underpaid, yet cannot get yourself to ask for a rise or a job at the right level, you may want to look at getting some help – perhaps through an assertion training course – in order to overcome attitudes which are undermining your financial responsibility to yourself.

Getting part-time work. If you have decided that you need to earn more but have not been able to find a way of doing so in your full-time job, ask yourself how much you need to make up a difference between your outgoings and your income. You will need to find some appropriate part-time work, but do you know what kind of part-time work you are willing to do, and when?

Marian K. had been off work for six months because of injury. During that time she had incurred enormous debts. When she reluctantly faced the facts of her financial situation, it became clear that it would take her about two years to pay off her debts. At the same time she knew that she wouldn't manage to do this unless she also had sufficient money to maintain her social life. 'There's no way I could see myself sitting at home drinking tea while my friends were round at the pub without me.'

Marian didn't greatly fancy the idea of extra work and at first she looked for work that it was difficult to find part-time – kidding herself by looking for the impossible. Then she got more serious and began to consider the kind of part-time job which she would be willing to do and that might suit her best. Did she want a job where she could mix with people? Did she want some peace and quiet? What did she want? She worked out that baby-sitting was the best all round choice for her because she would be completely on her own (assuming her charges went to bed), she could catch up on her TV viewing, or do some studying. If she babysat on Friday and Saturday nights, she would be able to go out on Sunday and Monday nights.

On the other hand, James M. did not want to work in the evenings, but he needed some extra money to cover the costs of the car he had just bought. As his daytime job was mentally very demanding he needed his evenings to recharge his batteries. But he never got any physical exercise. So he solved the problem by going out and washing cars. He does this only on Saturdays, together with a friend, which makes the work both quicker and easier. They do it street by street in an area at some little distance from their own, and just knock on doors.

Do you want to meet people? You may choose to be either behind the bar or in front of it; you can either bartend or wait on tables. If you bartend you earn less. But some people prefer that because they like the opportunity for talking to others and welcome the physical boundary which the counter gives them. If you have got an outgoing personality and enjoy being with people, this can be the answer.

Or is the idea of part-time work completely unacceptable to you? Are you in a job where you rarely see your family anyway, or hardly have the energy to carry you through to the next day? What about working during your holidays? There is some truth in the saying that 'a change is as good as a rest'; and you are probably not talking about every holiday anyway.

> *Jacqueline H. has recently changed teaching jobs. She is earning a lot more and this has enabled her to clear her debts. But she still finds herself short of money at the same time every year when she needs a quick injection of cash. Her work is too demanding to do anything about this during term time – and she feels that she is way past the age, and disposition, when babysitting or waitressing are options for her. Then she realized that there was a demand for summer courses in her subject which she was well qualified to run and which would bring in the extra money that she needed.*

There are many ways of earning some extra money. Sometimes the difficulty is not so much in finding the job but rather in accepting the fact that working 'after I've finished work' is both necessary and possible.

Work overtime – or quit working overtime. On the other hand, you may not have any time after work or at weekends because you are already working long hours. If you are in a job which will pay you for work after completing your basic hours, then this is a way to increase your income as and when you need to. But if you are in a job that does not pay overtime and you find that you are already working extra hours, you will need to cut down on this, if you are to have the time to pursue other options.

If your firm or organization does not pay overtime but you nevertheless choose to work extra hours voluntarily, that is fine. But if you need to earn more money, then you may have to look closely and critically at your workload, your work management, and your attitudes.

22

Summary

As an employee, having financial control of your working life means having the information you need – about your income as well as your spending. Armed with this information you will know your position and what your options are. Remember that your income is fixed but your options are not.

THE 5 STEPS

1 Acknowledge where you are – and what you want

Are you satisfied with your present situation at work?
  How would you like to see your working life develop?

2 Know the facts – your figures *and* your feelings

Do you actually know whether you are getting the best financial deal for yourself at work?
  Do you know whether you are living within your income, spending more than you are earning, or needing extra money for plans you have?

3 Consider the *real* options

If you need extra money, what could you do to earn it?

4 Make choices – live for today *and* plan for tomorrow

Are there changes you want to make at work?
  If you want or need extra money, will it be easier for you to cut down on your current expenditure, get some part-time work, or get a promotion or rise?

5 Do it – and review it

Do you have the confidence to initiate the changes you want to make?
  Do you need help to review your plans regularly? If so, where could you go to get it?

Further information

Chapter 4 Planning for a Quality Retirement

Workbook Chapter 2 Working for Someone Else

Workbook Chapter 9 Planning a Quality Retirement

The Practical Guide to Arranging a Pension

2. Working for Yourself
You set the boundaries – you're the boss

It requires a particular kind of courage to take the risk of backing yourself. And this is what you are doing if you work for yourself – you are the boss.

People who are employed by someone else have many of their boundaries drawn for them – what they do, the hours they work, where they work, what they are paid. If you work for yourself, you have to draw all these boundaries yourself. If you are less than honest with yourself about this fact, any oversight is likely to be reflected in the loss of quality and profitability in your work.

This chapter considers some of the more common financial implications which face those who are self-employed – at the stage of deciding whether to work for yourself, getting started (on your own and with partners), organizing your work and organizing your financial back-up.

Deciding whether you *really* want to work for yourself

Most people believe that working for yourself means choosing your own hours and doing work that you would like to do. That is only part of the picture. When you start working for yourself, you are likely to be working 6 days a week and 12 hours a day. You will also probably accept any reasonable offer that comes along rather than turn it down. Only when you are established and successful will you acquire the luxury of reducing your hours and choosing your clients – providing you have planned properly.

There are pitfalls to being self-employed – being available to anyone, any time, any place, anywhere; not valuing yourself sufficiently to charge enough for your goods or services; nobody paying you for holidays; not taking control of your accounts, so you can pretend that you don't know how much you are earning – or losing.

There are also bonuses – the fact that you pay less tax and National Insurance, the control you have over your work, the flexibility you can exercise over the time you work.

If you are considering becoming self-employed – or 'going freelance', you need to give yourself time in which to discover whether your idea of working for yourself is wishful thinking or based in reality. This is a situation in which you cannot lose.

Amanda B. was working as a temporary secretary but she really wanted to be a full-time astrologer. She was very good, she said, and there were lots and lots of people who wanted to pay for astrology. When pressed to say how many people would be interested in having her read their chart, she had to admit that she did not actually know because she hadn't asked anyone.

Amanda is not yet clear about her market. And what about her costs? Setting her basic expenditure for rent, other regular bills and food against her estimated income from reading charts, she found she would need to cast 400 charts a month just to remain solvent. Anything less than this and she would be in debt to the bank within a couple of months.

Casting 400 charts per month is not realistic, as it takes her five hours to cast one chart. She would need to charge a higher fee than the one she had had in mind. So before she went any further, Amanda needed to do some homework, like checking with others in the astrology business on their going rates. She would also need to ask some friends whether they would be interested in having her cast their charts, and at the fee which she now had in mind.

When she returned two weeks later to see her financial consultant, she had asked a couple of friends but they had not been interested, and 'the ones I really thought would be interested are away right now.' Nor had she asked any other astrologer about their rates because, 'I've really been very busy . . .'

How serious is she about being self-employed? This is not clear. What is clear is that Amanda is not yet ready to work for herself.

She has now decided to test out her intentions by saving

*with a building society by regular standing order, so that
by this time next year she will have built up some capital.
During that time she will also be able to develop her skills
further, including perhaps her speed in casting charts, and to
check out the market, both for costs and clients. At the end
of the year she will have some back-up capital to get started,
provided that she still wants to go ahead and provided that
her market research has shown that she has a fair chance of
making a go of astrology as a business. If not, she will have
faced up to the reality that her dream is not viable, at least
for the present, and will also have some capital to enable her
to do something else. Either way, she will have won.*

If for some reason you are not ready to work for yourself
full-time, or if you cannot bear the thought of abandoning the
security of a regular wage, then it is perfectly feasible to be
both an employee and self-employed. Job shares and part-time
work can offer these opportunities and more employers are now
amenable to such arrangements.

Getting started

No matter how talented, skilled and enthusiastic you are, there
is some groundwork you need to do before you start off. What
is the market you are aiming at? Is there, in fact, a market? What
support can you expect to get, and from what source? How much
capital will you need to carry out your plans?

*Joe and Gaby S. were fed up with living and teaching in
London. They had a dream of running a health food shop,
so they sold their house, found a place in a city they liked,
and started their business. It is not yet clear whether or not
they will be successful: they have struggled for several years
now and have, from time to time, changed their services to
meet changing demands.*

*But what they ignored was the money and help that might
have been available to them in getting started. They could,
for instance, have investigated government schemes aimed at
helping people who want to start up their own business. Or
they could have approached banks which offer advice and
free services during your first year in business. There are also
resettlement plans and special offers.*

Read it! Consider the issues

To be your own boss you do not have to be master or mistress of all trades, but you do have to be willing to obtain specialist help when necessary – and to pay for it. And you have to be prepared to be selective about the help you get.

> *Jane T. knew that she had a very marketable talent for making fine jewellery, but 'I wouldn't be any good at running my own business because I simply don't have a head for figures.'*
>
> *But she could run her own business if she got herself a good accountant. Her skill is in making a product for which people will pay; she only needs someone to help her organize and manage the business side of things.*

You must first know where you are going and what you have to offer. Then you can employ an accountant to cost your plans and a bookkeeper to look after your figures. What you do need to remember is that they are there to help you but that ultimately you are still responsible.

When you are planning to work with somebody else, whether full-time or part-time, there are additional preparations you need to make. You need to ensure that both of you understand and agree on your individual and joint responsibilities. It is also sensible to have a legal agreement drawn up between you. Do not assume that your ethics and priorities are necessarily the same as those of the person with whom you are planning to work. It is crucial that, in any proposed agreement, anything with which you disagree even slightly is discussed and resolved before you enter into the partnership.

> *Celia N. recently started a company with three partners. Her understanding was that as they would all put the same amount of start-up capital into the venture, they would all be entitled to share income equally and in addition would be holding shares. Although she was not totally clear about, or indeed comfortable with, the shareholding agreements and contracts of employment, she went ahead and signed them. She believed that everything could be sorted out later. Nor did she worry unduly as she felt that all partners shared the same point of view about running their business. She was wrong.*
>
> *She found that her partners had agreed on various financial benefits in which she did not share, and that this*

had been done on the basis of the original shareholders agreemen which enabled three out of four partners to approve such arrangements. An amended agreement is now being drawn up at her insistence which will remedy this situation.

Having to sort this out after rather than before they had started the business has been difficult and damaging to their partnership. And Celia realised that she had been responsible for allowing arrangements to slip through with which she did not agree.

The most solid foundation for starting up your own business is the preparation you do before you get started.

Organizing yourself

Working for yourself requires you to know a lot about the ways in which you work best. Most of us have habits which can entice us into avoiding work. When you work for yourself, such habits cost time and money.

One common area is that of 'proliferating peripherals' – doing first what is not central to your work. For example,

Barry R. was setting up an interior design business. He knew that all good businesses had computers and fax machines, so he wanted them too and was going to spend a great deal of energy looking for the right ones. This before he even had his first client.

Nancy G. needed to get organized before she could get on with her writing. Unfortunately it always took her one or two hours to tidy her desk and deal with her correspondence. By the time she had finished, her energy and inspiration had evaporated.

Instead of spending time with his client, Jim E. liked the feeling of always keeping his account books in perfect order. So instead of being out front dealing with customers, he left that to the salesperson he employed and spent most of his time in the back room – at a cost to both the image and profit of the business.

All of these tasks are necessary – getting the right equipment, getting organized, keeping the books. But if you get them back to front, you are undermining your work, because peripherals proliferate. And if you give them your peak energy time, they drain your creativity.

If you are self-employed, you are often your own secretary, bookkeeper and handyperson. This is essential back-up – but it does not earn you money. So do your productive work in the day – or whenever your creative energy is highest – and your back-up work afterwards.

Organizing your time. Let's face it, people who are employed can often waste a lot of time, while maintaining that it's not really their time or their money which they are wasting but their employer's. When you are self-employed, time wasted is money wasted – and the money is yours. Unless you know what you are doing with your time, you will not know how best to go about earning money.

If you are uncertain or puzzled about the way your time just seems to disappear, you may find it helpful to keep a Time Diary for a while, in order to get the facts about the way you spend your days. *Workbook Chapter 4 Being Self-Employed*, gives details of how to keep a Time Diary and assess the results.

It is important to be honest with yourself about how you work. But don't assume that some ways of working are automatically right or wrong. For instance, it is not 'bad' to start work at 10 am. But if you break for an hour at lunch and knock off at 5, don't kid yourself that you have done more work than you really have.

You may be just starting your business and want to work five and a half days a week to get it going. Or you may only want to work three days a week. The choice is yours, but you have to find out the facts – how much money you need and how much time you are willing to work – before you can make a choice and understand its consequences.

Drawing some boundaries. When they start to work for themselves, many people are willing to take on work *any time, any place, anywhere*. This may make sense in the short term, while getting your business off the ground – but it may not be cost effective in terms of either your time or the money you need to earn.

> Brian H. did various kinds of personal consultancy work. Looking at his bills and commitments, he had worked out how much he needed to earn. He also knew that there were

limits to the number of hours which he could work effectively in one day. With the kind of work he did, the limit was five hours a day. Brian also needed a day each week for his administration, and he wanted a full weekend, to relax. So the maximum number of days he could actually work was four. That gave him twenty hours a week during which he was going to earn money – four days at five hours per day. Given these facts, he was able to calculate how much he needed to charge in order to meet the standard of living he had chosen at this point in his life. He had dealt with both his time and his money.

If you had trouble drawing boundaries when you were an employee – if, for example, you consistently worked overtime or took work home at weekends – you will probably have the same difficulties when you are your own boss. Remember: you are the one in charge. It is you who says, 'I don't see people on Mondays,' or 'My hours are 10 – 4'. Of course there have to be exceptions – but drawing clear boundaries allows you to choose when you want to make exceptions.

It is not only unnecessary to work seven days a week, it is also unhealthy – and unsustainable. When you work for yourself, nobody else pays you when you are ill. In fact, as you are your business's major resource, it pays you handsomely to take good care of yourself.

After a long patch of seven-day weeks followed by a scare about her health, Casey K. now disappears four times a year to a health farm. 'I spend my money and take my time to spoil myself which in turn makes me more productive – and a lot easier to live with.'

If you are busy all the time, and not making significantly more money, something is wrong and you need to stop and find out what it is.

Treating the telephone seriously – and honestly. The telephone, backed up by an answer machine, is an invaluable resource for any self-employed person – and a danger.

The telephone can be a trap. You may find it quicker and more cost effective to seek new business by phoning your contacts rather than by arranging to meet them in person. But watch your behaviour. Do you always get to the point of your business first? Or do you start with an extended social chat, at the end of which you mention business, briefly? There is nothing wrong with having a social chat and, if you work on your own, the telephone may be a way of giving you support when you need it. But be honest with yourself about what you are doing. Check your phone calls, how much time you spent on each call and what was achieved.

Deciding where to work. It may seem a good idea to work from home. You can claim a lot of tax advantages if you do so – but it may not be the most profitable place for you to be working.

> *James McF. was a graphic artist working from home. As long as he worked there he felt that he was busy, all the time – yet he had no clear idea about the number of hours he was actually working. When he finally moved out to a studio, making a real separation between his home and his work, he tripled his income within a year and took on more staff. He admits he doesn't have a super talent, just that having a clear work space gave him the chance to focus on work away from home, and on home away from work – with profitable results at work and better relationships at home.*

You may find that working from home suits you, but it will require you to set clear boundaries about when you are working and when you can be interrupted. And try and negotiate these times amicably with anyone else who is at home.

Organizing your financial back-up

You don't have to do all the book-keeping and accounting yourself to keep your business efficient, but you do have to be in control of it – from the fees or price you charge to the way you keep receipts and whether you are planning for your future. Ignoring these matters is like building a house on quicksand. The talents and interests on which you have based your business will quickly be undermined.

Valuing your work. If you work for yourself, you have to set a price on your labour. You are earning money directly for your own endeavours – and this often brings about a conflict. A lot of people, particularly women, find it very difficult to put a realistic market price on their skills and their time. There is a tendency for them to undercharge for their services or to work over and above what is reasonably required. Consequently, some self-employed people are underpaid, overworked, greatly appreciated, much loved – and very frustrated.

> *Frank P. was a pioneer in his field of management
> consultancy. Many of those whom he trained now charge –
> and get – more than he does. He is reluctant to put up his
> prices and to make himself less affordable to the lower end
> of the market. This also means he has no back-up savings in
> the bank. He has therefore never really come to terms with
> his feelings. He thought he had two fundamental choices:
> either to stop feeling sorry for himself and to accept the fact
> that he prefers to work in the lower paid end of the market.
> Or to charge more and move up, leaving the lower end of the
> market to newcomers. There is also, actually, a third choice:
> he can move up and still retain some clients at the lower end
> of the market. Frank P. has not accepted that the buck stops
> with him; he has three choices, not a dilemma.*

If you have a social commitment plus a wish to be paid more for your services – find a way to meet both feelings, such as varying your fee scales for clients with different means.

The important thing is not what you charge but that you should be clear with yourself, and with your customers or clients, about what you are asking for your time and skills, and what you are offering in return.

Getting paid. Setting a price on your work is the first step. Collecting payment for work done is the next. Experiences vary depending on the sector in which you are working. Many self-employed people find that most people pay within a reasonable period of time – say, within the month. But this is less true for those producing or manufacturing goods. In that sector, it is not uncommon to wait 30, 60, or even 90 days for payment; a spate of recent bankruptcies among small businesses resulted not from any lack of business but from the fact that they were not paid promptly by clients.

Some self-employed people find that it is sufficient to state on their invoices, 'Payment within 14 days.' Others require a deposit. And some have found that, when quoting or tendering for work, it is useful to check a company's payment practice in order to manage their own cash flow accordingly. It is also

33

worth considering whether you could or should adjust your price downwards if a quick payment time is guaranteed.

Whatever approach you choose, time needs to be set aside each month to phone around to those who have not paid their bill. Strategies vary: 'Hello, the post here has been appalling, and I wasn't sure whether you had received my invoice because I have not yet received your payment. Could you check and phone me back, please'. Next send off a second invoice and ring every day for a week. Finally, threaten legal action – provided you are prepared to take that step.

You also need to consider how you want to be paid. Do you require a deposit, or a cancellation fee? Do you wish to be paid on the spot or to invoice your clients? Different methods of payment are appropriate to different businesses and conditions – but remember that you need to take your own needs and preferences into consideration.

Getting help. People who work for themselves do so because they have a particular skill, interest or talent which they want to use. They are often less skilled and less interested in the financial side of the business, preferring their accountant to take care of this. They take the view that while they themselves are knowledgeable in their own area, they just don't know enough about accounting to ask the right questions or check the accounts.

Accountants are there to help. Responsibility for your finances is always yours – both practically *and* legally.

If you don't have a knack for organizing your finances, there are other ways of putting that right.

Terence W. is someone who has a talent – but not for finance. He had worked as a tailor for an old-fashioned menswear shop and was at last ready to go to work for himself. A friend who could keep the books and accounts offered to join him as a partner, and offered to put a small amount of money into the business. Terence designs the clothes and markets them. The pair of them meet regularly to discuss all aspects of the partnership. His partner already runs several businesses of his own and is not in the same office, so these meetings are important. They tend to plan a year ahead: his partner ensures that available funds match the year's plan. Terence organizes sales. They have been in business five years: Terence still does not understand facts

*and figures and has no interest in that side of the business,
but he now has an extremely successful custom tailoring
company.*

It can also be tempting to feel that you must have a secretary
to deal with the finances and other administrative matters. Do
you really need someone like this? Or will a short course in
word processing, access to a nearby photocopier, and an answer
machine do instead? Check whether what you really want is
status: secretaries often fulfil that need. And will a secretary
be cost effective? If the answer is yes, fine. If not, reconsider
your options.

Planning for emergencies – and for retirement. It can be easy to let
your personal affairs slide when you are trying to set up your
own business. Remember that you are your business's major
asset. Insurance, which provides an income in case of illness, or
accident or disablement, may be the last thing you want to think
about; in case of emergency, it will be the first thing you need.

Look around you at the number of self-employed people
who are past the statutory retirement age. Some continue
to work from choice. But others will work until they drop:
they can't afford to stop work because they failed to plan for
their retirement. Employees are often part of a pension or
superannuation scheme, but if you work for yourself, no one
else is going to plan ahead on your behalf.

Organizing time for your finances

Whether you are doing the day-to-day book-keeping yourself or
paying someone else to do it, you and you alone are responsible
for controlling the financial side of your business. That means
that you have to make time to sort out your figures yourself or
to review them regularly with your accountant.

How, you may wonder, can you possibly find the time to do
this while you are trying to keep the business running? There
are many time management courses and books which offer
advice. They are only useful if you are honest with yourself
about two things:

- the importance of being in control of your finances,
- the fact that you can only do so by making time to
  review the situation regularly.

Read it! Consider the issues

If you want to be clearer about all of this, then further advice is given in *Chapter 10 Managing Your Own Money* and *Workbook Chapter 17 Managing Your Own Money* which help you to design ways of doing so that are best suited to your own working pattern.

Summary

In order to benefit from being your own boss, you have to accept, and carry out, the full responsibilities that go hand in hand with being in charge. Be honest with yourself about your own talents – and your limitations. The buck stops with you.

THE 5 STEPS

If you are thinking of becoming self-employed,

1 Acknowledge where you are – and what you want

What do you want to do?
  What kind of life do you imagine that this would help you to make?
  How far have you gone towards making a decision?

2 Know the facts – your figures *and* your feelings

Do you know if there is a market for what you want to do?
  How much would it cost you to set yourself up in business?
  Could you earn enough to meet the costs of your present lifestyle?

3 Consider the *real* options

What do you need to do in order to decide whether you actually want to take the step of working for yourself?
  Do you have the skills and confidence which you need at this point in time?
  If you have already made your decision, do you know what you need to do in order to get started?

4 Make choices – live for today *and* plan for tomorrow

When do you want to make the change?
  Where would you get the support which you need in order to get started?

5 Do it – and review it

Can you arrange further training? Or, if appropriate, seek advice from a consultant?
  What is the state of your financial and systems organization?
  Have you reviewed everything you have done at least once every three months?
  Have you made any necessary changes?

Further information

Workbook Chapter 3 Thinking about Working for Yourself

Workbook Chapter 5 Creating Financial Security

THE 5 STEPS

If you are already self-employed,

1 Acknowledge where you are – and what you want

What developments would you like to see in your business?

If you work with partners or have employees, do you all agree about what you expect to get out of the business – in terms of money and satisfaction?

How satisfied are you with things at present?

2 Know the facts – your figures *and* your feelings

How is the business doing financially?

What is it costing you to live?

How much time are you spending at work – and how are you apportioning that time?

3 Consider the *real* options

Are there any changes which you would like to make in your work in order to develop your business and to refine your own working pattern?

4 Make choices – live for today *and* plan for tomorrow

Can you see ways of building up your work and your income while maintaining your required lifestyle?

5 Do it – and review it

Do you make time to review regularly the state of your business?

If you work with partners or have employees, do you make time to review the business together?

Further information

Chapter 10 Managing Your Own Money

Workbook Chapter 4 Being Self-Employed

Workbook Chapter 17 Managing Your Own Money

The Practical Guide to Book-keeping and Taxation

for the Self-Employed

3. Managing Changes in Your Earning Life

Manage changes – or they will manage you

You are likely to face changes during your working life. These may be voluntary or they may be forced upon you. You may choose to take a new job or make a sideways move into a new career. You may lose your job, inherit money or find that you have to depend on government benefits for all or part of your income.

With any of these changes you have two choices, either to manage them or allow them to manage you.

To avoid being out of control of your finances, remember that no one has job security, but everyone has the chance to create some financial security. If you find yourself facing changes outside your control, and you have little or no financial back-up, there are steps you can take to gain control quickly over the situation.

This chapter looks first at how you can give yourself some financial security, so that you are better prepared to face whatever changes occur in the course of your working life. It then considers some of the issues you may face when planning changes or having to deal with the unexpected in your work and/or your income.

Creating financial security

If you have got money, you can choose where and how to spend it. If you do not have it, you have left yourself with no choices. Everyone needs 'fall back money' – money that you have put aside for contingencies and emergencies. This 'fall back money' will let you take control of the various changes which you are likely to have to face more easily and quickly.

Do you feel that you will be working in your present job, or one like it, until you retire? In the middle years of a working life people often wish to move sideways into a new career, or towards early retirement. Others are susceptible to losing their jobs, through no fault of their own.

> *Frank N. made enough money in five years in the Middle East to put down a deposit on the house of his dreams on his return home. He found work nearby with a thriving electronics firm, but the decline in the economy has recently put him out of work – 'last in, first out'. His wife had started a small dress shop in the nearby town, but that was hit by the slump in retail spending. So now they are left with a large mortgage and four teenage children to support. They hope that he can find alternative work and that her business will pick up. Until then their main worry is to find ways of generating income to cover their outgoings.*
>
> *Jim D. was a member of the senior management team of a firm that made food under franchise for a large company. After several complaints from customers about the quality of the product, the whole senior management team was sacked. His wife had just started a well-paid job that was important to her, but in the area in which they lived there did not seem to be any immediate prospects for him. They were therefore faced with the question of what was more important to them – the immediate financial security of her work or his need for a senior management career.*

Others 'know' that their job is not forever because they have an unfulfilled dream. This is the 'going to New Zealand' syndrome. Many people have dreams – to change jobs, to return to the home of their birth, or to emigrate. As in, 'We're going back to New Zealand to raise the children in better surroundings', or 'One day we'll retire to the country and open a tea shop'.

Who is to know whether these are dreams that are meant to come true? The secret is to *live for today and plan for tomorrow*. Then you are in a position to make the change when, or if, the opportunity arises. Plan ahead and make adequate provision for going back, or emigrating, or changing jobs. But do not put your day-to-day life on hold. Either way, you will be the winner.

Finally, you need 'fall back money' for your retirement. You do want money in your old age, don't you? If so, what are you doing about it? Old age is unavoidable. But if you've ever said, 'I'll be dead before then . . .' Or 'I'm never going to retire', you are really saying that you are neither facing your old age, nor preparing for it. People live longer: 60 is now coming to be middle age, and many of us can expect to live into our 80s and even 90s. As longevity increases, you have to address your need for financial security after you give up work, and you must address it *now*.

Start with the pennies and the pounds will take care of themselves. Many people pretend that the only reason they do not put money aside for their old age is because it costs so much. It does not have to. And putting aside something, anything, is better than putting nothing aside, as any retired person with only a state pension will confirm.

If you have been convinced that you need 'fall back money', how do you go about accumulating it? This can take several forms, the most common of which are savings plans and pensions. To young people, setting up a personal pension scheme may seem absurd, particularly when there are so many other things on which they could spend their money. So it may help to think of 'fall back money' as money which you have put aside for any contingency, not just for your retirement. You always need to have a small reserve tucked away for your future – even if you are not sure what you want to do with it. For instance, by the time a savings plan matures, say after ten years, you may prefer to continue with small monthly payments because, at that point in time, you do not need a lump sum in cash. Or the available lump sum will help towards that new car. Or it could finance retraining. Or subsidize a long holiday.

And what if it all goes wrong? What if you become redundant, lose your job, or lose your health? The money that you had set aside for a holiday can be used instead to keep up your mortgage payments during a difficult patch, or finance additional help if you are ill.

The next statement may appear to be contradictory, but it is not. Don't rush out straightaway and arrange a pension or a savings plan. Sound financial moves which are not made at the right time, may turn out not to be sound moves after all.

Helen K. decided that it was time to set up a pension scheme because she had the money for it and knew that it was the sensible thing to do. In fact, what was really bothering her at the time was that she hated her job and wanted to work part-time and write. Yet she felt that she ought to be in a job because she needed to provide for her retirement. The key word is 'ought' – and that is why, right now, she should delay arranging her pension until she has sorted out her options.

And she does have options. She already has low overheads, as she owns her house outright. If she lets her spare room, the income will pay all her bills and half her car loan, and she would be able to work part-time. That would enable her to leave a job she hates and begin to write.

Yes, of course she needs to have a pension plan, but it is wrong for her to do anything about this until she sorts out the underlying issues.

People often get stuck with what they 'ought' to be doing. They forget what they need and want – both today and tomorrow. Make sure you know what you want and what you feel before you do any financial business.

Planning for changes in your working life

Many people find they would like to move in new directions – but cannot quite find the way of making the change. Test yourself for honesty and realism. Are you sure that you really want to make a change? How much will it cost? If you really want to make the change, there are many options. If you own a house or flat, you can remortgage your property to subsidize your retraining. Or you can stay in your present job and train part-time, which will be less of a strain on your pocket. What do you *really* want to do next?

Barry M. was discontented with his job and thought that he would like to run his own business. He took the time to talk to people who ran their own businesses. He discovered that what he really wanted was recognition and prestige, but he did not really want the responsibility and risk of running his own business. He wanted to be a big fish in a small pond so that he could acquire the prestige without taking too much of a financial risk.

You cannot plan for the next step until you know two things: what you really want to do, and how much it will cost. Then you plan.

Matthew S. wanted to do an accountancy course, and felt that it would be best to do it full-time. He remortgaged his house to finance the training, cut down his budget, and lived exactly within the boundaries which he had set himself. He chose to have no new clothes, no car, no holidays – and accepted that that was his choice in the short term.

He reached the point when he needed to earn money. He got himself a part-time job but found that there still was not enough money available to pay all the bills. So what could he do? He knew that accountancy was the career he wanted and that his practice would build up to the point where it would earn him a good income. What he needed in the short term was to find a way to finance his decision. He worked out exactly how much he needed to live on for six months – the length of time he gave himself to get his business running profitably. He then further increased his mortgage by that amount. At the end of six months he will review his situation.

If you want to make a change in your career and have the opportunity of doing so, beware of the following trap.

Carolyn P. wanted to change career. When she was offered a job in a new field, she jumped at the chance. The job was advertised at £12,000 – £20,000 based on experience and other factors. She had been earning £16,000 but was advised by the interviewer that she should consider accepting £12,000 as she was lucky to have the chance of changing career and would have to make some sacrifices. Fortunately for her, she was encouraged not to undervalue herself and she decided to ask for £18,000 – she got the job. When she started her new work, she discovered that salaries for her job ranged up to £22,000, even though the people

43

involved all had similar experience to her own. The only difference was that those who were paid at the highest rate had had the confidence to ask for what they were getting.

Carolyn had advice from her financial consultant, who got her to cost her figures realistically. When planning major changes, it is advisable to check out your plans with someone whom you trust and who knows enough about your and/or their area of expertise to fill the gaps in your own thinking and experience.

And you do have to be honest with yourself in order to plan effectively. Some people can plan quickly; others need to plan meticulously over a period of time. Neither approach is right or wrong: you just need to learn how to manage changes in a way that is comfortable for you. If you think that you are taking 'too' long in coming to a decision, check out your feelings. They may be telling to you that, deep down, this proposed change is not really what you want.

Dealing with unexpected changes in your work

If you are faced with the loss of your job, there are two areas to which you need to give immediate attention – your finances and your reactions, even though your confidence is likely to have been dealt a severe below.

Faced with the loss of their job, people often have a tendency to do something hasty – or nothing at all. The important first step is to recognize clearly what has happened. Most of us will have heard stories of people who have lost their jobs, yet continued to go through the motions of going to work for months, because they could not face telling their partners, or admitting to themselves, what had happened. That is not a satisfactory solution, either financially or emotionally.

Even before you have picked yourself up, you need to check quickly that your firm has played fair with you. Many companies, when they dismiss a worker, for whatever reason, treat the situation professionally and sensitively – and some offer help with managing the transition. Other firms mishandle the process badly. If you have any suspicion that you have not got the financial deal to which you are entitled, you will need to take urgent legal advice, from your union and/or a solicitor.

> *Karen B. lost her job when her firm was bought out by another company. The terms of her redundancy had been negotiated and agreed – then the firm refused to pay her the full amount due to her. The new company was itself facing financial difficulties and acknowledged that this was one way by which they were cutting costs. 'The new management assumed that I would accept their revised offer and cut my losses. I consulted a solicitor so that I knew exactly where I stood. Then I decided to try to hold them to the original agreement even though, after paying legal fees, I would only be a little better off if I won my case.'*

Others in that situation might have chosen to cut their losses. The point is not what action you take, but that you take responsibility for knowing the situation and making your choice.

After you have cleared up any loose ends with your old job, look at your financial situation. Good advice may be on offer – from your bank manager, from one of the special consultants whom your firm has recommended or from your own financial adviser.

But before dealing with them, it can be helpful to use the 5 Steps to keep control for yourself. Going through the three basic analyses in *Workbook Chapter 1 The Basic 5 Steps Analysis* will help you to find out what you have and what you can afford to spend – and how much time you have. If you have received a lump sum, the best thing to do in the short term is to put it on deposit with a building society or bank for six months while you are sorting out your next steps. Your confidence may have suffered a blow, you may have been living under a great deal of stress – so a good holiday, or buying something special, may help you to deal with this period of change in a more constructive and relaxing way.

Finally, make a plan – about what you want to do next, and how you are going to manage your resources while working towards your goal. This all sounds more straightforward than it will be in practice. The loss of a job can be quite devastating. So much of our self-image and self-esteem is bound up in our career that being rejected at work can be a major catastrophe, especially for men – and it needs to be treated as such.

Given time, however, these experiences can also open doors

to new opportunities. Obviously you will have learned a good deal about yourself and about your reactions to adversity. You will probably have become more resilient to ill fortune and you will know about the choices, in both your personal and financial dealings. You may not have wished for the change that has overtaken you, but you do have choices in managing the consequences.

Managing unearned income

There is an area which can confront you with particularly complex issues – when you receive monies for which you have not worked, either through government benefits or through an inheritance.

Whether such monies are all or part of those on which you live, you need to come to terms with your own feelings about them. It is worth remembering that when we work, we pay taxes so that, if we fall on hard times, we can claim benefits to which we are entitled.

Kevin D. was on government benefits. When he and his partner split up she left him with their two young children. He decided to quit his job and stay at home to raise the boys. His only income was benefits from the government but he refused to recognize this fact. 'I liked being with the kids, but I felt guilty about their mother walking out on us. So I used to buy the boys anything they asked for. And I spent money as if I was still on my old salary.'

When a letter came from his bank about his overdraft, Kevin began to face up to the changes in his circumstances. He was not used to counting pennies and he would now have to do so. But he has found that by saving even a few pence each week and by cutting down on his smoking, the pounds are beginning to accumulate. 'I don't plan to have to live like this forever, but at least I can now see that there's something I can do about all this.'

Sarah T., on the other hand, inherited some money from her grandfather. Because inherited wealth contradicted her political beliefs, she kept quiet about this fact. She had a low paid job and a couple of rooms in a shared flat and she prided herself on living on her salary. Nothing is wrong with any of that – except that when she finally came to look at her financial situation, she discovered that she was spending £900 a month on 'extras'. Extras included eating out – and paying for her friends and buying extravagant presents.

Sarah realized that she was living by a double standard, 'and I needed to do something about it. I considered giving the money away, which is what I'd always thought I would do. But then I realized that I had grown to like these extras, a lot.' She finally decided that she would live on her salary and pay all her bills from it, but that out of the inheritance she would allow herself a small amount to pay for treats. This was a resolution with which she was comfortable.

Of course Sarah and Kevin have very different financial options. But the step both have had to take is the same – to accept their situations and to know the precise figures with which they have to deal. Now that they know, they can begin to see their choices and to adapt their feelings to their new situations.

Of course, it is more comfortable to manage on more money rather than on less. But the fact is that whatever situation you are in, the way to take control of your finances is the same whether you are handling pennies or pounds.

Summary

Managing any change in your work and your income means managing both your finances and your reactions to your changed circumstances. This is true, whether you now have more money to spend or less.

THE 5 STEPS

1 Acknowledge where you are – and what you want

If you would like to make changes in your work, are you clear what you want to do?

If you have been faced with unexpected changes in your work or your income, how are you managing?

What 'fall back money' – reserves – do you have?

2 Know the facts – your figures *and* your feelings

Do you know your current financial circumstances precisely?

What is the financial cost of any changes you would like to make or are being forced to make?

What are your feelings about your present situation and future prospects?

If you are facing redundancy, are you sure that you are getting the best deal for yourself?

3 Consider the *real* options

Are there different ways in which you can reach the goals you have set yourself? If so, what are these?

If you have been faced with unexpected changes at work, what can you see yourself doing in the short term to adjust to these new realities?

4 Make choices – live for today and plan for tomorrow

What are the first steps which you need to take to manage planned changes or to deal with the unexpected?

Do you have the confidence to do so? If not, what can you do about this?

5 Do it – and review it

Are there any loose ends you need to clear up, financially or emotionally, before you feel able to tackle your choices?

Supposing that, for the present, your personal finances have had to be severely curtailed, can you see ways of rewarding yourself for the changes you are handling?

Further information

Workbook Chapter 5 Creating Financial Security

Workbook Chapter 6 Planning Changes in Your Working Life

Workbook Chapter 7 Dealing with Unexpected Changes in Your Earning Life

Workbook Chapter 8 Coming to Terms with Benefits or Inheritance

The Practical Guide to Saving and Investing

4. Planning for a Quality Retirement
Live for today – and plan for tomorrow

During your working life you have some very serious decisions to make about the time when you are no longer earning an income. *When* you make these decisions will influence the quality of the rest of your life.

Ask yourself:

- When do I want to stop work?
- What kind of life do I want to have in retirement?
- What will I do if either I or my partner falls ill after we've retired?

Be honest with yourself. Have you faced the *fact* that you are getting older – or did you find yourself turning away from answering the above questions?

Whether you plan to retire at 50 or 75, unless you want to be poor when you retire, you need to make contributions to a pension scheme for at least 25 years. If you delay, you will pay more to reach the same goal – though it is never too late to start.

Dealing with myths about retirement

Planning realistically for a comfortable old age tends to be bedevilled by the existence of a number of myths. One of these is that life will be cheaper when you are retired.

Saul H. had been a taxi driver. He had always thought that any talk about pensions was rubbish, since 'you can live more cheaply when you are not working, can't you?' What he discovered was that it can cost more to feed yourself and keep yourself warm when you spend a lot of time at home. He had also dreamed of travelling, seeing places he had always talked about with passengers, and playing a bit of golf. But he finds that he does not have any spare money for these anticipated extras, and he feels bitter about the kind of life that he is now having to live.

In fact, if you want to do things for which you never had the time while you were working full-time, your life in retirement is likely to cost you more.

Another myth is that, in the kind of world in which we live, there is no point in planning for tomorrow because:

- there is going to be a nuclear war and we are all going to be wiped out;
- we could hit a depression like the 1930s and our money will be valueless;
- your parents are quite well off, and you expect that they will leave you enough to provide for your old age;
- you might die early.

Yes, all of the above could happen – or none of them.

If you have made no provision, you have got nothing going for you either way. Whereas if you make some kind of provision, then, if there is a future, you will have the money necessary to fund it.

A variation on this theme is the feeling that you are too young to be thinking about retirement. You are never too young. The earlier you start contributing to a pension scheme, the more likely you are to end up with a respectable pension. If you still can't imagine yourself worrying about retirement, an alternative is to contribute to a savings plan which will give you a lump sum at the end of a specified period of time. You will then be able to invest this lump sum in a pension plan or in some other major item of expenditure. Whichever way you get there, the point is to live for today but also to plan for tomorrow.

Deciding when to retire

Would you like the option of retiring early? In these days, when health and leisure are figuring ever larger in people's minds, many people are choosing to retire, or semi-retire, at age 55 or thereabouts, depending on whether early and good enough planning has given them this option.

If you would like to aim for this – remembering that you

can always change your mind and carry on working for longer
– check out your existing pension and monetary provisions.

The facts of your financial resources will clearly indicate
whether you have made sufficient provision for retiring early
or whether, in order to do so, you need to start investing heavily
now, while you are earning and in good health. If you need more
money, decide how much you can comfortably afford to put away
for your pension. Do not lock all your money away where you
cannot touch it until you retire: there are such things in life as
emergencies.

Check whether the amount you plan to put away each month
will provide you with the retirement income that you require.
If not, do your calculations again, allowing a little more time,
perhaps five years, to top up your pension. But make sure that
you are being realistic. Somebody aged 40 who has only paid
for a pension for three years and then announces that he or she
wishes to retire at 55 is not being realistic.

If you have correctly calculated the sum which you will need
to save in order to retire at 55 but are baulking at the prospect
of having to set that much aside then, maybe, you need to check
again whether you actually want to retire early. Perhaps you
are really thinking about building in more choices for yourself,
perhaps working slightly less and having a lump sum for a few
major extras. If that is the case, you may want to accumulate a
tax-free lump sum of money by 55, not a pension. *Workbook
W5 Creating Financial Security* will give you the details of how to
do that.

Deciding where to live in your retirement

If you own property, think about whether you might want to
move when you retire. Calculate the amount of income you think
you need to support the way of life you have in mind. Do you
have a dream of moving to the South Coast or the Yorkshire
Moors or the South of France? Take a one month holiday and
stay there during the least auspicious time of the year. See how
you like it – and how much it costs.

It is never too late to start

Many of us are reluctant to think about the end of our working
lives. If you leave it too late to make adequate provisions for

your retirement you will have to cut down on your standard of living now in order to achieve the quality of life you want in retirement.

> *William S. had made no provision for his retirement because he believed that he was never going to retire. At age 55, however, he had to recognize that he would have to retire from his firm in another ten years, by which time he would receive only a small pension. He and his wife decided to cut their expenditure dramatically for the next ten years so as to enable him to build up a reasonable pension.*
>
> *Now he has retired. His wife has chosen to earn a bit extra by working one day a week. They have time, a car, a cottage and a boat. He goes hang-gliding and water-skiing and they go to Spain for a cheap month in the winter every year. They have a super retirement – but only because he got smart just in time.*

On the other hand, it may be that you just haven't been clear enough in your mind about what kind of life you would want when you retire.

> *Margaret D. desperately wanted to retire when she was 59. She had reached the end of the road in teaching. Having calculated her figures, she realized that she could retire and have a modest lifestyle on what she had. But she also discovered that two other things mattered to her: enjoying some luxuries, and keeping her mind alert. So she decided that she would need to earn some money working part-time, though definitely not in teaching. She retired early and found a job in which she can work part-time and which keeps her involved. She now has time to go to galleries, visit friends, become active in community life, and is relieved and delighted that she took two calculated risks – leaving teaching and taking on a new job at her age.*

It is never too late to start – if you are willing to be honest and realistic.

Changing plans if everything goes wrong

Supposing that, after you have retired, you or your partner becomes ill? If you have planned for a comfortable leisure in your old age, then you are well placed financially to handle ill health. Money will not of itself cure illness, or protect you from gradually 'wearing out', but it will make the circumstances of living easier.

> *Edna and Len M. had enjoyed 10 years of the kind of retirement they had wanted – visiting their children and grandchildren, travelling in their caravan to warmer countries in the winter, walking. Then he had a stroke which left him unable to walk. The only way in which she could keep him at home and look after him herself was to have a chair lift installed, to get him to and from the bedroom. 'The local authority wouldn't help us with the costs. But luckily we had the money we had put aside for travelling, so we were able to pay for it ourselves.' The extra they had enabled Len to stay in his home for the remaining three years of his life.*

If you have got the money, you can choose where and how to spend it. If you don't, you have left yourself with no choice at all.

Dealing with retirement

Many people were raised on the principle that you ought never to touch your capital. Yet, as you get older, your capital is there to provide for two eventualities: to give you security in case you need care, and to spend and enjoy it. You will need to review both your own feelings, and the well-meaning advice you are likely to receive, so as to make sure that what you are doing with your money is what you wish to do.

> *Gemma D. is 78. Several years ago, when her husband died, she received a large lump sum from an assurance policy. She decided to sell the family home in which they had lived, as she felt that she didn't need that much space any more. She was advised by her bank manager to buy a smaller house and to invest the rest so as to give her a small income. This did not seem quite right to her, so she discussed it with her financial consultant. She finally decided that she did not really need another house – a flat would do – but she did need some financial security and she wanted money to spend on herself and on visiting her daughter in Canada.*
> *Having rented a small flat in a block with good security*

arrangements, she put a lump sum in a building society, to act as back-up if she needs care and, if not, to fulfil her wish of leaving something to her daughter. The rest of the money provides an income.

And Gemma is having a ball for however many years she has left. If it is ten years or if it is twenty years – her money is making money and is there to provide for her. If she lives for only a few more years – fine, she is enjoying herself and what is left can go to her daughter. By using some of her capital, Gemma is able to have big treats, not just small ones. It cost her £10,000 to go to Canada for three months, but she could afford it. She is also able to treat her friends, travel around the country, fly first class, eat out in restaurants, and go to the theatre. And every six months she reviews her budget, just to make sure that she stays in control of this new experience of spending money on herself.

Our difficulties with money are not just financial, and in retirement it is our attitudes as much as the amount of money we have that will determine the quality of those years.

Summary

On the whole, people no longer wonder how to fill their time in retirement. There are so many things most people can imagine themselves doing, some that cost nothing, others that cost quite a lot – travelling, more time for sport or other leisure activities, studying, gardening. And nobody wants to lose their home – or have no back-up if they fall ill. This all requires money – and planning.

It's never too late – but it does get more difficult, both emotionally and financially, to sort things out the longer you leave it.

THE 5 STEPS

1 Acknowledge where you are and what you want

What do you imagine your life will be like when you retire?
　When do you want to retire?
　Do you think you are too young to be bothered about this?

2 Know the facts – your figures *and* your feelings

What pension and savings arrangements have you already made?
　If you have not made any plans, why not?

3 Consider the *real* options

Will the provisions you have made give you the kind of retirement you want?
　If not, are there ways by which you can put that right?
　Are there any other things you need to consider and plan for now, in addition to future financial security?

4 Make choices – live for today *and* plan for tomorrow

How can you balance the cost of financing your retirement plans with the kind of life you want to live now?

5 Do it – and review it

As retirement gets closer, are your ideas about it changing?
　If you think you are not yet ready to sort this out, when will you be willing to review your feelings and circumstances again?

Further information

Workbook Chapter 5 Creating Financial Security

Workbook Chapter 9 Planning for a Quality Retirement

The Practical Guide to Arranging Life Cover

The Practical Guide to Arranging a Pension

The Practical Guide to Saving and Investing

II Money and Relationships

Be honest – with yourself

Introduction

From birth to death – and even beyond – money affects our relationships.

There are two sides to this coin. On the one side, there are practical ways in which, with friends and family, we can better manage our money, in order to have the kind of relationships we want. On the other side, money is a tool, and sometimes a weapon, in developing our relationships. Conflicts about money are often like the tip of an iceberg, a sign that a lot more is going on beneath the surface.

Have you ever said, or heard, 'We have a good relationship – except when it comes to money'? The 'except . . .' means that something isn't right between you: at the very least, that you haven't come to terms with your different approaches to dealing with money; or that, when it comes to money, you are hiding many issues which you would rather not face.

The first step to sorting out money in your relationships is to sort out your own relationship to money. That's where honesty *is* the best policy. After that, what you choose to reveal about money – what you feel about it, how much you have, and what you do with it – is up to you and depends on the kind of relationship you want.

Understanding Childhood Messages looks at how our own financial behaviour is influenced by our family's style and traditions, and what we might do to make our messages clearer and more positive for our own children.

Few of us go through life without borrowing money from, or lending it to, a friend or another member of our family. *Borrowing and Lending – between family and friends*, discusses ways in which awareness of your motives, and of the practical arrangements, can protect your relationships from damage.

Living with another person throws up particular financial

issues, whether you are friends or a married couple. The chapter *Living Together* looks at healthier ways to start off, carry on – and split up, if it comes to that.

At some time in our lives, most of us will live alone, whether by choice or by circumstance. *Managing on Your Own* considers particular issues for you when you are the sole adult managing the finances in a household.

And finally, *Looking at Death* brings us up against the inevitable. We have to decide what we want to happen to our assets – and to our remains – after we die. The way in which we handle this can affect our relationships with others, and especially those closest to us, both now and after our death. The chapter presents some of the emotional and practical issues which you need to take into account when preparing your own Will and when dealing with someone else's death.

5. Understanding Childhood Messages

Know your money style – and let your ethics be your guide

Most of what we know about money we learned when we were growing up, by observing how it was treated in our family. We learned what it would buy, whether we had plenty of it or never enough, and who was in charge of it. By the time we were ready to manage our own money, we were full of other people's messages about what we ought and ought not to do.

Some of these messages will be inappropriate for us today; some are still sound advice; others are matters of personal belief and choice. All, however, affect our attitudes towards, and our use of, money. What is important is that we are aware of the messages and learn how to make our own choices.

Your family's money style was neither right nor wrong, but it will be part of your own behaviour.

When Eileen M. was a child, her parents charged her a penny for any phone call that she made. This didn't cover the cost of the call but it was a token, so that she learned that a call cost something. In Victor F.'s home, a lock was put on the phone so that the children couldn't use it at all. Eileen learned that you could have what you wanted but that you had a responsibility to pay towards its cost. Victor on the other hand learned that in order to get what you wanted, you had to figure out a way of overcoming an obstacle – and he learned to open the lock. Neither is right or wrong – but they did learn very different lessons.

Try and be aware of your family's money style – but do not judge it. Then look at how you can adapt those patterns to suit your own habits and preferences. There is no right or wrong way with money, but there are choices – and these choices need to be made by each of us as we grow up so as to ensure that our money style is the one that suits us.

Family styles and messages

Think back. What is your earliest money memory? How did money 'feel' in your family – taboo, central, matter of fact, plentiful, tight? Who controlled the money in your family? How did it figure in your parents' relationship with each other and in their relationship with you? What was their attitude to debt?

Jeannette R.'s mother felt strongly about teaching her and her sisters the value of money and how to manage it. Meetings were held around the dining room table, where the amount that each child would have to spend on clothes and some non-essentials was set for the year. 'But dad never really took any of this seriously and would always bail us out if we overspent. Therefore, the family meetings never had any sense of reality': Jeannette knew she would be rescued. And even now, when she is earning a comfortable living, she finds herself more often than not in a financial mess because she can't make the link between what she earns and what she spends. She expects her bank manager to rescue her, just like her father did – and is having to face the reality that that is not the way banks operate.

Having become aware of what you learned, you need to sort out which of the lessons are the ones that will help you to make a healthy relationship with money and which are the ones that are not helpful – bearing in mind the kind of person you are, the kind of life you lead, the beliefs you hold, and the social and political circumstances in which you function.

Patsy P. can still hear her father's voice: 'There are two things that are inexcusable – running out of petrol, and being in debt.' As a result, she has never had an overdraft, nor bought anything on credit, nor had a credit card. She avoided getting a mortgage for a long time by not buying a house, but continued to pay rent.

Patsy's father was raised to pay all bills promptly and never buy anything on credit. He also grew up in times when many more people rented their homes. Patsy on the other hand lives and works at a time when 'intelligent debt', through credit cards and hire purchase, is considered good money management. Only when she realised how some of her parents' ways with money were not right for her did Patsy begin to feel that she was making her own decisions. 'I also

59

realised that I had learned some really good habits from them. Now that I do have a credit card, I pay it off each month and I never overdraw on my bank account. Those are good habits for me – and I learned them from my parents.'

Nowadays women are, as often as not, earners too and are as likely to be heads of household as men. Despite these changes, many of us are still bound by the expectations we inherited.

Alice T. remembers that her mother was always the one to do without in order to make sure that the children had enough – although her dad had a new car every two years and enough money for nights out with his friends. Alice only became aware of the way that this had conditioned her when her husband gave her an expensive jacket for their first Christmas together. She felt that he had spent far too much on her, and changed it for a cheaper jacket – even though she never questioned the money which he spent on his hobbies of collecting compact discs and restoring old cars.

On the other hand, Phil. W. remembers that his dad was often out of work and that his mother always managed their money. 'Even when my father had a job, he would give his pay packet to my mum and she would give him back enough for his cigarettes and beer.' It was only when Phil and his girlfriend Connie started to live together that he realized how little he knew about managing money. Because of her family background, Connie expected him to take care of their finances – and he expected her to do the same. They both had to learn and understand the different traditions and expectations which they brought to their partnership.

These examples may help to illustrate how and why children receive different messages about the ways adults should manage money. The important thing is to be aware of what those messages were in your own family and let this awareness help you to make your own choices.

Money and morals

The baseline for our relationship to money is the same as it is for the rest of our lives: what are our values and beliefs and how are these reflected in our choices and behaviour?

Money presents us with moral and ethical dilemmas at every turn. Do I invest in a company with interests in South Africa or in one which is involved in ecologically damaging activities? Is it a fiddle to make private phone calls from work, take home paper clips, pad the expense account? Is it right to buy shares?

How you answer these questions will depend on your values, whether these are informed by politics, religion or family tradition.

Money is neither good nor bad – but what you do with it is not neutral. The way you use it affects others, besides yourself.

Janet T. found that as she became an adult, she could love her father but not respect him. 'I learned that he was a crook – I can't honestly use any other word – in his business dealings. He cheated people and he made shoddy goods at the same time as he was making a comfortable life for my mother and my brother and me.'

The contradictions in her father's professional and personal life gave her a great deal of trouble in her own relationship to money. She came to think of money as 'dirty' and lived a life of great political commitment where spending money on yourself was considered wrong. Eventually she realized that money wasn't the problem, her father was. She also came to realize that having money meant that you could choose how to use it and that, politically speaking, this enabled you to support causes in which you believed.

What are the alternatives? Are there ways to be 'clean' in business? Where do you draw the line? The answer is that there are always alternatives – and it is up to you to draw your own line. But there is no way of avoiding such decisions.

Richard R. was selling his flat because he and his girlfriend were planning to buy a house together. He had accepted an offer from a young couple who were first-time buyers. Then a man, who wanted the flat as a base while working in London during the week, offered him several thousand pounds more, a figure the young couple could not match. Richard's principles told him that he wanted the flat to go to the couple – he had already given them his word, and he would prefer the flat to go to first-time buyers. But financially, the extra thousands would be useful to put toward the house he was planning to buy.

What would you have done?

Many people are becoming more aware of their responsibility for the uses to which they put their money, and of the social and environmental implications of both consumer spending and personal investments. 'Ethical' or 'green' have become labels which indicate a moral high ground. Yet nothing is as straightforward as it seems. 'Ethical' or 'green' as descriptions do not guarantee that the purchase or the investment is either ethical or green. And certainly few investments are pure: those companies which do not invest in South Africa may experiment on animals, exploit workers in some other country, or pollute your local river. Charitable giving poses similar dilemmas. Do you know where your money is going? What causes do you believe in? What kind of support do you believe helps people?

Your choices will reflect your own values.

The messages we pass on to our own children

We in turn influence our own children's attitudes towards money. The first step in accepting responsibility for this is to be aware of what you want them to learn – and then to practise it, both by your own example and by the way in which you help them to develop their own responsibilities for managing money.

Helping children to achieve a knowledge of money is as much a part of their development as learning to read or sharing chores around the house: you make choices that are appropriate to their age and circumstances – and to your own financial circumstances.

Pocket money is probably the central tool in this process. What do you do now? Do you give your children a fixed amount that is theirs and with which they can do as they like, with no strings attached? Or is it conditional on their good behaviour, like cleaning up their rooms or drying the dishes? Or do you have a system whereby some of the money is theirs no matter what, but they can also earn extra for doing jobs like raking the leaves in the autumn or helping you with the shopping?

Remember, there is no right or wrong, but there are different messages. If you feel strongly that children should help around the house, then you may not want to pay them for what you think is a basic responsibility. It is for you to choose. Whatever your choice, it is important to be clear with yourself and consistent with them.

The age at which you begin to let your children handle money will vary, but it is probably not much earlier than five and not much later than seven.

Every Monday at school Emily R.'s class has a collection for a different charity. Initially she donated money which her parents gave her. When, at the age of six, she started getting pocket money, her parents told her that if she wanted to support charities, she would now have to do so from her own money. She could not, at first, understand this reasoning. Her parents simply made the point that she did not have to give but that, if she chose to do so, she was now old enough to make that decision on her own. For a year she resisted donating any of her pocket money to charity. Then, when she was seven, she began to understand that the point of giving was to help those who had less than she did. This made sense to her and she began to donate a small amount of her own money voluntarily.

Where money is concerned, it is helpful to allow children to understand the consequences of their own actions, despite the temptation to 'put things right' for them.

At 10 Jerry W. was two years older than his friend Andy P. At Jerry's instigation, they made a five penny bet on who could hit more targets in the shooting alley at a funfair – and shook hands on it. Jerry won and demanded that Andy pay him his five pence. Andy was outraged: he had heard about betting but he did not yet understand that this might mean losing his money. It would have been easy for Andy's mother to put things right by appealing to Jerry or by giving Andy the money herself. Instead, she made Andy hand over his five pence from his pocket money: she felt that it was important that he should learn at first hand what gambling really meant and to accept his responsibility for decisions he made about money.

By the time children are teenagers, they are able to take on more responsibility for their own spending – and to understand the realities of the family's financial circumstances.

When Tessa K. was 14, her father and stepmother gave her a yearly clothes allowance. It was her responsibility to negotiate any advance she wanted or any increase if she felt

63

the amount was not sufficient. Once the amount was set, it was hers by right, and if she spent it all on a single item and couldn't afford new underwear, then she had to live with the consequences of that decision.

Children who no longer live with both their parents are some-times subject to further 'messages' – when money is used as a device by either parent to buy affection, ease their own guilt, or show anger. It is responsible parental behaviour to be aware of these difficulties and to be especially alert to the dangers of imparting mixed messages. Try not to put a 'right' or 'wrong' tag on your different styles but explain that what you do and how you do it is your personal choice.

Summary

There is no right or wrong way with money, but there are choices. These choices need to be made by each of us as we grow up, so as to ensure that our money style is the one that suits us.

THE 5 STEPS

If you want to understand some of the reasons why you manage money in the way you do,

1 Acknowledge where you are – and what you want

How would you describe your own style of dealing with money?
   If you are living with someone, how would you describe theirs?
   If you have children, what messages are they picking up from you?

2 Know the facts – your figures *and* your feelings

How did your parents deal with money?
   Do you feel that the messages which you inherited affect your present day dealings with money? If so, how?

3 Consider the *real* options

When dealing with money, can you identify aspects in your style which appear to limit your options?
   If your income is linked to that of a partner or friend, can you identify the ways in which his or her style either helps or hinders the making of joint decisions? Or have you agreed on a joint approach, and does this work?

4 Make choices – live for today *and* plan for tomorrow

Where money is involved, would you like to change any of your present habits?

5 Do it – and review it

As they grow older, do you ever review the types of expenditure to which you expect your children to contribute from the money you give them?

Further information

Chapter 10 Managing Your Own Money

Workbook Chapter 10 Understanding Childhood Messages

Workbook Chapter 17 Managing Your Own Money

6. Borrowing and Lending – between family and friends

Examine your motives – and get your ground rules clear

There is an old saying about money, 'Never a borrower or a lender be.' Whatever we may feel about this, few of us go through life without, at some point, borrowing money or lending it to a friend or to another member of our family.

At first sight, either act may seem straightforward. Someone asks for a sum of money, usually for a stated purpose. The other person only has to consider whether they have enough money spare to meet the request and, if they have, to produce their chequebook.

If the transaction were between you and your building society or bank, it would be straightforward, and the contract between you would be clear and precise – and legally binding. But when borrowing and lending takes place between people who know each other well and, more particularly, between members of families, the idea of some sort of contract is often acutely embarrassing. Yet the failure to make some ground rules may be a recipe for disaster, or at least for misunderstandings, in your relationship.

Even with a contract, your relationship may become muddled because of the assumptions and expectations that one or both of you have. If you are the lender – are you just being helpful and generous, or are you 'buying' yourself a bit of cooperation, or approval, or forgiveness, or simply some peace and quiet? Or are you just afraid to say 'no'? If you are the borrower, do you actually intend to pay back the money, or are you asking for a loan but planning to treat it as a gift? Does borrowing make you feel somehow inferior to the person whom you have had to ask for the loan, and if so, how will that affect your friendship?

Sorting out money matters among family and friends means being clear about the arrangement into which you are entering and your feelings about the deal. You may not want to *do* anything about your feelings – you do need to acknowledge them.

Money between friends

If you decide to lend money to a friend, you need to consider in advance what you would do if he or she failed to repay the loan. Would you be willing to take a friend to court? Or ask them to put up a collateral? If not, then you have to be prepared for the possibility that it is your friendship that will be the price you have to pay in the event of something going wrong.

> Frances J. was put on the spot when her friend, Lucy K., came to her one day to say that her bank manager had refused to lend her the final £150 which she needed to cover the costs of car hire for a holiday which she had already booked. Lucy promised that if Frances would lend her the money, she would repay her as soon as she got back home and had her next pay cheque. Frances knew that Lucy was desperately in need of a holiday and felt she couldn't really say 'no', even though she knew that lending Lucy the money might cause her some short-term financial inconvenience.
>
> Lucy never mentioned the money again, and the longer this went on the more embarrassed Frances became. She just couldn't believe that anyone would borrow money and not pay it back. She felt that Lucy had betrayed their friendship. Months later, when she desperately needed the money, she wrote to Lucy but never got a reply.

As happens between friends, Frances had never considered what she would or could do if Lucy failed to repay the loan. The possibility of this was never discussed between them. And that is hardly surprising.

Ground rules for borrowing and lending between friends rarely involve a written contract, though there is no reason why that should not be the case. But, depending on the nature and closeness of your relationship, you can, as the lender, at least make it clear when you want the loan repaid, whether instalments are acceptable to you or not – and you need to understand that your friendship may be at risk if you can't get your money back at an agreed point or when you need it. And it is your responsibility to do any chasing up that may be necessary.

If you are the borrower, you too need to be clearly aware of the consequences of what you are doing. If you make a verbal agreement – stick to it. If you run into problems about repayment, make sure that your friend knows about them at the earliest moment. If you don't, the gulf between you, and the embarrassment, may become too great to bridge and you will damage or destroy your relationship. Remember that if you had borrowed from a bank you would have had to repay – or suffer the consequences. Failing to meet your commitments really means that you are trading on goodwill, and exploiting your relationship.

Money and family

Within families, the process of parents lending and children borrowing is inevitably influenced by our own childhood experiences and expectations. When we were young, most of our parents gave us what financial security they could. As we grow up, relationships change. As children achieve independence, the financial links weaken. But often the first people we approach when we need money will be members of our family. Because of our expectations, we may feel that members of our family 'should' give us money, or that they 'must' lend it to us – assumptions that can cloud the issue.

> Sam C. is in a position in which many parents and children find themselves. He owes his parents £8,000 which they advanced to him towards the deposit on his house. 'They lent it to me', he says – but he also admits that he doesn't really intend to pay them back.
>
> Who is at fault here? When challenged, Sam will say, 'If they need it all they have to do is ask.' His parents are of two minds: they feel that it is healthier to regard the money as a loan, but they also feel embarrassed about asking for their money back. After all, he is their son.

How can you respond to requests to borrow money so that you will not damage your relationships? There are several choices. The first is simply to say 'no'. Or you may decide to make it a gift – and make it clear that that is what it is. If you are asked for a loan which you yourself don't really expect to see repaid but which, for the sake of appearances, you call a 'loan', then you are being less than honest. You are almost certainly building ambiguity and perhaps stress into your relationship.

You also have the option of arriving at a clear arrangement between yourselves – a contract, whether verbal or written.

After all, the money for which you are being asked is yours. You have a right and, more probably, an obligation to make clear on what terms you are willing to give. You cannot lend money and complain when it is not repaid if there were no ground rules between you in the first place.

If, as adults, you want to achieve an adult relationship, being clear about the basis of your money transactions is important. A contract will guard you against the uncertainties, and possibly the unhappiness, which can arise when neither party is clear about the rules.

> *When Kathleen P. needed a car her father lent her the money at no interest, but on condition that it should be repaid over an eighteen month period. Dealing with money in a businesslike way has always been the rule in her family.*

But you as the lender, whether you are parent, child, or friend, have the responsibility to follow through on the terms of the contract. This is true with any contract; within families and between friends. The emotional relationship and patterns can make this more difficult, but no less necessary.

> *Stan K. did a deal with his father. Because he himself was too young to borrow from the bank, his father agreed to make the monthly payments on Stan's motorbike, and Stan agreed to reimburse his father. When Stan lost his job his father continued the payments, but Stan didn't.*
> *'My father goes on and on about what I owe him but he doesn't stop making the payments. If he did, I'd find some way of paying the instalments myself – or give up the bike.' Stan knew his father – he would moan but wouldn't act. Neither of them honoured their side of the contract.*

An aspect that complicates money transactions between parents and children is the expectation that 'one day our parents' money will be ours anyway', therefore we are entitled to it as a gift. But changing circumstances and attitudes are ensuring that children can no longer count on inheriting a house and/or some money, even though they may be expecting to do so.

Nowadays more people live longer, stay healthier, and aim at a lifestyle in retirement which comes as near as possible to the standard of life which they enjoyed when they were at work. To achieve this, they may use their assets, including their home, to produce the necessary financial resources. Some parents also prefer to give their children a 'good start' in life. Rather than bequeath money, they will choose to contribute towards their children's further or private education, or towards the deposit on a first home.

As long as we believe that we are entitled to inherit money, or to financial help from our parents, we are not taking full responsibility for our own finances.

> *Justin R. and his wife want to leave London and settle in the country, somewhere where they can run a small business and have a house with some land. Justin's mother is quite well off; he does not see why she cannot just give him some of her money to which he feels 'entitled'. He has never discussed this with his mother, but his expectations are preventing him from taking financial control of his own life, and may eventually seriously damage his relationship with his mother.*

The issue in families is not whether our parents do or do not give us money. What matters is the effect that our assumptions can have on our own life and on our relationships with each other.

Summary

Money transactions among family and friends do not have to end in tears, and often don't. But separating them from other aspects of your relationship may be difficult. Better, therefore, to be honest about the feelings and motives of all concerned, and clear about the practical arrangements, so that relationships may be preserved rather than harmed.

THE 5 STEPS

1 Acknowledge where you are – and what you want

When you give or lend money to someone, do you ever attach strings?

When you accept money from someone, as a gift or a loan, how do you feel?

Do you consider a loan from family members or your partner a debt? or a gift?

2 Know the facts – your figures *and* your feelings

Do you know how much money you are at present lending to others?

Do you know how much money you owe at present to friends or family?

3 Consider the *real* options

Are you able to say 'no' if, when asked, you don't want to lend money – or accept it?

Can you collect monies due to you?

4 Make choices – live for today *and* plan for tomorrow

Do you make 'contracts' when you lend or borrow money?

Are you always clear when a gift is a gift?

5 Do it – and review it

What would you do if you lent money to a friend and they failed to keep to the terms which you had both agreed?

Further information

Workbook Chapter 11 Borrowing and Lending –

making a contract with friends or family

7. Living Together

Share it – in a way that suits you both

People who live together usually share the costs of their domestic and social lives. The issue is not so much money in itself but rather how you deal with it between yourselves.

This chapter is about people who share their domestic lives, whether as friends, as partners or as a married couple. Whether we are men or women is not important. It is the roles we play in our partnership, the different financial contributions we bring to it, and our individual money styles that really matter. Whatever the relationship, the elements of financial good practice are similar. It's just that the closer your physical and emotional relationship, the more layers you may have to work through in order to achieve a healthy financial partnership.

The focus of this chapter is on ways of making the money aspects of your domestic lives healthier, and what you need to do if, at some stage, you decide to split up.

Starting out

Talking about money is, as often as not, a taboo subject. Yet, if you are going to share day-to-day financial responsibilities, the familiar saying, 'prevention is better than cure', truly applies. It is easier to start out with some clear ground rules than to have the bother of clearing up a muddle when things have gone wrong.

In the first throes of enthusiasm about sharing your domestic lives, it can be hard to imagine that anything will ever go wrong. 'We're friends, aren't we?' or 'We love each other; we'll be able to sort things out.' But it is very easy for emotional and financial issues to become tangled up. By being as clear as you can be about financial issues at the start of your life together, you may be helping your friendship or partnership to stay healthy – or, if it comes to that, to end more cleanly.

There are many ways to work out practical arrangements for paying bills, maintaining the house or flat and dealing with joint expenses. Start as you mean to go on. There is no point in agreeing to a system and to assume that things can always be changed when you have been together for a little longer. It is one thing to compromise; it is quite another thing to go against your better judgement. This is both foolish and asking for trouble.

Probably the major decisions you will need to make are how you will share your financial responsibilities and whether each of you will have any personal money of your own.

One way of doing this is to have a joint account for expenses which you have agreed to share and separate accounts for personal spending. If you are earning different amounts of money, you may want to consider contributing equal percentages of your income, rather than equal amounts, to the joint account. Where personal spending is concerned, you may want to pool, and share equally, the money that is left after you have both paid your share into the joint account. Or you may each choose to keep what is left to you, to do with as you please.

Another way is to have a joint account for everything – and if that suits you both, fine. Just be very honest with yourself. Accountants and financial consultants know that in such cases it is not at all unusual for one partner quietly to open another account, for their private use. Most of us need privacy and some financial independence. If that is true for you, your financial arrangements need to reflect this.

It is, of course, not necessary to have a joint account at all.

Cordelia and Gareth A. have been married for 20 years and have never had a joint account. Cordelia says, 'We are agreed about the expenses we share, but we each pay whatever comes up. Then at the end of the month, we compare our expenditures and if they don't balance out, one of us writes a cheque to the other for the difference. We knew from the beginning that our styles of dealing with money were so totally different that if we tried to have a joint account, we'd probably kill each other – or split up quickly.'

Even if one of you is not earning, but giving more time to shared commitments, or is, at present, unemployed, the principle should still be the same – agreed joint expenses, and some spending money for both.

Terry R. quit his teaching job when his daughter was two years old. He and his wife Nancy decided that she could earn more money from her work than he could, and that the time he spent at home would also give him an opportunity to fix up the house they'd just bought. Nancy's salary is their sole income at present and not only supports Terry and their young daughter but also his two teenagers from a previous marriage. Their financial situation is such that each of them feels like an equal partner because they consider themselves a 'corporation'. She says, 'We even talk about The Corporation when we discuss joint family finances and commitments. Then it doesn't feel to me as if I'm earning and he's not, but that together we both do what it takes to run this business we have created.'

These ways of sharing are not the only possibilities – and it may take you some time to work out a way of sharing which makes sense for the two of you.

Sorting out difficulties

Money is often the acid test of a relationship. If you are squabbling about pennies or pounds, you may need to look at what is happening in your relationship. The way in which you handle your financial affairs will often give you some clue to the state of your partnership.

If there are money tensions between you, one of you has got to make the first move. Whether, as a result, your relationship gets better or worse will, in part, depend on your partner's willingness and ability to respond.

Rosie S. did a little part-time work but the main family income came from her husband, Ted. She also looked after their three young children. Although he kept withdrawing money from their joint account for expensive clothes and nights out with the boys, he still took her to task for overspending – on things like food and cleaning materials. When she raised the issue of opening separate accounts for personal money, his response was: 'What do you need that for? It's all our money, isn't it?' And that was the end of the discussion. Rosie is still unhappy but has given up – at least for the time being. 'Right now I don't have the energy for arguments. I'm just waiting until I feel more like tackling him, and clearer about how to do it.'

Difficulties in working out our financial relationships may also arise from the particular, and different, ideas we have about what a partnership should be like and what each person ought to be contributing. Many of our expectations and feelings are still based on the tradition that men and women have had different roles in partnerships – men to earn, and women to stay at home and care for the children.

Attitudes and circumstances have both changed a great deal and domestic partnerships today are seldom as clearcut as they may have been in the past. More women work. More families have a single parent at home. And in two parent families, more partners have previously been married. Any changes in the way in which we live together and work inevitably have financial and personal consequences. But adjusting to change is seldom straightforward. Our feelings often change more slowly than our actions – and what we do, and how we do it, often seesaws between the two.

> *Frank H. had managed to get into quite serious debt with the business he ran. But Tamara H. acknowledged that she was in part responsible for their situation. 'He always had these outrageous schemes for making money, and I wanted to believe that they would work, So I'd encourage him to take out another loan or remortgage the house. You see, there are two sides to me. On the one hand, I want to be independent, earn my own money, do my own thing. On the other hand, I don't want to work, I just want him to take care of me and make lots of money so we can have this wonderful life. So I colluded with all his grand schemes.'*

Money issues often get so confused because we have such tangled feelings about both the money and what we want in our relationship.

> *Philip W. was pleased when his wife, Carole, began sorting herself out financially and asked to share responsibility for their joint monies, of which he had always been in charge. He was less prepared for the fact that sharing financial responsibilities would cause him to lose his total control over the family's financial affairs – and he finds it difficult to come to terms with this. His logical mind tells him that they*

> *are going in the right direction – but his deep-rooted attitudes*
> *are sending him different messages. 'I know my desire*
> *to keep control is wrong – but that doesn't stop me from*
> *sometimes feeling the way I do.'*

Nevertheless, they are likely to be fine, because he really does mean it when he says that he is happy for her to take responsibility for herself. It will just take him a while to work through all the consequences, both practical and emotional.

The best thing we can do in a relationship is to be honest with ourselves and with our own mixed-up feelings. And to understand that our partner is probably just as confused. That sort of awareness, plus some healthy shared financial management, is likely to keep you making progress – together.

All this is well and good, but what if you each want different things? And how do you take into account your children's needs and wishes? It may be possible to have different things – just not all at once. The practical work in *Workbook Chapter 12 Living Together* may help you to see ways of meeting your personal needs while also staying committed to your family.

Starting out – again

It is not unusual these days for at least one party to a new marriage or partnership to have been married before and to be receiving, or paying, support for the children of the previous marriage. This brings a whole new set of tensions to questions of money – and opportunities for resolving them constructively.

Vera M. reflected on the situation that almost wrecked her second marriage. 'Gerry and I had both been married before. I didn't have children, but he had three teenagers. We loved each other so much that it never occurred to me we would have difficulty sorting things out. Of course we shared everything financially; I certainly expected to, since one of the conflicts in my first marriage was that he kept secret everything to do with money.

'Then I found that I started to get upset by the fact that the cost of outings and gifts and extra food for his children came out of our joint account. My resentment almost ruined our marriage. It wasn't so much the money that was the issue, but the fact he seemed to be taking me, or at least my money, for granted. Finally I got up enough courage to

raise this with him. At first we rowed. 'If you don't love my children, then there's no future for us'. But eventually I got the point through to him that it wasn't the children at all, or even the money, but the fact that we hadn't cleared things between us.

Once he was willing to take my feelings seriously, I was happy to compromise. I know that having to pay child support makes things tight for him. Now he contributes a little extra to our joint account and we also have separate accounts for personal spending. I feel that I am back in control of my financial life without having destroyed what we are trying to build between us.'

Vera's story shows how easily financial and emotional issues can become confused. Financial clarity between partners may not immediately lead to greater emotional tranquillity, but it can help to pinpoint issues which are troubling you, and indicate what you might be able to do about them.

Part of our reluctance to get to grips with financial conflicts will be due to an understandable fear that, by bringing such issues into the open, we may at best damage, and at worst break up, a relationship. Then what?

Getting out

What if your marriage or partnership has ceased to be okay – and you know that divorce or separation may be unavoidable? Breaking up a partnership is never easy. Financially speaking, it is seldom totally satisfactory for either partner because the money available is usually not enough to allow both parties to maintain, at an individual level, the standard of living which previously they shared. But if you can get to grips with your financial situation immediately, things may become bearable and reasonable.

The financial situation in separations is more acute when there are children, simply because their financial needs are such an important factor. Couples who have no children may have to contend with other worries. In either case, there are decisions to be made. Who gets the house? Who gets the children? What about the possessions which you bought together in happier days?

Sorting these things out is difficult. How difficult will depend on whether you want to make the separation and the eventual settlement amicable or not. So decide first how you want to play it. What advice do you want? Do you want to know how to hold your ground? How to be fair or generous or ruthless? And be honest when you answer. When it comes to financial settlements and divorce proceedings the people who advise you, such as your solicitor and financial consultant, will take their cue from you. So give them a clear lead. *Workbook Chapter 13 Splitting Up* takes you through the practical steps you need to take in order to get the best deal for yourself – and decide on the kind of deal you want to offer to the other person.

If neither you nor your ex-partner is clear about the kind of financial settlement you want, the natural tendency of financial and legal professionals is to opt for confrontation in divorce or separation proceedings – rather than resolution. If you can, sort out your feelings and decide on the kind of relationship which you hope to have with your ex-partner, the children (if any) and possibly other members of the family – before starting the legal process. If you find this too difficult, a consultation with a counsellor may help. The address of RELATE (formerly the Marriage Guidance Council) is listed in *Resources for readers*.

Summary

If you are living together and sharing financial responsibilities, it is quite likely that, at some point, you will encounter difficulties which hinge around money. The issue is not whether this will happen, but how you will handle it when it does.

THE 5 STEPS

1 Acknowledge where you are – and what you want

What do you share?

How did you decide on these arrangements?

What agreements, if any, did you make about sharing the financial costs?

Do you ever lie to your partner about your earnings, or about what you do with your money?

Do you have conflicts that are, at least superficially, concerned with money?

How would you describe your money style? Your partner's?

2 Know the facts – your figures *and* your feelings

What percentage of your earnings do each of you contribute to a common pot?

Who pays for what?

Which expenses do you regard as shared expenses, and which as personal ones? Does your partner agree?

3 Consider the *real* options

Would you like to share joint financial responsibilities differently?

Do you feel you know enough about your joint finances?

4 Make choices – live for today *and* plan for tomorrow

Would you rather not confront your partner right now about difficulties you are having in dealing with your joint financial affairs? If so, why not?

If you feel that the only way forward is to live apart, how do you plan to sort this out?

5 Do it – and review it

Can you talk with your partner about making changes to your financial arrangements?

Do you make time to talk things through when there is a change in you or your partner's circumstances?

Further information

Workbook Chapter 12 Living Together

Workbook Chapter 13 Splitting Up

Resources for readers

8. Managing by Yourself
Deal with your attitude as well as your finances

At some point in our lives, most of us will live alone and/ or manage our finances by ourselves. We may be on our own by choice or through the death of a partner or by divorce or separation. You may in fact not be strictly on your own at all but sharing your home with your children. If you are the only adult in your household with responsibility for day-to-day financial matters, then the general points in this chapter may be relevant to you.

Although individually each of us is ultimately responsible for our money, friends or couples sharing will usually have more joint resources to run a household, and greater combined financial reserves in cases of crises. It can be true that two can live more cheaply than one.

If you are managing on your own, there is usually no one to bail you out, no one on whom you can immediately rely for help. It also becomes easier to let your financial affairs drift, and to avoid facing up to this. Yet it is precisely because there is no one else around to come to your rescue that you should be particularly accurate with the figures.

Your attitudes towards being on your own will have a major effect on the way in which you deal with your money.

Managing your attitudes

There are several ways of looking at life on your own. One is 'I'm so glad that I don't have to bother about anybody else's whims, wants or needs!' Another is 'Isn't it awful that I have no one else with whom to share my burdens.' For those with children, it is often, 'I'm glad the fights have stopped, but I don't know how I'm going to manage financially.'

Whichever response reflects your attitude, the end result is still that it is you, and you alone, who has total responsibility for your financial situation. There is no one else – at home – to share the burden. And, depending on your attitude, that is tough or exhilarating or sometimes both.

When you are on your own it is easy to refuse to do anything about getting your financial affairs in order. No one is looking over your shoulder and it is easy to think that what you do or do not do does not really affect other people. So why bother? If you can honestly say to yourself that you are managing your finances well, fine. Otherwise, it is important to sort them out. Not taking responsibility for your finances may block many other aspects of your life. If you can see that your situation is a mess, it may mean that you are not happy about it. For instance, if your bank account is overdrawn and your income does not cover your outgoings, you alone must choose between sorting this out or sinking further into debt: there is no one else to help.

Or is there? Some of us have parents to whom we can turn if we need 'a bit of a loan' or friends who will tide us over. The question to ask yourself is whether asking for their help is just a way to avoid taking control of your own financial life.

Some people prefer to live on their own. Others see it as a temporary state from which they long to be rescued. They often finish statements about their financial problems with 'Unless of course I get married . . .' or 'This might change if . . .' – whether or not they are currently in a relationship. There is nothing at all wrong with wanting to share your life with a partner: the problem is in using that expectation as an excuse for not sorting out your finances, and perhaps other aspects of being on your own.

Edward B. is single and earning good money – and longing to be in a partnership. He does take care of his material and financial needs, but neglects himself physically and emotionally. He has been caught in the 'if only . . .' syndrome and, as a result, has been accumulating both money and unhappiness. He spends most of his time at work and this limits the opportunities for meeting people. Besides, he feels unattractive – and looks unattractive. Recently Edward took a good look at himself – and neither liked what he saw nor how he felt. He knows he is extremely fortunate to enjoy the income he does, and has belatedly decided that he deserves more of its benefits. He is now spending both more money and time on himself: he has joined a gym, is buying clothes that he likes and is generally enjoying life more. The 'if only . . .' hope will never go away, but he is now a lot happier with himself – and, incidentally, more likely to be able to have a relationship when the opportunity comes his way.

Starting out on your own

When starting out on your own, whether it is your first job after school or your first home of your own, it is usually your family to which you will turn for the financial advice you need – about banking, borrowing and finding accommodation. Remember, however, that their method of dealing with their finances may not suit you. Take on board the information they give you, but do speak to others as well, such as a bank manager or a friend who is managing comfortably already.

Adjusting to death, divorce or separation

The financial situation which faces you when your partner dies or you are separated or divorced depends a great deal on how you shared your money management while you were together.

Because bereavement or separation usually brings in its wake deep emotional trauma, you need to buy yourself time for reflection, at least six months if at all possible. If you have children, you will also need time to take account of their emotional needs, particularly during the early period.

Ideally you should involve yourself in only two pieces of financial business during that first stressful period: find yourself a financial consultant whom you trust, and make sure that you know all the facts of your financial position. If you handed over control of your financial affairs to a partner, it may come as a huge shock to find how ignorant of the facts you are.

Two chapters offer more detailed advice about what to do financially during this period: *Chapter 9 Looking at Death*, and *Workbook Chapter 16 Managing after the Death of Your Partner*. Some of the information will also be relevant to those of you who are experiencing divorce or separation.

There are always people around who know what is best for you when you are on your own, and even more so when you are experiencing loss. In fact, what is best for you at this stage is to have time for your feelings to settle down before considering the financial implications. During these first months on your own, what is best for your money is a safe secure haven. This may not always be possible, if you do not have any extra financial resources or if, in the case of divorce, you are now having to manage with less than you did before. Nevertheless, the basic principle is to put off making major financial decisions, if at all possible, until you feel emotionally ready to do so – or until you are forced to do so financially.

And don't forget to treat yourself!

When her divorce came through, Carole S. took her credit card and went out shopping. When she saw a dress she particularly liked, she said, 'I'll have both the green one and the blue one, and those shoes and that bag to match.' She ended up spending the next year paying it all off, but 'it felt good – and did me good.' So that was fine. It was worth it to Carole, at a time when she had been feeling neither cared for nor glamorous.

To have treats without jeopardizing your future financially, you need to know your total income – and then to set aside a sum which you will feel comfortable about spending.

If you have children, you may want to set aside a sum for special things for them too, while being careful not to overdo things.

Frank T. and his partner had separated, and the two children had stayed with him. He says, 'I found myself buying them things because I felt guilty that they didn't have their mother around and I also felt guilty because I wasn't around more. I felt guilty that maybe I was not taking care of them as I should.' Finally it was one of the children who said to him, 'Look, dad, we love you even if you don't take us out for a hamburger every night.'

The time will come when you will find that the initial trauma has lessened and you are ready to start on the next stage of life on your own. That is the time when it is important to look at your goals and resources and decide how to tackle your new life. For that is what it is, whether you wanted it or not.

Living alone as you get older

As you get older you could have the choice of living on your own, living with members of your family or moving into residential accommodation, provided that you have done some financial planning. If you have not done so, you might find that you will not have the luxury of these options but may have to take whatever is affordable, even though it may not suit you at all.

With financial planning, you will be able to choose between paying for help in your own home, or paying your own way within your family, or selecting a retirement home of the quality that suits you. Your choices will depend both on what you want and what you can afford.

> *Edna H. lives on her own in council property and feels increasingly vulnerable. She is now 75 and would like to move into a particular residential home. It is in a nice area and she has friends there, but it is expensive. She has money but is terrified of spending it. Her worst fear is that she will outlive her money – and what will she do then? Where would she live? For a long time she has had some of her money in a building society account and the rest lying around her flat in cash. Recently, however, she has taken steps to increase her capital by investing part of it. But she resolutely refuses to spend any of the income which this investment is giving her. When she was younger she never quite got around to putting money into a pension scheme, or to investing it in a way which could provide her with an income as she got older. Now she only has her capital. She is unhappy with her present life and frightened about what the future may hold.*

For Edna the issues lie as much in her attitude as in her finances. She is right to be concerned about what would happen to her if she outlived her resources. That is a possibility. She has had a great deal of financial advice about the options which are open to her. But her unhappiness and fear are preventing her from living as best as she can for the present, and planning for a more congenial future. And only she can deal with her attitude.

Even if you do have family, be aware that as you get older your family's feelings about your choices will change. Many children, while not looking forward to their parents' deaths, are aware of the possible financial gains for themselves. Advice to parents is often influenced by their own mixed feelings. As one son said, when his widowed mother started to take holidays which she had never been able to have when his father was alive, 'It's nice that she's enjoying herself, but don't you think she's being a bit extravagant? With each trip I see our inheritance dwindling.' Remember – the one thing of which you can be sure is that it is you who will serve your own interests best. Be clear in your mind what these are.

Getting help

If you are managing your financial affairs on your own, you may be in greater need of help from people such as financial consultants, bank managers, accountants and solicitors. They are important supports, especially during times of stress. One difficulty is that they can also tend to think that they know what is best for the client, particularly if she is a woman and more so if she is older. Many people find, as they get older, that professional advisers rarely listen to what they tell them. Instead, advisers operate on the basis of what they think is right for your money, without necessarily taking into consideration the most important factor – your needs and wishes. Children who have ageing parents sometimes fall into the same habit.

> *Dorothy T. is now 94 and is determined to stay in control of her life for as long as she can. Her sight is going, she cannot walk far – but her mind is still sharp. She has found that it takes considerable vigilance to remain in control as even loving family and friends seem to equate old age with increasing incompetence. She knows that she now needs more help with the practical management of her finances, but refuses to give up her chequebook or her right to make decisions about what to do with her money. A template from a charity for the blind allows her to continue signing her own cheques despite her failing sight. She says, 'I have found that the art of growing older is to adjust to new circumstances and decreasing physical capabilities without simply giving up.'*

Summary

If you are managing financially by yourself, you must be much more precise with your figures, because, in all probability, there will be nobody else to support you, or to bail you out if you go wrong. Only you can work out what you will need to do to organize your life in order to meet your wants and needs.

As you get older, you may find that practical financial details become a bit overwhelming and that you need practical help from your children and/or professionals in order to manage. Even then, you are most likely to get the kind of life you want by accepting that, whatever the help, it is still *your* money and *your* responsibility.

THE 5 STEPS

1 Acknowledge where you are – and what you want

How do you feel about living on your own?
Are you in control of your finances?
Do you live on your earnings, or does anyone else contribute to your income?

2 Know the facts – your figures *and* your feelings

Do you know the precise details of your financial situation?
Do you have any money in reserve for emergencies?

3 Consider the *real* options

Considering both how you live and how you want to live in the future – what kinds of things do you need to do to move in the direction in which you want to go?
If you have children, how do you plan to provide for their changing financial needs?

4 Make choices – live for today *and* plan for tomorrow

If your earnings are your only income, are there any changes you want to make to ensure that you are managing your finances effectively, for the present and for the future?

5 Do it – and review it

Do you get professional help in dealing with financial issues?
Do you have someone you trust with whom you can talk over money matters?

Further information

Chapter 9 Looking At Death

Workbook Chapter 16 Managing After the Death of Your Partner

Workbook Chapter 14 Managing On Your Own

9. Looking at Death

Prepare for your death to help those whom you leave behind

To quote Benjamin Franklin, 'In this world nothing can be said to be certain, except death and taxes.' And most of us would rather deal with taxes than death.

We will all die sometime. The point of preparing for your own death is to lighten the financial burden for those whom you have left behind at a time when they will feel especially vulnerable. Dealing with death financially really means facing up to your feelings about, and relationships with, people who matter to you now; and making the legal and financial arrangements that will affect them when you die.

The idea of death itself is sometimes less threatening than the fear of a lingering death. You might, therefore, want to consider ways of conveying your wishes should you find yourself in that situation.

Making a Will

Making a Will is the only way of exercising choice about money, belongings, and relationships after death. Wills are about confronting your feelings about people today, which is one reason why many of us do not like making a Will.

You cannot know the reactions of friends and family to the decisions you have made in your Will – should you decide to tell them. You can, by careful planning, leave as few opportunities as possible for the shabbiness that sometimes intrudes into the grief that follows a death. Doing things properly need be neither time-consuming nor costly, and while it may not be enjoyable, it can be illuminating.

The details of making a Will are mentioned in *Workbook Chapter 15 Making a Will*. But the Will itself is actually the last part of what is a lengthy, often unsettling and demanding process. You will need to identify your assets, decide who will – and who won't – inherit from you, actually make the Will, and inform your executors where you have placed it. And finally, you will need to decide what – or whether – you will tell your friends and family about its contents.

Deciding about your assets. Before you can make your Will, you will need to identify all assets, those primarily of monetary value, such as your house or car, and those to which you attach personal value, such as your photograph albums or your favourite jewellery. When you have that information, you will need to turn to the trickier task of deciding among whom you want – and don't want – to divide your belongings.

Unless you are going to abdicate responsibility for deciding what happens to your assets, you will have to confront your feelings about people and what do to about them in your Will. In general, we do not feel the same about everyone in our lives, be they family or friends. If you feel that you *should* give someone money or belongings, regardless of what you are feeling about them at present, ask yourself why? It might be because, 'it makes me feel better to be fair' or 'I can't bear the thought of causing anyone hurt after I die.' Fine. Or you may decide, 'Yes, she's family, but we've never got on, so why start pretending now. I don't want her to have anything and that's how I feel.' That's fine, too.

> Len M. admits that he came to the task of making his Will most reluctantly and only after his partner refused to fly on holiday with him until he did. 'Then I found that I really enjoyed deciding which of my family and friends and godchildren I'd like to benefit from what I've accumulated. My partner has no need of my computer equipment, but I have a friend who would really appreciate having it. The trickiest thing I found was deciding what to do about my sister. I get on with her very well and I've never made a secret of the fact that I don't like her husband. I don't want him to be able to touch a penny of my money, but I didn't want to cut her out. Finally I decided to leave her my fancy car, which she has always loved, and some money earmarked for its running and maintenance costs. And I also left her all my premium bonds.'

What is important is that you are honest about your feelings. Then it is up to you to do what you want to do.

Which of your possessions should go to whom may seem obvious. Hasn't your sister always admired that ring, or your best friend your wardrobe of clothes? But are you really sure that you know that this is what they would most like? Or might they have commented so enthusiastically just to please you? It may be best to ask. One mother had her children choose the furniture which they would like to have while she was still alive and then taped their names to the bottom of each piece.

Remember that your money does not only have to go to people. Have you thought about giving to causes or places which are important to you? Many charities and other causes depend for their survival on the bequests made to them.

Making provision for your children (under the age of majority). Most people find making a Will difficult enough in itself, but thinking about what should happen to their children is even more difficult. Yet without provision for your children's care written into your Will, you may have no say in who takes care of them should both of you die, either simultaneously or within a certain period of time.

It may be helpful – though painful – to imagine the situation on the day when both you and your partner have died suddenly. Climb onto on a cloud and look down on what you have left behind. How are your children? Is someone whom you can trust taking care of them? Do you feel relief that at least financially things are in order? Or are you distressed at the mess which you have left behind?

You may be clear about whom you would trust most – or least – with your children, but if you do not make the necessary legal arrangements to name them as guardians, members of your family whom the children may not know, or like, could have first, and often competing, claims. You also need to choose Trustees, who may or may not be the same persons as the Guardians, in order to oversee the financial interests of your children until they reach the age of majority.

It can seem obvious that any parent would want to make sure their children's interests were protected, but even as you read this chapter, do you find that you are still reluctant to act? Are you still convinced that nothing untoward will ever happen simultaneously to you and your partner – or can you simply not bear to think about this?

Nathan H. and Molly T. had been divorced for some years. They had made generous financial provision in both their Wills for Susan, their mentally handicapped daughter, who was still a teenager. What they could not bring themselves to do was to talk about guardians and trustees. It was only after the sudden death of friends who had young children that things changed. As Molly said, 'They left three young children. Because they travelled a lot, they had made a Will, and the friend they'd asked to be guardian was able to move into their home straight away. I saw what a difference it made to the children. It was then that I realized how selfish Susan's father and I were being. After that it took us about five minutes to agree on guardians and trustees.'

Planning your own funeral and deciding what happens to your body. If you have strong feelings about the kind of funeral you would like to have, and whether you prefer to be buried or cremated, your Will is also the appropriate place in which to state your wishes and to make financial provision for these to be carried out. Funerals cost money – and people seldom realize how much.

Joe S. wrote into his Will that he wanted his valuable cello to be sold immediately after his death so that his sons, whom he had named as executors, would have the necessary cash to deal with any immediate expenses. 'Although I know they could manage financially, I've never wanted to be a financial burden on them or their families, and making this provision has left me feeling much better about this.'

Do you want parts of your body to be of use to others on your death? If so, you need to have signed a donor card, carry the original with you always, and give copies to those who are most likely to be notified first in case you are critically injured or die – and state this in your Will. Or is it just as important to you that *no* parts of your body are used on your death? State this in your Will but also inform your next of kin.

Deciding what to tell your family. Many people feel that their families have a right to know what is in a Will. Take a deep breath and think again before you do anything about this.

> *Joanna R. has two daughters, both in their thirties. She thought they were mature enough to discuss what she had put in her Will. She discovered that that was not true at all. 'When I tried to tell them that, because of their different circumstances, I was leaving them different amounts of money, Nesta was outraged. She is quite well off, which is why I wasn't worried about her financially. What I had not taken into account was that she had always felt herself to be the less favoured. The idea of her getting less just confirmed in her mind that I loved her less. Gloria is running her own business on a shoestring and I would love to be able to give her some extra help to make a go of it.*
>
> *At first I could not stand the tensions and decided to change my Will. But after a week's reflection, I knew that I wanted to stick to what I had decided in the first place. The Will represents my money and my feelings. What I have done is to write each of them a letter, to be left with my Will, so that they should know that I loved them both equally, and why I made the decisions I did.'*

The decisions you make in your Will are you own, but if you do decide to tell your family of your provisions, be prepared to deal with their reactions.

Knowing that there is an inheritance can alter young people's ways of living. If you want them to make their own way in life, it may be unwise to let them know too much too soon about future inheritances. Some parents, for example, make it a condition that their children will not inherit any money until they are 25, except in an emergency, and state this in their Will.

Selecting and informing your executors. In addition to deciding on money and possessions, you will also need to name executors – persons who will undertake to make all the necessary arrangements connected with your Will after your death. It is easiest – and cheapest – to name friends and/or partners or other family members to be the executors. You may want to name your solicitor instead of, or in addition to, a family member or a friend, although it will then cost your estate money to pay the solicitor's fees. If you know that there is conflict in the family and/or that your estate is complicated, a solicitor's involvement may be helpful. Don't forget to ask those whom you would like to act as executors if they are willing to do so, and also to tell them where your Will is kept.

When you die, those closest to you will need to make many quick decisions about arrangements. If you have made a Will, it will help them if they know who the executors are and where your original Will is kept. The more you can leave things in order, the easier it will be for them.

Reviewing your Will regularly. Your feelings about family and friends will change over the years, your circumstances will alter, and your money and belongings will grow or diminish. A Will can be reviewed when some major change occurs in your life, or as often as you want. For instance, if you marry or remarry, any previous Will you have made is no longer valid.

Making, and later changing, your Will may sound expensive, but it need not be. The majority of us have straightforward estates: using a Will Form, which is available from many stationers, is both adequate and legal. If your situation is more complex – if you have remarried or if you have children who are minors – get the help of a solicitor even though it will cost you money. It will buy you peace of mind and make things easier for your family.

What if you face a lingering death?

Most of us hope for an 'easy death' – going quietly in the night. But what if this isn't the way for you? What if you fall ill or become senile and cannot manage your affairs? What then? There are several things you can do, some of which hold force under the law, some of which are simply statements of intent.

If you become unable to manage your own affairs, you can give Power of Attorney to another person who will then be able to decide what to do with your money, and when it is time for you to go into a hospital or home. (See *Chapter 12: Getting Professional Assistance*, for further information about Power of Attorney.)

Joanne T. did not just give Power of Attorney to her only child, John, but also to her solicitor, Janet F. 'I remember how bad John's father was in dealing with his sister's illness before she died, and I feel that a lot of men don't cope very well with age and illness. So in addition to Janet's legal

*expertise, I simply feel more comfortable knowing that a
woman is sharing this responsibility.'*

Ageing and illness can be upsetting and disruptive to those
nearest to us. So think about your situation carefully. Who do
you feel would be most trustworthy should you no longer be
able to manage for yourself? If they do not have the necessary
legal skills it would probably be wise also to involve someone
who has.

Many people are afraid of being kept alive technologically
beyond a certain point. A 'Living Will', or 'Advance Declaration', is an increasingly acceptable way of indicating how
you want to be treated if you become senile or terminally ill
or injured, and whether you want to be kept alive artificially
and, if so, for how long. It is a document which you can sign,
stating when you would like all but the most basic support to
be withdrawn. You then give this to your executors, your family
and your family doctor. Although a Living Will does not carry
clear weight in a court of law, it will give those who are entrusted
with your care at that time a clear indication of what your wishes
were when you were able to make a choice. This information may
at least help them to respect your interests at a time when they
are being forced to take difficult decisions.

> *Aileen H. and her sister-in-law Rosa S. had both made
> 'Living Wills' because they were anxious not to be kept
> alive artificially in circumstances in which their quality of
> life could no longer improve. Rosa became increasing senile
> and Aileen had to place her in a home. By the time she
> contracted pneumonia, she was also suffering from kidney
> failure and no longer recognized her family. The home, in
> which she had been happy and well cared for, wanted to
> treat her to get her 'well', but Aileen was insistent that her
> sister-in-law's wishes should be respected and that she be
> allowed to die a dignified death. 'I could not have argued
> with the doctors, who all cared a great deal for Rosa, if I
> had not known her wishes with certainty and if she had not
> written them down.' Finally Rosa was moved to a hospice
> where she was able to die with her pain under control and in
> surroundings which brought dignity to the end of her life.*

The 'Living Will' is a separate document to the legal Will which
provides for the disposal of your assets. Information about where

to obtain copies of the 'Living Will' form is in *Resources for readers*.

Dealing with the death of someone close to you

The death of someone who has been close to you and with whom you have shared your day-to-day – and financial – life, will leave you with the task of handling the immediate arrangements for their funeral and associated details. No one can relieve your physical and emotional pain. But knowing that your partner has left a Will which states his or her wishes, and which makes financial provision for all those immediate arrangements, can make the initial tasks facing you easier to bear.

There are many expenses connected with someone's death, burial or cremation, and it is the responsibility of the deceased's estate to bear those expenses, provided that the necessary resources are available. Usually the last thing that you yourself will be thinking about will be the retention of receipts for all expenses incurred. Nevertheless, you must do so. It is not callous to do so; it is dealing with finances sensibly and will help prevent misunderstandings at a time when you and those around you are under particular pressure.

In addition to dealing with all the immediate arrangements, you will also have to cope with the emotional and physical shock of living on your own, and managing financially. When you are in this situation, there are some practical financial steps you need to take, at a time when you will least feel like doing so. These issues are discussed in *Chapter 8: Managing By Yourself*, and the practical steps are spelled out in more detail in *Workbook Chapter 16 Managing after the Death of Your Partner*.

Dealing with those who refuse to deal with death

What if your nearest and dearest refuses to deal with any of these matters, doesn't make any financial or legal arrangements, or won't even discuss the issue with you? You know that this attitude will leave you in a mess when she or he dies. What can you do if the only response you ever get is, 'Why are you being so morbid, always thinking about death?'

Being prepared for death is not being morbid; it is about leaving no muddle and less pain for those who are left behind. But what if you cannot get this across? The fact of the matter is that you cannot actually *make* anyone else *do* anything until they themselves are ready for it. What you *can* do is to deal with your own side of things, over which you *do* have control – your figures and your feelings.

> *Simone P. was concerned about the way she and her husband would be buried. But he refused to talk about it. Despite this, she called together their three adult children, hoping that this might induce him to join in a discussion. But he stayed away. The discussion made it clear that two of their children could not handle the prospect of cremation. So Simone purchased two plots in a cemetery of her choice, under some lovely trees. 'I feel comforted by the knowledge that when either of us dies, the other one won't have to make a quick decision about this – and if I go first, I hope he'll then appreciate my foresight!'*

Summary

The more you and your partner know about your joint financial arrangements and share responsibility for these while you are alive, the better prepared you will be to manage the practical arrangements when one of you dies.

But because death is such a difficult thing for most of us to handle emotionally, preparing the legal and financial arrangements also becomes difficult. Whatever your own situation, do not let someone else's reluctance to act be an excuse for failing to put your own affairs in order. It is true that 'you can't take it with you', but you can say what is to happen to everything you leave behind.

THE 5 STEPS

1 Acknowledge where you are – and what you want

Have you made a Will? If not, why not?

If you have children under the age of majority, have you arranged for guardians in case you and your partner die simultaneously or within a short time of each other?

Do you know what to do and how to manage financially if the person with whom you share your life dies? Have they made a Will?

Do you know or care what kind of funeral you have and how you are buried?

2 Know the facts – your figures *and* your feelings

What assets do you have?

3 Consider the *real* options

To whom do you want to leave something?

Is there anyone, right now, to whom you definitely do not want to leave anything?

4 Make choices – live for today *and* plan for tomorrow

How can you best make your Will so that it acknowledges your present relationships?

5 Do it – and review it

If you have already made a Will, when did you last review it?

Have any of your circumstances or relationships changed?

Further information

Workbook Chapter 15 Making a Will

Chapter 8 Managing by Yourself

Workbook Chapter 16 Managing After the Death of Your Partner

The Practical Guide to Taxes and Tax Returns

III Pinning Yourself Down

Sort it out – practically

Introduction

Understanding your attitudes toward money is of limited use unless you can also find practical ways of managing your finances which suit your particular money style.

Although the message throughout this book has been that there are no hard and fast ways of dealing with money, most financial professionals would not agree. The financial world has some very traditional and blinkered ideas about the right way of dealing with money. Financial professionals also use a great deal of jargon which can be sufficiently intimidating to persuade you to accept their ideas – or to make you feel hopelessly inadequate if you don't.

The aim of this section is to help you to increase your competence and confidence in your own money management, so that you will be able to work in partnership with the financial professionals when you need their help – and to remain in control.

Managing Your Own Money helps you to design a system for your own financial management and gives you the basic ingredients which need to be included in this system, whatever your personal style.

Dealing with Debt faces the fact that debt is a state of mind, and offers practical ways of dealing with both your debts and your attitudes.

There is no way of avoiding the financial professionals unless you keep your money under your mattress. You have to find the right person to give you the particular help that you need – while still retaining responsibility for, and control over, your financial affairs. *Getting Professional Assistance* describes the roles of different financial professionals and offers guidelines on ways of using them appropriately and effectively.

Once you have worked out a way of managing your finances

which suits you, you have to keep at it and be prepared to review it – for the rest of your life. *Maintaining Your Progress* suggests ways in which you can do this.

What all these subjects have in common is the fact that *the buck stops here* – with you – and that taking full control of your financial choices also means taking full responsibility for your attitudes.

10. Managing Your Own Money

Develop a system that works for you

The idea of keeping your money in tins on the mantelpiece is usually good for a laugh – but do you *really* know how to organize things differently?

Few of us were taught how to manage our money. And if we were, it was probably in ways which did not quite suit us. Traditional ways of organizing and dealing with financial matters are not always right for the majority of people. Yet, instead of questioning tradition, we are usually made to feel that, if we don't 'get it right', something is wrong with us.

Many people, for instance, were raised on the principle, 'only buy what you can pay for in cash.' Yet this is not always the most practical or financially advantageous way of going about things. Today we need to look at a range of possibilities – credit cards, loans, hire purchase, paying cash – before deciding which form of financial management suits us best.

There are many ways of 'getting it right'. What will work best is what you custom design to suit yourself. When you design a system of your own, it not only has to be efficient: you also have to understand it.

Your system needs to make it possible for you to undertake the basic tasks of the financial year efficiently:

- paying bills as they become due
- keeping control over your spending
- making an informed decision before borrowing
- filling out a tax return once a year if one is sent to you and, if you are self-employed, completing your profit and loss accounts
- making decisions about major expenditure
- saving, whether pennies or pounds.

Whatever system you set up needs to include a method for filing relevant correspondence and records, for keeping

up-to-date with your bills, and for giving yourself time to deal
with these.

You will need to allow time to make adjustments while you try
out alternatives. Needs change, financial circumstances change,
relationships with money change. You will only get it right by
trying out different ways of dealing with your money, seeing
what works for you, and then 'fine tuning' your approach.

Look for the key which can not only transform your relationship to money management but which will also be your way of
unlocking that area of money management which is giving you
most trouble.

*For Connie J. a turning point came when she confirmed
that, despite criticism from others, she was in fact managing
her money well enough but in her own way, and had, in
fact, been doing so for years.*

*'I am an absolute idiot with money, and my husband, his
accountant and the bank manager have always told me I
was wrong – and hopeless.'*

*She could never stick to a budget which told her how
much she had to spend each month; she never even took
it seriously. She would go for months buying nothing at
all beyond basic necessities, then hit a patch where she
suddenly spent a great deal. Not a binge, but simply a
way of catching up on things she had neglected to replace,
or on treats she had denied herself for a while. Of course
her monthly accounts never balanced in a way which her
husband found acceptable. Yet, she was never in debt
because, over a period of six months, her figures always
balanced. Somehow she had an internal calculator that kept
her accounts.*

*This meant that her money management was a bit fuzzier
around the edges than most financial professionals would
have liked. Eventually she thought that maybe she should
be doing things a different way. But luckily the financial
consultant to whom she had been introduced, recognized
that what Connie was doing was not wrong, as long as she
stayed out of debt. Recognition of the fact that her style was
different, not wrong, has given Connie more confidence in
herself and a greater sense of being in control of her finances.
Admittedly, she would like to be a bit tidier: 'I know that
we need to manage our joint money in a way that is more*

comfortable for both of us. But now that I no longer feel I'm hopeless, it's easier for me to meet my husband halfway.'

This is not a recommendation for keeping your books in your head, unless you know that that is truly the way which works best for you! But it is a reminder that you first need to find out what is the right way for you, and not be too influenced by what others think you ought to be doing.

For Frank W. the turning point was a much more practical one. He worked for himself and was sloppy about keeping receipts. He suspected that, during the first four years of his business, he had probably 'given away' hundreds of pounds to the taxman through not keeping accurate records. But he travelled a lot and just couldn't be bothered to collect and sort out receipts. Then he discovered that he could get some pages for his Filofax on which to record his daily outgoings. And an envelope in which to keep the receipts. This meant that more receipts for parking and snacks on the trains got noted – all those little things that would have slipped his mind by the time he got around to writing up his accounts. At the end of the year he now has the necessary raw materials – his receipts and a record of his spending – to enable him to produce his accounts without 'giving away' money to the Inland Revenue.

The key for you may be in your attitude, as in the case of Connie, or in finding a practical aid to money management, as in the case of Frank. Look honestly at what trips you up when, and if, you are trying to get your financial affairs into some sort of order. The answer may come from talking to friends about their experiences, or while browsing through a stationers to see what is available to make money management easier.

A method of keeping relevant records and correspondence

'Doing your own thing' is important. But do not mistake style for content. Whatever your style, you need to keep the following information in order if you want to have the figures to be in control of your finances – and have the necessary evidence in case of a dispute:

- bank statements and correspondence

- records of the bills you pay and copies of all letters you send when dealing with your affairs
- information for the Inland Revenue: a copy of your tax returns, your P60 and pay slips for the current year
- mortgage information and correspondence
- copies of all insurance and assurance policy documents and of all correspondence
- your credit card statements and correspondence
- If you are self employed, information for your accountant
- any other information that is relevant to your circumstances: when in doubt, save it.

In general, it is most efficient to make a file for each of the above items and to keep your filing up-to-date. You are likely to find it easier – and quicker – to trace information when you need it; but only if this method suits you. If you have never been able to get on with files and filing systems and have always tossed anything that looked relevant into a drawer, that's fine too. The baseline is that you need to save that information – somehow. It may take you a bit longer to locate the papers you need if you keep them in a drawer, but that doesn't matter – as long as they are there.

A way of keeping up to date with bills

In order not to overlook bills when they are due and to ensure that you have enough money to pay them, you need to find a way of keeping track of both. This is also trial and error territory. One person's 'bills pending' file is another person's black hole.

> 'I have tried a dozen ways of keeping track of bills and I've learned one thing – if I put them away, in a drawer or a file or even into one of those fancy racks, I forget all about them till the warning letters come,' Jill R. said. 'Now I write the cheque immediately and put it in an envelope on which I write the date on which I am going to post it – the date by which I know there will be money in the bank to cover it.'

You can deal with your regular bills in a variety of ways. Some of them can be paid yearly, half-yearly, or monthly. If you have enough money to pay a yearly bill when it comes and you prefer to do that, fine. But if you do not have that much money available at any one time, or if you have a tendency to get into debt, then it is crucial to work out a regular, monthly system for paying bills.

> *Rachel S. found that her money problems were 'a spectre draining my energy'. 'I had this terrible fear of getting any letters because one was bound to be a bill and I couldn't face it. The biggest change in my life came when I was taught to put a fixed amount straight from my salary into a separate bank account for bills. Although I still say, "Oh bloody hell, the phone bill," my fear of facing the letter box has gone.'*
>
> *All Rachel's regular bills are now paid by standing order from her second account for which she declined a chequebook, so as to avoid the temptation of withdrawing money for some other purpose. She found this was cheaper than the bank's Budget Account system for which she would have been charged. Now she simply has two current accounts, one used exclusively for her bills and one for everything else. This works perfectly for her.*

Dealing with your bills includes checking their accuracy before you pay them: look at the way the total has been made up and phone to ask if you are in any doubt about the sum. Never assume the total is correct. There is a great deal of credit card fraud and human and computer error: you are more likely to protect yourself from it by catching any mistakes early and then writing or phoning immediately to sort them out.

Making time to deal with your money

Managing your money is no different from managing your car or your wardrobe: things will be fine for a while, then you'll need to take stock and decide what needs to be done. Whether you use a shoe box or a filing cabinet, you cannot be in control of your financial system if you don't keep it up to date – and review it regularly.

When trying to figure out the best time to do this, keep in mind that the longer you let things go, the longer it will take you to sort them out.

There are many options for how and when to make the necessary time. If you are convinced that you 'simply don't have the time', you need to be honest with yourself about why that is. If you don't know the answer, it may help you to keep a time diary for several weeks. How to do this is described in detail in *Workbook Chapter 4 Being Self-Employed*.

> *Sarah H. admitted that she never found time because she had such a block about dealing with money anyway. Of course she was busy, but she found time for other things she wanted to do, didn't she? 'I used to lie to my accountant that I'd never received his letters. I built up all this money stuff into a huge monster – yet when I got down to it, it never took very long. It was my fear of not being able to do it that freaked me.'*
>
> *Recognizing her difficulties, she has worked with her accountant and her financial consultant to find a system that suits her – into which she has built regular reviews to keep her honest. This has taken her almost 10 years: she is still reasonably erratic about her bookkeeping, but she is no longer afraid.*

The key is to be honest with yourself and then to get the help you need to devise a system that works for you. There is nothing wrong with putting some of the tasks into someone else's hands – as long as you are clear that the final decisions and responsibility are yours.

> *John T. is a film maker who travels a lot – and he hates dealing with his finances. After years of getting into hot water – and almost into court – about unpaid bills and tax demands, he finally made the decision that he was never going to manage any of this himself. He just wasn't interested and, besides, he could afford to buy help. He now pays someone to deal with everything and says, 'I know the final decisions are mine. And the relief, when I quit pretending I was ever going to do any of this myself, was enormous.'*

Most of us cannot afford to pay someone to do everything for us. What we can do is to work out ways to compensate for our weak spots.

Things that may get you into a mess

From the beginning, the message of this book has been 'there are no right or wrong ways with money: it is your attitudes that make the difference.' Or 'do your own thing, find your own style.' And that is true. But in organizing your money on a day-by-day and month-by-month basis, there are some things you may do – or fail to do – that will almost certainly get you into a mess.

You might, for instance, keep meticulous accounts which show that you are getting into debt because food expenditure has risen sharply over the past couple of months. It is now up to you to do something with this information to stop yourself sinking further into debt. It is no good saying, 'After all, it's not my fault there's so much pressure on me at work that I didn't have a thing to eat in the house and had to go out to eat three times that week.' No, it may not be your fault. But it is your responsibility to re-evaluate honestly the way you allocate your time so that you do not spend money which you don't have.

Other common routes to trouble include:

- refusing to open bills when they land on the mat;
- ignoring letters from the bank/tax office/credit card company – and then getting angry because they charge you additional interest on what you owe;
- refusing to talk to someone when you know that you are in a financial mess.

Remember: most mistakes can be put right, but it may take effort and patience. Never despair. The sooner you can admit your mistakes to yourself, the quicker you can put things right, and with least loss to yourself and most goodwill and help from people like bank managers and mortgage lenders.

Summary

The aim of good money management is for you to feel in control of your money and to be aware of the choices available to you. This can be achieved in many different ways – and it is the result that is important.

THE 5 STEPS

1 Acknowledge where you are – and what you want

How would you describe your style of managing your money?
   Does it work for you? Does it cause friction with others?

2 Know the facts – your figures *and* your feelings

How do you manage your day-to-day finances at present?
   What records do you keep?
   Are there any areas in which you feel that you don't have a grip on your money?

3 Consider the *real* options

What promises could you make about improving your money management?
   Which promises would you be able to keep?

4 Make choices – live for today *and* plan for tomorrow

What is your biggest concern about your money management?
   How can you tackle it?
   What small thing could you change that would give you a real sense of progress?

5 Do it – and review it

How can you make sure that your good intentions last for more than a week?

Further information

Workbook Chapter 17 Managing Your Own Money

The Practical Guide to Book-keeping and Taxation for the Self-Employed

The Practical Guide to Taxes and Tax Returns

11. Dealing with Debt
It's never too late to sort it out

Debt is a state of mind.

It has nothing to do with how much you earn, how much you have to spend, how much you owe. The problem is your attitude.

Does this sound outrageous or offensive to you? If debt is an issue for you, give yourself a break. Read through this chapter, then decide whether you are ready to sort out your situation. If so, the practical help available here will enable you to begin to think about your debts differently and to start to put things right.

What is debt?

Financially, debt is when you owe money to someone else. Whether or not you are comfortable about this is a state of mind. Some people can have a £5000 overdraft with which they are perfectly happy. Others, earning much the same, worry if they are £150 overdrawn.

A debt is money you have got to pay back, in the end, without achieving any financial gain. You have the gain first, such as a holiday or new carpets. Later you have to pay for it.

Some debts are different from others. Your mortgage, though technically a debt, is not really one – unless it is too large in relation to your earnings. If you did not have a mortgage, you would have to pay out rent. It is best to think of a mortgage as a living expense, like gas, telephone, electricity and food bills.

If you fall behind in paying your bills for basic living expenses, then you do not have a debt but you do have a spending problem. You are spending more than you are earning, and you can choose either to cut down on your spending or to increase your earnings.

Of course, if you have taken out a mortgage in excess of your repayment capabilities, or if your idea of 'basic living expenses' means that you are paying a rent far beyond what you can afford on your salary, then you are creating a debt.

What causes debt?

In two words, you do. You have wanted more things – *right now* – than you have either been able to afford or are able to pay back over a period of time. Or your financial circumstances have deteriorated and you have not yet readjusted your expenditure to the new situation. We tend to be better at spending up to a new, higher limit than at adjusting downwards.

It is up to you. Check out your attitude right now. Are you angry, or are you convinced that you are an exception, and that it is not fair to be hard on people who have been caught up in circumstances beyond their control? If you are convinced that it is not your fault, then presumably it must be your parents' or your employer's, or the lack of available work or life in general. Apportioning blame will only sidetrack you from the major question, which is how you are going to get yourself out of debt. Whatever the facts, only you can resolve your problem.

Many people have found that they can no longer afford to keep up payments on their mortgages. Some are falling behind. Others have walked out and left the keys with the mortgage lender because they could not see any other way of dealing with their situation. If you had approached the lender when the problem first arose you would have found that, for good business reasons, he or she might have been prepared to help you sort things out by extending the life of the mortgage or accepting reduced payments. Of course, there is always the exception, but don't think you are necessarily it. Check it out first.

In dealing with debt, the buck stops with you. The responsibility for getting yourself into a situation – and now for getting yourself out of it – is yours. Can you accept this?

If so, it is safe for you to read this paragraph. Financial institutions and organizations which lend money bear a huge share of the responsibility for creating an environment in which you were tempted and able to get yourself into a mess. They make their money by lending to you at higher rates of interest than they pay to investors. That is the payment you make for using their money. They make even more money if you do not pay them back on time. Nevertheless, and this is extremely important, the problem remains yours. You chose to borrow.

It takes a great deal of discipline – financially and emotionally – to resist attractive offers even when these are clearly not right for you. Have you noticed how much unsolicited mail you receive offering to let you borrow any amount (or so it seems) in order to buy anything you want? Wouldn't you like that luxury holiday? Or how about paying off all your debts in one go, with just one easy signature? Don't you care about your kids? – surely you owe them this additional insurance protection? These offers are temptations. Even the most down-to-earth person may be caught off guard, and could succumb. What, then, can you do? First, take control of your money situation – know yourself and what pushes your spending button. Then when an offer comes through the door or the post, look at it, read it, indulge in a bit of wishful thinking (*that* comes cheap) – and finally bin it. If you are really tempted, try out the 5 Steps on the offer. Look at the figures, your feelings, your goals, and then decide whether this offer is realistic for you.

Remember: the current financial climate and the behaviour of financial institutions may have set the scene. But you – not they – are responsible for your financial choices and any debts with which they leave you.

When you are about to get into debt

There is an early stage when your debts are not yet a mountain, only a molehill. For instance, all of a sudden you have a small bank overdraft which you have never had before and it seems to be getting a little bit bigger each month. Or there is an outstanding balance on your credit card which you always used to clear at the end of each month. But this month you just can't afford to do it. How about looking at why this happened?

Was it that you simply had to have that new compact disc player so you took out a loan or paid for it with your credit card? Of course you intended to pay it back . . . next month. Funny the way the debt keeps building up every month. How long has this been going on?

Stop right now. Get out your old bank statements. Find the month when you started to get into debt. Were you surprised when you found the date? It wasn't last month or even the month before? Now get out your chequebook and your credit card statements. What do they show you about the way you have been spending your money?

If you can see that you are at the beginning of the slippery slope, or not too far down it, that is the time to cut down or stop spending – depending on how far you have already slipped. 'It's only a small amount so it doesn't matter'. Repeat that every month and the monthly molehills will have become mountains.

Once you are in debt

People cannot bear to look at how much they owe. Once they are in debt, there is a tendency to hide under the bedclothes and hope it will all go away. The agony of sitting down and seeing what you have done to yourself is very difficult. But if you are able to face the reality, life gets a lot easier.

People to whom you owe money will usually listen to repayment offers as it rarely makes good business sense for them to take you to court – and this includes everybody from the taxman to the loan company. They will try and help, but *you* must approach them, and *you* must calculate your debts and accept that you have to cut your spending dramatically.

The longer you ignore things, the more unmanageable they will become. Debts do not go away; they increase. Most people who get into debt manage to maintain their liabilities at a level that is just about sustainable. Those who get into serious debt are the minority – but you could be among these unless you face up to reality – and fast. There is no other first step.

Then what? *Workbook Chapter 19 Dealing with Debt*, offers a step by step way of dealing with your debts. It is a way of planning which will help you to identify which expenses are fixed, which are variable, and what choices you have. For example, we need to eat to stay alive. After meeting that basic need, we have choices about what we eat and how much we spend on food.

Pat C.'s story shows you how someone in serious trouble was able to deal with her debts.

Pat C. had a reasonable income but was nevertheless poor. She had no money, she could not afford to buy anything, and she was always in debt. The only glimmer of light in her situation was that she lived in a council house at a reasonable rent.

When Pat decided she wanted to do something about her debts, she went to her financial consultant for help because 'I didn't have a clue where to start. When I had to list them, I discovered I had 16 different debts – including three credit cards, my bank, the store from which I'd just bought carpets, and a video and tv shop.'

Pat admitted that she often feels bad about herself and her life. Working as much as she does, she does not feel that she is being a good mother; she does not have money to buy clothes, and she has let herself go physically. She often buys expensive presents for her children and her mother.

It took Pat a while to recognize how large her debts were. Then she needed to agree a time limit by which each debt would by paid off. This was crucial, 'So by March next year that will be gone and I'll only have 15 more to go; by April this one will be settled and there will only be 14 left.'

She also worked out what she could spend. At one point this was £25 per week for food and extras, for herself and her two children. Before going shopping she made a shopping list and only bought what she had written down. Going to the supermarket without a list – or deviating from it – is dangerous.

Pat is now down to the last three debts and she is in credit at the bank – 'for the first time ever'. To get this far has taken her 18 months – but in that time better financial habits have gradually taken root, helped by the prospect of clearing all her debts. She now keeps her chequebook up-to-date. As the debts ease, she is able to keep in credit – because she has kept her spending under tight control. And she can now afford to spend a little on herself – as a reward.

Pat has given her financial consultant all her cards – every single one: her loan card, her credit cards, her electrical shop card, her three cards for major department stores. She has not asked for the cards back nor is she yet willing simply to cut them up.

She is now buying her own council house – something that she thought she could never achieve. As an occupant she gets a special discount, and with the right financial advice, she was able to start on the purchase. Pat needed something really big to work towards, in order to keep herself to her three year debt-clearing plan. Owning her own home was the great goal that has kept her going.

Other tips for clearing your debts

You need to have a plan for clearing your debts. Nothing can substitute for this. Once you have made your plan, ask yourself in what ways you are likely to undermine yourself. You may not find it easy to be honest about this. We are so bound up in our ways of spending that it is often hard to see how we can cut down. But if your goal is to deal with your debts, then you will need to be quite creative in matching your figures and your feelings.

> *Michael T. discovered that one of his biggest expenditures – and the easiest one about which he could do something – was taxis. The amount he spent each week was quite evident, and outrageous. But he worked in a business where most of the clients earned more than he did, and it made him feel important to be able to hail a cab when he left a meeting. He had a choice: would he stay in debt or would he face his pride? He dealt with his pride and thereby dealt with his debts.*
>
> *Terri M. works very hard but is not very confident about her cooking. So when friends come around, it is easier for her to take them to the nearby Indian restaurant or to the pub. Of course she pays – she would feel awkward asking them to share since they prepare meals for her when she visits them. When she got into debt and began to think about ways of economizing, she realized that she could invite her friends for tea, not dinner, and offer them tea and biscuits. And if she does want to offer dinner then even the relatively expensive prepared meals from supermarkets are cheaper than going to a restaurant.*

You may also find that your plan can be undermined by a partner who refuses to do anything about his or her debts or financial behaviour. If this is the case, be careful that you don't let his or her reluctance divert you from putting your own finances in order. And separate your money affairs from your partner's.

Budgeting

Do you believe that budgeting will help you to avoid all these pitfalls? Our ideas about traditional budgeting mirror our traditional views about money – and neither works very well. In traditional budgeting, you take the amount of money with which you are left after paying bills and allot set amounts for set things such as food or clothing. This leaves your money in little 'boxes' and usually provides little understanding as to why your money has been going out of control.

> *Francis C. budgeted in the traditional way. Figuratively speaking, she had all her money in little biscuit tins. 'I worked out what each item cost: clothes, holiday, spending, insurance . . . but something always went wrong. Money somehow escaped from the 'tins' to which I had mentally consigned it'. And she genuinely believed that it could not have been her that had taken it. 'I have everything neatly arranged, then it all just goes. It's the oddest thing.'*

People delude themselves, feeling that they have a budgeting system that works, and when it fails – 'it's not my fault, it's the system's'. If you are willing to accept that the buck stops with you – that it is your responsibility to get things straight – then there is an alternative system that really does work.

Instead of keeping tins on a shelf, visualize yourself as a lock-keeper on a river. There are several locks which you control by raising the gate, just enough to let out the right amount of money. After you have let out sufficient to cover all your bills and other fixed expenses, you are left with a sum of money. That sum is yours to spend as you will – but that's all you've got. You then face the choice of spending less in order to live on that amount, or of earning more if you can't, or of staying in debt.

Treats or rewards are important to this system. As you clear each debt, it is a good idea to divide up the sum you had previously been paying monthly toward that particular debt. Put part of it towards clearing another debt and a part towards 'treats' – as recognition for the progress you are making. These rewards will encourage you to keep going with your debt clearance plan. Remember, the plan is the first chapter in your success story, not a punishment.

The issue with debt is not a matter of *how much* – how much you are earning, how much you are in debt or how much you can afford to pay back. Clearing your debts involves the same planning – and discipline in carrying out your plans – whether you are clearing them with pennies or with pounds.

'Wanting' and 'needing': overcoming the language of debt

Confusing 'what I want' with 'what I need' is a trick which we often play on ourselves. If you find yourself in financial difficulties it may help you to look at the difference between situations in which you use the term, 'what I want', and those in which you use the term, 'what I need'. If you feel that you 'need' a new pair of shoes when you already have one pair in good condition, then you are stating a 'want', not a 'need'. It is a signal that you are *spending* your money rather than *buying* a necessity.

In order to prevent yourself falling into this trap, you may find it helpful always to ask yourself, 'Do I need this or can I do without it?' If the honest answer is 'I could do without it', then, no matter how reluctant you may feel, do not *spend* your money on an item that you do not actually need.

Do you really want to get out of debt?

The point at which you start to clear your debts and avoid new ones is when you put away your credit cards. Credit cards are simply another way of building up debts. They are also very convenient – unless for you they are lethal. They are lethal for those who have spent to the absolute limit of their credit, have been at that point for some time, and seem to be unable to reduce their debt. If you are not clear whether you fall into this category, the best check is to look at your past credit card statements. Then you'll know.

Even if you are in financial deep waters, you may be reluctant to cut up your credit cards. If you can cut them up, fine. If you can't, put them away. Or, if you know that your willpower is weak, give your cards to someone whom you trust, such as your accountant or financial consultant, but who is not too close to you. Ask them to hold on to them for you, until you either feel that you have re-established control over your own spending habits, or have reached a point where you are able to cut them up. Do not give your credit cards to your bank manager, as returning the cards to you then becomes his or her choice, not yours. Remember that a bank manager does not work for you; an accountant or financial consultant does.

Being in debt can become a way of life. Do you really want to change it? Your reaction to your credit cards is one test to your answer. If you can cut them up, then you know that you want to get to grips with your financial mess. If you can neither cut up your cards nor put them away nor give them to someone else for safekeeping – then you are not yet being serious. You aren't taking responsibility for your finances if you keep an escape route open! So start by facing that fact.

What if, having done your calculations, you are left with so little spending money that life hardly seems worth living? There are only two choices: earn more, or remain in debt.

Anna E.'s debt-reducing plan left her with so little that she knew she would not be able to stick to her intentions. Going out socially was terribly important to her. 'I've just broken up with my partner and I need to get back into the social scene. The money I'm left with after I pay my bills is a laugh – I need more money now, not less.' Anna was being honest with herself: to her, her social life was as high a priority as reducing her debts – maybe higher. She had ruled out the option of spending less, so she was left with two choices: stay in debt, or earn more money, in order to fund her social life.

She calculated the cost of her social activities and the additional income she needed to fund them. At first she baulked. 'I didn't much like the idea of cutting down on my social life by having to work evenings, but then I came back face to face with my debts.' Eventually she concluded that she could work an extra three nights a week, earn the money she needed, and still have four nights left for socializing. She would have a clear financial conscience and money in her pocket.

Only you know whether you are ready to face the prospect of dealing with your debts. If not now, keep coming back to it. If you can at least acknowledge that you created your debts yourself and that it is your responsibility, and yours alone, to clear them, then you are getting closer.

Taking risks

You can choose to put yourself in debt by taking risks which are disproportionate to your resources and your income. Again, there is no right or wrong way about this – the decision you make is about the level of risk with which you can feel comfortable, both financially and emotionally.

> *Winston and Avis B. have almost paid off the mortgage on their house which has increased a great deal in value since they bought it. If they can raise £40,000 he has a chance to go into business. They decided to borrow the money against the security of the house. Both are quite clear that if the business were to fail, they would stand to lose the £40,000. Before they went ahead, they both had to be certain in their own minds that they could handle that risk and not blame each other if anything went wrong. Between them they decided that their relationship, and their confidence in each other, was sufficiently strong to allow them to take this step.*
>
> *Charles W., on the other hand, would also like to go to work for himself. But his wife cannot bear the thought of risking their money in a new business. She knows that she could not handle the additional stress and uncertainty which this would cause, let alone the possibility of financial failure – no matter how little money they had invested. Knowing this, Charles is now looking at other options that would be acceptable to both of them.*

When you are making up your mind whether to go into debt or not, it is as well to be realistic about the possible consequences of your decision. Ask yourself, 'What is the worst that could happen?' Sit down and spell that out, not just in words but also in figures. It can help to doublecheck your conclusions with a third party, such as your financial consultant. Then decide whether, financially and emotionally, you (and your partner) can handle the risk. If you are being honest with yourself, you will know whether you are taking a calculated risk or whether you are about to throw yourself off the cliff.

Summary

Avoiding debt in the first place is always easier than getting out of it But if you think that your situation has got out of control, you are probably wrong. Most situations can be retrieved. Whatever stage you are at – whether small debts are just beginning to build up, whether you can just about manage your debts, or whether you are drowning – the first step in reversing the process is to stop and face it.

Read it! Consider the issues

It is hard to deny yourself and your family a lifestyle which matches your, and their, expectations, especially when everything around us encourages us to aim high. Yet debt is bound to undermine your chosen lifestyle. It is a drain, both on your emotions and your finances. And it prevents you from building up the reserves which you and your family need in order to cope with unforeseen demands or emergencies.

It is never too late to change. If you can face the facts honestly, however painful that may be, there is a way out.

THE 5 STEPS

1 Acknowledge where you are – and what you want

Do you know whether you are in debt – or about to get into debt?
  Do you know how you got there?

2 Know the facts – your figures *and* your feelings

How many debts do you have?
  How do you feel about the position you are in?

3 Consider the *real* options

What would be the consequences of continuing to be in debt?
  Are you able to live on the amount remaining to you after paying all unavoidable monthly bills?
  Do you need to think of ways of earning more money?

4 Make choices – live for today *and* plan for tomorrow

What changes do you need to make in your pattern of living and spending so as to avoid sinking further into debt?

5 Do it – and review it

What occasional treats would help you to sustain a debt clearance programme?
  Where will you find the support to see this through?

Further information

Workbook Chapter 18 Avoiding Debt

Workbook Chapter 19 Dealing with Debt

Chapter 3 Managing Changes in Your Earning Life

Workbook Chapter 5 Creating Financial Security

Workbook Chapter 7 Dealing with Unexpected Changes in Your Earning Life

Workbook Chapter 8 Coming to Terms with Benefits or Inheritance

12. Getting Professional Assistance

Ask for help – but don't let them manage you

Getting assistance from the various professionals who can help you with your finances is fine; feeling at a disadvantage with them is not. They may be experts in their field, but you are the expert about your needs and the person with final responsibility for your finances.

Their work is based on arranging for you the four basic products of the finance industry – investments of lump sums, savings plans, pensions and mortgages – and servicing your accounting needs.

The aim of this chapter is to help you to be clear about whom to ask for assistance, how to find them and how to make use of their expertise – and what to do about mistakes they might make. It introduces the main financial professionals and looks at what they offer – and how you can go about getting the best deal for yourself.

Who they are and what they offer

There are five major professionals in relation to financial matters – bank managers, accountants, solicitors, mortgage lenders and financial consultants. There are also tax specialists, mortgage brokers and Trust specialists.

There are two sources of free advice: the Inland Revenue, who are advisers even though they are rarely seen as such, and the national network of Citizens Advice Bureaux. The CABs offer free advice and support about some financial matters, particularly if you are in debt.

Although in recent years the services that are offered by different professionals have expanded and often overlap, you can in general assume that: a bank manager lends you money; an accountant deals with your tax; a solicitor handles your legal matters; a mortgage lender lends you money to buy a house or flat; a financial consultant deals with financial planning and makes your money work.

It is always good to have a choice of advice available, according to your needs. Each professional has a service to sell, and their own perspective from which to advise you. Remember, for instance, that when the bank offers you a 'one-stop' financial centre, you are in fact going to see a different person for each of your different requirements.

How to find them

The best way to find any financial help is usually on the recommendation of someone who is happy with the service they are getting from the person with whom they already deal. Do not assume that if someone specializes in the area in which you need help – such as, a solicitor who deals with contracts – they will necessarily suit you just because you need a contract checked. Always interview them first. Nor should you assume that someone who suits a friend would suit you: it's just a good starting point.

It is necessary – and appropriate – to interview a person before you give your business to them. *Workbook Chapter 20 Getting Professional Assistance* gives a list of detailed questions for you to ask in order to help you to make this decision. The two basic criteria are that you like them and that you trust their professional expertise.

There are some things to keep in mind when you are on the look-out for one of these professionals.

Bank managers. Most people select a bank that is near their home or place of work, and change to another branch of that bank if they move. They therefore acquire a bank manager along with the bank. If you are only doing normal banking, you may not need to vet the bank manager, although you may judge the bank by the service which you get over the counter. It is only when you are asking the bank for a loan, or using other financial services, that the manager, himself or herself, will become important. Banks use the money which you deposit with them to make more money for themselves, and will charge you interest on any money they lend you. They will make judgements as to your ability to meet their interest charges and repay any loan, and they are usually correct in the judgements they make. If you truly believe that your bank manager is wrong, change banks.

You no longer have to go cap in hand to a bank. Banks realize that they are no longer the paternal institutions that they once were. They are big business. But be aware, and beware, of the less palatable remnants of their traditional approach. Where women are concerned in particular, bank managers have a habit of thinking of themselves as substitute fathers or husbands, and the expression, 'my dear' is one that most women both expect and dislike. The other side to this is that a long standing contact with a particular branch and a good relationship with its manager means that you are more likely to get extra support in times of crisis.

Accountants. The accountant is the exception to the advice about accepting recommendations from friends. A personal recommendation is not always the best as most people do not understand what their accountant does except produce figures for a tax return. The job of an accountant is to assist you to declare your income and expenditure to the Inland Revenue in the most tax efficient way, from the information you provide.

The best way to find an accountant who suits you is to get several recommendations and to go and have a chat with each one, which should be free of charge. Remember, the accountant is looking for business.

Solicitors. Solicitors handle legal matters. Many of them specialize, so that a solicitor who is good at conveyancing – house purchase or house selling – is not necessarily going to be the one who would be best at drawing up your Will or checking over a new job contract for loopholes. Be wary of the solicitor who claims that he or she can do it all themselves. Many solicitors work in a firm which has different specialists or partners. Just because you deal happily with one solicitor in a firm, don't assume that you ought to, or want to, deal with someone else within the same firm. Make sure you interview anyone else in the firm first, rather than handing them your business by referral.

A recommendation is very definitely necessary in finding a

solicitor. Ask friends first, then family, or your mortgage lender or financial adviser.

Financial consultants. A financial consultant will generally take a detailed overview of your finances and match the figures with what you have specifically requested them to do, or with what they recommend you ought to do, e.g. pensions or life assurance. Most financial consultants earn commission from the products that you buy from them, such as a savings plan or a pension. When banks operate as financial consultants, they also receive income in this way. A growing number of consultants charge a fee; some deduct the fee from their commission, others charge the fee only if you do not buy a product from them. Always find out which way a consultant works before you give them your business.

There are two kinds of financial consultants

- those who are independent of any particular investment/life assurance company and can offer you the products of any company;
- those who are 'tied' to a particular company and its products.

Neither one is better than the other, contrary to much media comment which tends to equate 'independent' with 'best'. Although an independent consultant may be able to offer you a wider choice of products, it will still be your responsibility to decide which company's product you wish to accept. It's really a matter of the individual consultant and your relationship with them – with one proviso. If a consultant is an agent for a particular company, check that the company which they represent is a reputable company. As long as the company is in the top 50% of all the life assurance and other financial organizations which have recently entered the investment market, such as banks, you are as secure as you can reasonably expect to be.

The simplest means available to you for checking this information is a fund performance record which your financial consultant should have readily available. You want to look at the actual performance chart and note the growth percentages listed on it, i.e. by how much the fund is growing per year. These figures will speak for themselves. Do not bother with comparison charts between different companies, as figures can be made to say almost anything.

MONTHLY FUND ANALYSIS AS AT 1 JANUARY 1991
LINKED FUNDS

ACCUMULATION UNITS	DATE OF LAUNCH	SIZE OF FUND (£M)	CURRENT PRICE (pence)	% PRICE CHANGE OVER:					
				1 MTH	6 MTHS	1 YR	2 YRS	5 YRS	10 YRS
FLEXIBLE (MANAGED)	1.1.72	90.1	378.2	0.7	−5.0	−4.9	17.3	50.3	181.0
FIXED INTEREST	1.8.79	9.6	222.3	0.6	6.9	4.1	7.8	33.0	116.0
EQUITY	24.4.82	75.7	333.9	0.8	−4.3	−3.3	23.3	69.1	N/A
INVESTMENT TRUST	1.11.68	81.7	570.5	−0.3	−13.6	−16.7	6.2	43.6	205.2
INTERNATIONAL	24.4.82	11.1	238.6	1.4	−13.2	−15.6	10.3	38.8	N/A
JAPAN	1.8.85	3.8	178.6	0.3	−17.8	−29.5	−19.8	42.1	N/A
AMERICAN	1.8.85	5.2	123.9	5.0	−11.2	−9.3	16.0	16.8	N/A
EUROPEAN	1.3.86	7.0	127.5	−0.3	−16.9	−12.2	22.2	N/A	N/A
PROPERTY	1.1.71	15.9	256.1	−0.4	0.0	1.1	21.3	86.9	143.7
GUARANTEED DEP.	1.8.78	3.1	223.0	0.8	4.7	9.5	17.2	36.1	85.1
EXEMPT FLEXIBLE	1.1.72	24.2	643.6	1.1	−6.7	−7.5	19.0	76.8	317.7
EXEMPT FIXED INT.	1.1.83	8.5	215.5	0.7	8.1	6.8	15.2	57.3	N/A
EXEMPT EQUITY	1.1.83	41.1	372.2	1.1	−7.6	−7.1	25.2	98.3	N/A
EXEMPT INV. TRUST	1.1.72	38.8	1138.8	0.2	−16.0	−20.9	5.5	74.0	367.7
EXEMPT PROPERTY	1.1.72	7.4	475.6	0.0	2.0	7.4	25.1	97.9	240.2
EXEMPT GUAR. DEP.	1.1.83	4.6	228.0	1.1	7.0	14.3	28.9	70.0	N/A
EXEMPT INTERNATIONAL	23.3.87	11.5	84.0	2.2	−19.1	−24.5	2.8	N/A	N/A
BALANCED	18.5.84	54.1	253.7	1.1	−7.8	−8.5	18.3	90.8	N/A
MONEYMAKER	1.1.72	14.8	306.9	0.5	−4.8	−5.5	15.1	46.8	159.0
CAPITAL GROWTH	1.1.74	9.1	1035.4	1.0	−4.6	−3.4	24.5	73.7	271.4
FT ACTUARIES BRIT. GOVT ALL-STOCK				−1.2	3.0	−1.8	−4.1	−2.1	15.0
FT ACTUARIES ALL-SHARE				0.0	−11.9	−14.3	11.4	51.1	253.2
FT ACTUARIES INV. TRUST				19.8	−1.5	−7.3	29.7	85.2	326.4

Notes:
1. London and Manchester Assurance Company Limited's linked fund prices contain no bid to offer spread.
2. Management Charge bands used are Non-Exempt 1.5%, Exempt 0.75%. (Except for Balanced which is 0.5%).
3. The Percentage Price change figures do not relate to annualised growth rates.

London and Manchester Assurance Company Limited
Registered Office: Winslade Park Exeter EX5 1DS Registered in England No. 4599
A member of LAUTRO A member of the London and Manchester Group

UNIT TRUSTS

	DATE OF LAUNCH	SIZE OF FUND (£M)	CURRENT PRICE		% PRICE CHANGE OVER:			
			BID	OFFER (pence)	1 MTH	6 MTHS	1 YR	2 YRS
INCOME	3.12.84	25.3	45.61	48.94	0.3	−14.1	−15.4	3.9
GENERAL	15.11.83	119.7	55.36	59.40 XD	0.5	−9.6	−10.6	17.0
INTERNATIONAL	3.12.84	59.3	35.46	38.05	1.5	−18.9	−25.0	2.3
JAPAN	1.11.86	5.7	34.51	37.03	1.6	−23.9	−40.9	−32.7
AMERICAN	1.11.86	16.2	32.69	35.08 XD	2.6	−17.7	−18.6	13.6
TRUST OF INV TRUSTS	1.11.86	53.2	36.02	38.65	0.1	−18.1	−23.8	0.7

Unit trust growth rates are calculated on an offer to offer basis.
It must be remembered that the price of units can fall as well as rise and past performance should not be taken as a guarantee of future returns.

Mortgage lenders. There are a variety of financial professionals who can arrange mortgages. You can either find your own mortgage through building societies or banks or via a financial consultancy or mortgage broker, preferably one recommended to you by a friend.

All of them offer different mortgages. You must ensure that you understand what is being offered to you and what the penalties are. If there is a plus side to a mortgage scheme, there has to be a minus side. It will be your responsibility to be clear about your own needs and circumstances. Get information from any of the above sources, and then decide on the scheme which, as far as you are concerned, best balances out the pluses and the minuses. For further details about the different kinds of mortgages, see *The Practical Guides Setting up a mortgage*.

How to use them

In order to make the best use of the expertise that a financial professional has to offer, you first need to be clear about what you want from them. At the very least, know the questions you want to ask them. Then deal with them in a way that gets you what you need.

The first facts you need to know are your own: why it is that you want to undertake some particular financial business, and what do you need to know in order to make a responsible decision? It can help to take yourself through the relevant chapter in *The 5 Steps Workbook* so as to be clear about your own needs and choices and also to refer to any of *The Practical Guides* which are relevant.

In doing this, you will be able to identify things you cannot answer yourself and things you do not know, but feel you need to know. Go to an appointment prepared with a list of what you require and the questions you need answered. This will help you to get what you want – and save time for both of you in the process.

One difficulty you may face when doing business with a financial professional is that you may not understand what they are talking about! Don't assume that there is something wrong with you. Financial professionals, like other professionals, often lose their ability to communicate with people outside their own circle. They also forget that the whole point of the exercise is that you should be able to understand, since you, not they, are ultimately responsible for your financial decisions.

Get them to speak a language that you do understand. For example, if your accountant or financial consultant asks you, 'What accounting records do you maintain?' you may have to ask several times until you can get this translated to, 'How do you keep a note of what you earn and what you spend?'

So gather your information, consider the financial details and your feelings, and choose the route you want to take – or choose to delay further in order to get more information.

But don't expect this process to be straightforward. It is easy to know that you ought to check around in order to cover yourself; it may be harder to do so. Gathering your own information may seem to your adviser like a vote of 'no confidence' rather than what it really is – a sign of how seriously you take your responsibility for your financial affairs. You can only make clear why you are doing what you are doing – and change advisers if you continue to feel uncomfortable.

You may also find that when you try to get information by yourself, you meet with a less than helpful response. Even the authors of this book, when trying to verify some of the facts included here, encountered individuals who were obstructive, rude or simply wrong in the information they gave. Getting the information you require, from any source in the finance industry, requires you to be persistent, to ask clear and concise questions – and to keep asking until you get the answer to your questions. Quite often it pays to put your questions in writing. Then, if the answer you are given is wrong, you may have a case for compensation.

Ask whether you really need their help

Sometimes we pay for help because we are afraid that we cannot manage on our own, or because we don't want to manage on our own. If you can be honest with yourself about your motives, you stand a better chance of getting the kind of help you need.

The most radical act of relinquishing responsibility for your own affairs is called 'Power of Attorney'. This means that you are authorizing someone else to use or spend your money in place of you. It does not mean 'on your behalf', as many people have found to their cost. If you want someone else to handle all your financial affairs – liaising with bank managers, accountants, the Inland Revenue, the mortgage company – then insist on six-monthly meetings to discuss and up-date your affairs. But do not give Power of Attorney to anyone unless you are truly unable to manage yourself.

On the other hand, you may be paying for help unnecessarily. Do you have an accountant even though accountancy fees may amount to a quite disproportionate amount of your income? Is this because you are not good with figures, or because you simply do not want to complete your tax returns, or because you genuinely do not have the time? Whatever the reason, if you have actively chosen, and are willing to pay for, professional services, that is fine.

Who is responsible?

Bank managers, accountants, financial advisers, and mortgage lenders are professionals. Therefore, aren't they responsible for your finances when you go to them for help? The short answer is 'no'.

Even though they are the financial experts, there are two reasons why you should not just let them take charge or 'get on with it'. First, even when they make mistakes, you are responsible for the consequences. Second, no one is as expert as you are about your own needs. Use their expertise; do not let the expertise abuse you.

If an accountant submits inaccurate accounts, you are the one who is liable, not the accountant. If you have not provided information because you were not asked for it, you are still liable. When you get your accounts, there is a sentence which reads, 'Accounts prepared by me according to the information supplied by the client.' The accountant is not liable – you are.

However unfair that seems, the person who for most of the time will bear the brunt of any errors is you. Even though there may be a slight chance of the professional being disciplined by her or his professional body or your being able to take legal action. The greatest protection that you have is always to be well prepared – and work in partnership with the professionals, which includes asking questions until you understand clearly what is being done on your behalf.

Jane T. recently had a long consultation with a tax adviser at one of the major high street banks. She was grateful for the trouble he had taken, though the implications of what she had been told caused her a great deal of worry. Months later

> *she approached her financial consultant who, on contacting the Inland Revenue, discovered that the bank's tax adviser had been quite wrong. It had never occurred to Jane to question the advice she had been given – or to check with the Inland Revenue herself.*

Jane had not yet realized that even experts can be wrong – and that, whether the news is good or bad, double checking can save worry and further errors. She simply assumed that what she had been told by a 'professional' had to be right.

> *John W.'s accountant informed him that he could include parking tickets on his claim for expenses. He queried this, but his accountant was adamant that the information was accurate. John still wasn't convinced and checked with his financial consultant. She knew that you could not get tax relief for breaking the law, and obtained a letter from the Inland Revenue to confirm this.*

John's instincts told him that the advice he initially received wasn't quite right. Despite feeling awkward about it, he challenged his accountant – and he pursued his enquiries until he felt that he had the correct information.

If you have a serious complaint about the professional services you have received, the different sectors of the finance industry all have bodies to which you can complain. A list of some of these is included in *Resources for Readers*. Make sure that you keep copies of all correspondence and notes of any meetings. This is good practice at all times, but essential if you feel that something has gone wrong.

Of course, most of the time your financial professional is likely to do a good job and do it right. This is more likely if you are clear about what you are asking for and prepare as much information as you can in advance of any meeting. You are more likely to receive sound professional advice if you yourself approach the situation in a professional way.

Don't be panicked by financial rumours

Most years the media will publish information which will panic you into wanting to take instant action on something affecting your financial affairs. The best – or worst – example recently was the abolition of double taxation relief on mortgages in August

1988. The papers, television, and some financial professionals themselves, were encouraging people to take out mortgages before the August deadline – even to purchase a property with someone else, whether they had previously been considering this course of action or not. The net result was that property prices soared and people purchased homes at unrealistic and inflated prices. Many are now paying the penalty for this panic, with mortgage payments they cannot meet or with shared arrangements which have not worked but where the property cannot easily be sold.

If there is a panic, and if the circumstances which are being predicted seem likely to affect you financially, look first at whether there is something that you feel that you ought to be doing about it. Then check with a financial professional whom you trust before you take any action. The right professional advice will spell out for you the pluses and minuses in direct relation to your circumstances. Then make up your own mind. Don't be panicked into doing something that does not suit you just because everybody else is doing it.

Summary

Many of us will find it helpful to consult one or other of the financial professionals at some stage in our lives. At best, they can offer invaluable support in getting your money to work for you in support of the kind of life you want – both now and in the future. Just don't let them manage you.

THE 5 STEPS

1 Acknowledge where you are – and what you want

Do you know precisely what kind of assistance you need with your finances?

If you are already getting help from someone, do you like them?
Do you know what is expected of you?
Do you know what you expect – and get – from each of them?

2 Know the facts – your figures *and* your feelings

Do you prepare your financial information and questions before you have an appointment with a financial professional?

Do you feel that your circumstances are understood by the professional/s you meet and that your needs are taken into account?

Do you find you get pre-packaged answers or personalized responses to your questions?

3 Consider the *real* options

Would you have the confidence to change professionals if you were not satisfied with their work?

4 Make choices – live for today *and* plan for tomorrow

If you have a financial problem, are you sure that you have the right professional to help you deal with it?

Do you need to ask for assistance about your money from any other professionals?

5 Do it – and review it

Do you see your professional advisers at least once a year to review what you want from them and what they are doing for you?

Further information

Workbook Chapter 20 Getting Professional Assistance

The Practical Guide To Saving and Investing

The Practical Guide To Arranging Life Cover

The Practical Guide To Setting Up a Mortgage

The Practical Guide To Arranging a Pension

Resources for the Reader

13. Maintaining Your Progress
Do it – and review it

Changing the way in which you deal with money is not easy, nor is it likely to be quick or straightforward. Deciding that you want to have a healthier financial life is the first and giant step; keeping yourself moving in that direction is a series of small steps which you will need to take for the rest of your life.

Have you found that various attempts at sorting out your money have started well enough but fizzled out after a few weeks or, if you were particularly determined, a few months? Do you expect the same to happen this time? Yes, it's likely to.

Don't see 'backsliding' as a failure. Few of us can consistently keep our finances in order any more than we can work at the same pace all the time or keep on top of letters we need to answer. Circumstances change, and so do our goals and our moods. The important thing is to come back to your good intentions when you find that you have strayed.

The way to make progress is to get on with the plans that you've made and to make time regularly to check how you are doing. How often? Every three months is probably best, especially if you are at a stage when your life is changing rapidly. Otherwise, every six months is fine. Leaving it for a year is too long. The longer you leave it, the more likely you are to find that your figures and your feelings are in disarray.

Whenever you stop to review progress, you will need to look at what you have done in the past three months and where you see yourself going to next. Check the figures to see whether there have been changes in your life that will affect your choices. Once you have this information you will be able to decide whether you need to adjust your goals or your financial arrangements.

How long do you have to keep this up? Quite frankly, for the rest of your life. Money maintenance is no different from the maintenance you have to do on a house, or from regular check-ups with your dentist. Taking stock of where you are is an ordinary activity which is only likely to feel threatening while your relationship to money is dicey. The more you use the common sense 5 Steps, the easier and the more natural it will become to see money management as an ordinary part of your life. But how long it will take for you to feel completely in control of your finances depends on your situation now.

But don't scare yourself to death – or into debt. The secret of managing your money is that you do not have to know everything or always get it right. Instead, you need to know how to think about your situation clearly and then to make a commitment to do something about it.

So be honest with yourself and take care of yourself; then you'll get there.

THE 5 STEPS

1 Acknowledge where you are – and what you want

How are you doing with the good intentions you had?

If you have done some backsliding, do you know when that started and what were the reasons?

Are there any changes in your circumstances that affect your financial plans?

2 Know the facts – your figures *and* your feelings

Have there been any increases or decreases in your earnings or outgoings? If so, do you know the reasons why?

3 Consider the *real* options

Given your present circumstances, what adjustments, if any, would you wish to make to your goals and/or your financial arrangements?

4 Make choices – live for today *and* plan for tomorrow

What do you feel are the most urgent changes you need to make in order to regain or stay in control of your finances?

5 Do it – and review it

How will you get yourself back into action, if you have had a slip or a slump?

Further information

Workbook Chapter 21 Maintaining Your Progress

Workbook Chapter 1 The Basic 5 Steps Analysis

Use it!

The 5 Steps Workbook

The 5 Steps Workbook

Introduction

The workbook is designed to help you to take practical control of your money.

The 5 Steps are not a task which you do once only and tick off your list. They are an approach to managing your money. Use the 5 Steps for regular reviews. Also, turn back to them immediately your circumstances change, or whenever you begin to feel signs of financial stress. Working through them will help you to become clearer about what you may need to do.

Workbook Chapter 1 takes you through the basic 5 Steps analysis. The chapter is lengthy because it provides you with the opportunity to prepare the background information which you will need for the subsequent chapters.

Workbook Chapters 2 – 21 apply the 5 Steps to the specific areas discussed in the first section of *Money's No Object* – work, relationships, attitudes and money management.

Find a place where you can keep the work which you do in these chapters, such as a file folder or drawer. Then, when you come to review, or when you are preparing to see one of the financial professionals for assistance, you will already have, at your fingertips, a great deal of the background information that you need.

W1
The Basic 5 Steps Analysis

The Basic 5 Steps Analysis begins with a review of what you want out of life, and a gathering together of all the facts you need to know, in terms of figures as well as feelings. With this information, you should then be able to see how to manage your finances in a way that lets you live for today and plan for tomorrow.

As you work through the different tasks, don't take short cuts. The 5 Steps are systematic: you need the information from each of the previous steps in order to move on to the next. Take note of those parts that make you want to quit. If you can see where and when you feel uncomfortable, you may also begin to see the pattern which you have adopted in dealing with money in your life.

For the practical work in this chapter you will need:

- a pen or pencil
- some paper or an exercise book
- a small cash book for spending and cost-of-living analyses
- any financial records you have, e.g. pay slips, bank statements, bills
- a box file, or several pocket files, in which to store your work.

There are no 'right' or 'wrong' answers to the different activities. But there *is* a wrong approach – deceiving yourself. The Basic 5 Steps Analysis will be more effective if you don't begin by judging yourself, just work through it as honestly as you can.

STEP 1
ACKNOWLEDGE WHERE YOU ARE –
AND WHAT YOU WANT

In order to have some idea of any changes you might want to make in your life, you need to know two things:

- your present all-round situation, personal and financial, and
- what you are hoping to get out of life.

By comparing the two you will begin to get a feel for any changes you want and need to make.

Make a start by describing your life right now, in whatever terms are important to you. Don't limit your description to matters that have to do with money. You do not need to put in too much detail at this stage. Do remember that your circumstances include the ways you are handling your work, your domestic and social life, your leisure interests, as well as your financial health *and* how you feel about all these.

- *I don't like working such long hours*
- *I want to clear my debts*
- *A new car next year would be nice*
- *Buy a flat soon, I'm fed up living at home*

The following checklist may help to remind you of areas for review:

- *material circumstances*
- *work and income*
- *relationships with family, friends, partners*
- *other areas that influence what you do with your money*
- *emotional and physical circumstances*

Set these notes aside and take a close look at what you are hoping to get out of your life – in the short term, the medium term and the long term. The three tasks below approach your goals in different ways, so it will help you to attempt them all. Don't forget to put down your dreams in your plans for the future but don't, at this stage, worry about how you are going to finance them.

1 What are your financial objectives – for the short, medium and the long term? You may want a skiing holiday this year, or an additional week on some beach and, in the long run, three holidays every year. You may want to fix up a pension, get a mortgage, or make sure that you and your children all have new winter coats this year. Or you may be saying, '*I simply want to gain control of my finances and clear my debts. I can't see any further than that.*'

2 What are your personal objectives? Take your current age and add five years or ten years or 25 years. Think about what you would like to be happening then. Think of the things about which you now say, 'One day I would like to . . .' or 'Someday I will . . .' or 'By the time I am X I will . . .' For example,

> '*By the time I am 55 I want to retire or at least work part-time.*'
> '*One day I would like to go and see my sister in Australia.*'
> '*Before I reach 50 I am going to quit smoking and lose two stone.*'
> '*Someday I'd like to drive a Ferrari.*'

3 What are your wildest dreams and deepest fears? Take this opportunity to express those things which you may never have dared to say out loud – your wildest dreams and your deepest fears. Dreams make for the enthusiasm in life. Fears can poison many of your actions.

Some people, when they finally talk about what they thought was 'just a fantasy', discover that it is actually something they could make happen:

> '*I'd like to run a pub in the country.*'
> '*I'm longing to play the oboe.*'
> '*I want to work part-time and write that novel.*'

Talking about your fears allows you to step back and look at what may be stopping you from making progress now or in the future:

> '*If I do this university course, it may split up our marriage.*'
> '*If I spend my savings on travelling, I may not have enough left to meet the needs of my old age.*'
> '*I can't possibly leave this job, and start my own business. What will happen to my family if I don't make it?*'

Look at what you have got

Once identified, there are often practical ways to do something, both about your dreams and your fears.

First, look at your work in 1, 2, and 3 above. is there a mismatch between your present circumstances and where you want to get to in life – or are you on course? If you are on course, use the activities in Steps 2–4 below to ensure that you are giving yourself the best chance of meeting your expectations.

Otherwise, look at the areas with which at present you are dissatisfied. What changes do you need to make to move in the direction of your goals? Make a rough list of the changes that you need to, or are willing to, or feel you should make. On another list, set down the fears which may prevent you from making them. Then put these lists aside while you work through the figures and feelings in Step 2, below.

STEP 2
KNOW THE FACTS – YOUR FIGURES AND YOUR FEELINGS

Below are the three areas about which you need to have as much information as you can muster, in terms of your finances and your feelings about them:

- the financial analysis – bills and other outgoings
- the spending analysis – a record of your day-to-day expenditure
- the cost-of-living analysis – an investigation into your overall financial situation.

These tasks are likely to be difficult to tackle requiring, as they do, precise details of your finances and honest reflections on how it feels to look realistically at your circumstances. If you have been avoiding this whole territory for a long time, it may take you some time before you feel able to complete these analyses, or even to start them in the first place. That's fine, and if you have to stop for a while when doing them, that's fine, too.

Just don't give up. The fact is that without this basic information, you cannot move on to the next steps. Ignorance of the facts means that you are fooling yourself and hindering your plans for tomorrow.

So give yourself credit for getting started, get on with it – and don't be hard on yourself.

A. The financial analysis – bills and other outgoings

The questions below will help you to find out how much you know about your figures and how you react to them. Here is a financial analysis form, to give you an idea of the way a financial consultant would work through these issues:

Take this task in three stages:

- answer each question
- score your answers
- review your scores and reflect on your reactions to them

Answer each question. Note down the answers to each of the questions. You do not need to take the questions in the order in which they are presented, but you do need to find the answers to all of them. Use any of the material you have to hand – and make a search for what you don't know or can't find.

Score your answers. Using the list below, pick the letter that is closest to the way in which you answered each question and write it in the left margin next to the answer. Remember, it is no use lying to yourself. The point is not whether you got x's all the way through, but what the scores revealed about how much – or how little – you know.

x *I knew the correct answer immediately*
y *I thought I knew the correct answer but I was wrong*
z *I hadn't a clue and I couldn't find the information immediately*

Review your scores and reflect on what you have learnt. After you have answered as many questions as you can and scored your answers, look back at the feelings that all this has thrown up. Can you see any patterns in your knowledge (or lack of knowledge) and in your reactions? The commentary after each question may give you ideas about the way others have tended to answer.

The financial analysis – bills and other outgoings

1 Earnings and income
How much do you earn – per month, per annum; that is to say, your gross income before any deductions?

FINANCIAL
ANALYSIS

CONFIDENTIAL

NAME

Michael   TANNER

DATE

9/1/87

AGE

33

D.O.B.

24 - 6 - 53

TEL. No.

HOME ADDRESS

Flat 1
27 Aberdeen Road
London N.W.1

OWNED/RENTED

House: divided into flats

BUSINESS ADDRESS

Stoke Newington Council
183 - 187 S. Newington High St,
N 16

TEL. No.

254 - 6691 (direct line)

EMPLOYED/SELF EMPLOYED

OCCUPATION

Local Government Officer

INCOME GROSS

£16,400

TAKE HOME

£1071 p.m.

TAX %

BASIC

MARITAL STATUS

Single

NAME

AGE

D.O.B.

OCCUPATION/
EMPLOYED/SELF EMPLOYED

INCOME

TEL. No.

CHILDREN (Names & Ages)

n/a

OTHER DEPENDENTS

n/a

ACCOUNTANT

Howard Keaton
Portland House
4 Gt. Portland St. WC1

TEL. No.

636 0927/8

ASSETS

1. BANK

£

Midland - current personal a/c | 0
"   "   house a/c | 100
deposit | 402

Building Society
Mornington Crescent Building Soc. | 10

Others

2. INVESTMENTS

Investment from Fiat 2 : £70 p.m.

3. SAVINGS PLANS & ASSURANCES

CO.	DATE	MAT. DATE	PREM	TYPE	L/A	S/A
Liberty Life	1978	25 yrs ?	£10	Life Assurance		£25000
" "	1985	25 yrs	£5	— " —		£5000

4. PENSION SCHEMES

BENEFITS

Co. Scheme Name: London Borough of
Personal Pension Name: Haringey pension

Death in Service   1 year's salary

Contribution: 6%
Retirement Age: 65
Paid-up Schemes Name: None
Amount:

Flats :   1   £100,000

5. VALUE OF PROPERTIES

2   £70 - 85,000

3   £55,000

LIABILITIES

		£
Bank Overdraft	Presently £12,000 o/d in bank	
Credit Cards 1	ACCESS c/L £1000	1,000
Credit Cards 2		
Mortgage Amount Borrowed	Mornington C. Bld Soc.	30,000
Top-up		

(i) Lender ←

(ii) Type : L/C End / (Repayment) / Pension   Co. Name

(iii) Date Effected July '85   Term O/S   25 yr term

(iv) Interest Rate   Standard %   (v) Monthly Repayment   £ 250 approx

Hire Purchase 1		
Hire Purchase 2		
Credit Accounts 1		
Credit Accounts 2		
Bank Loans	Bridging loan from bank (Nov 85) for Car purchase	£5,400
Others	Owes Sister £10,000.	

OUTGOINGS	Weekly	Monthly	Annually
Rent/Mortgages		£ 250	
Fares/Petrol		£ 40 + £40	
Food		£ 145	
Loans/Debts		About to clear	
Credit Cards		About to clear	
Electricity/Gas/Phone		£100 average	
Rates/Poll Tax		£ 82	
Insurance		£ 65 (incl. property + car)	
Others		£60 (cigarettes)	
Others		£25 (subscription)	
Total Outgoings		£ 767	

1. Clear debts
2. Sensible use of cash : investment
3. Clear any tax liability
4. Purchase more property (long term)

Do you know what your net income is; that is your 'take home pay' per month, per week?

If you have just had a rise, what was your last pay cheque?

Do you consider yourself to be well paid?

If you are no longer working, what is your income – per month, per annum – from your pension/s?

If you have any unearned income, how much is that per month, per annum? What is the total capital on which that income is based?

> It is amazingly common for people not to know. 'Well . . . let me see, it's about £1000 . . .' when really it is £920 – or £1200.

2 Banking

How much is in your current account?

How much have you usually got in your current account on the day before you get paid?

How many accounts do you have?

Where are they and what kind are they?

What interest do they earn?

What are you paying out in standing orders/direct debit mandates each month – to whom and for what? When do they finish?

> Some people can tell you to the last penny what they have in four different bank accounts. But many of us can't even say what we usually have in one account. It's no good saying, 'I have got £400 at the bank today' when the fact is that, by the time your overdraft and standing orders have been paid, you are left with £20 at the end of the month.
>
> Do you know how much you are paying out in standing orders? Many people don't, and a large percentage don't even know how to read a bank statement in order to find out this information, or to locate the codes which identify standing orders and direct debits. If you can't find any of this information quickly, or at all, this is an immediate giveaway that you either don't read your bank statements, or that you read them incorrectly.

3 Savings plans and back-up money

Do you have building society or Post Office accounts?

How much is in them?

What sort of accounts are they?

Do you save regularly?
What is the interest rate on each of the accounts, if you have more than one?
Do you have any savings plans?
If so, with whom are the plans and when did you start them?
How much are you paying per month?
Are your savings plans index-linked?
Have you any life assurance? If so, what is the basic life cover on each policy?
Who is named as the beneficiary on each policy in the event of your death or when the policy matures?
If you don't have a company car, are you saving towards replacement costs of the car you own? Do you have other savings?

> *The one thing most people do know is what they have in their building society account(s) when the amount is over £500. With anything else, such as savings plans, most people do not remember much about the plan, not even the name of the company. If the amount they are paying out is less than £10, they quite often forget about it.*

4 Pensions

Are you contributing to a company pension scheme?
If so, how much do you contribute? How much does the company contribute?
How long have you been contributing?
Do you have 'death in service' benefit? Do you know what that means? Do you know how much it is?
Have you any funds left in the pension scheme of a company for which you no longer work?
If so, do you know the details of that scheme?
Do you have a personal pension plan?
How much are you paying in to this? When did it start?
Is it with-profit or unit-linked? Do you know what these terms mean?
What company are you using? (If you have more than one plan, answer for each company.)
At what age do you plan to retire?
Are you getting tax relief on the contributions?

> *Few people can tell you what their company pension scheme is. Could you? And 'death in service' – 'What's that?' Do you have a booklet? Do you know where you can get one?*

*If you are in a personal pension scheme, it's likely that
you do know how much you are paying and when you are
able to retire, but not necessarily what the eventual value of
your pension will be. And were you surprised that you could
not give the correct name of the company which operates your
scheme? You are not alone. When asked this question some
people name policies which they think are in force now and
which, on investigation, they discover they cancelled five
years ago.*

5 Property and other investments
(i) Property and mortgages
What is your house/flat worth – the market rate, not your own
valuation?
How much is your mortgage?
Who is the lender?
What type of mortgage is it?
What interest rate are you paying?
If yours is a pension or endowment mortgage, did you know that
when answering question 3 above? If not, go back and make a
note of it now.
How much longer does your mortgage have to run?
(ii) Other investments
Do you have any other form of investments? Stocks and shares?
Premium bonds? Unit Trusts? PEPs? Bonds?
With whom do you have these investments? How many?
When did you buy them? How much did they cost?

*Most people know roughly the value of their house or flat.
'Oohhh, I haven't had it valued, but a house down the road
in the same condition as ours sold last week for . . .' But
we don't remember whether our mortgage has endowments or
pensions attached.*

*Few people who have shares can say how many, or
quote the purchase price. If you can't, then you don't know
whether they are in profit or not.*

6 Debts
(i) Credit cards
How many do you have? Which ones?
What is your limit on each one?
How much do you owe?
How much do you pay off each month?

(ii) Bank overdraft
Do you have an agreed overdraft? What is it?
Are you over its limit? If so, have you phoned your bank to confirm that they are happy about this?
Do you know what you are being charged for the 'privilege' of having an overdraft?

(iii) Hire purchase and other loans/debts
How much are your monthly payments?
When did they start?
When will they end?

(iv) Any other bills
Review your commitments, look at your bank statements and chequebook stubs. Do you have any other bills, e.g. rent you owe, loans from friends or family, which you expect or are expected to pay back?

> *People usually can't work out what their debts are. Did you know accurately what your credit card debts were last month? Or how much you paid? 'I have a bill of, whew! about £500 . . .' and on checking it will turn out to be 'oh my goodness, £700 and something . . .'. Yet the same person may have £1000 in the building society but can't bear the thought of using that money to clear the credit card bill. Why? Because deep down they know it will quickly build up again. Does that sound familiar?*
>
> *Most of us don't know the limits on our credit cards. And it's no excuse that the credit card companies keep increasing the limit without our asking. Most of us spend closer to our limits than ever before but still underestimate how much we owe – and we don't usually pay this off in regular amounts. 'I usually pay about £100. Last month? Oh, that's different – I paid only £25, I was short.' And the month before? 'Oh, probably about £50.' Then if they look at their credit card statement, they see that what in fact they paid was simply the minimum amount, which is why that particular debt isn't decreasing.*
>
> *Do you have more than one credit card? If so, did you find real difficulty in answering these questions? Most people do.*

7 Regular bills
(i) Mortgage or rent
How much is your mortgage payment or your rent?

How much is your local tax and how is it being paid?
(ii) Telephone
What was your last phone bill?
(iii) Gas
What was your last gas bill?
(iv) Electricity
What was your last electricity bill?
(v) Other regular bills
What other regular bills do you have, e.g. water rates, car loan,
AA or RAC, house and contents insurance?
Do you know what each of these cost you?
Do you know when they are due?

> *Did you overestimate, underestimate, forget anything?*
> *Did you include any* annual *bills in here as if they were*
> monthly *ones? If you did, take them out. Keep a note of the*
> *annual bills for the cost-of-living analysis, but don't include*
> *them here.*

Review your scores and your reactions

Now let's review the way you have scored your answers and see
what they tell you about your relationship to the figures in your
finances.

X I knew the correct answer immediately. For most or all of the
questions, did you know the correct answer or where to find it
quickly? Were you one of those who were able to say, 'I'm not
quite sure what it is, but [flick, flick, flick], here it is . . .' or
'It's around the £400 mark. Just a second, it's £432.50.'

If you got the answers correct most of the time, you are clearly
in command of your figures. Excellent. But don't read too much
into this. People who keep meticulous records often have a hard
time knowing what their goals are and deciding about what to
do with their money: they lose sight of the wood for the trees.

If you knew most of the answers, which ones didn't you know?
Why? Could you answer that before you move on? Don't worry
if you can't – just admit it.

Y I thought I knew the correct figures but got them wrong. Test
yourself before you move on. When you got an answer wrong,
did a voice say, 'I should have known it but . . . I just changed

jobs *or* my husband/wife/partner/bank manager deals with that *or* it was so long ago . . .'? Can you hear yourself justifying your mistake and excusing it? Who is fooling whom – and why? Don't move on until you can answer that. Fooling others may be a choice you can afford to make. Fooling yourself means you can't make progress.

If you know that you've been making excuses and can admit that fact, move on – but watch your step!

Z I hadn't a clue – and couldn't find the information. Did you get out masses of papers but say 'I'm not quite sure where to look'? Are you someone who doesn't know that you can find your standing orders by looking at your bank statement? And did you have no idea what's in your current account? It will not surprise you to hear that you have a major problem.

Even though it may seem obvious that you have got good reason to despair – don't. Yes, it's going to be hard work, but you may find that in the long run you have an advantage over those who answered questions correctly. Many people who manage to keep their records in good order don't actually understand how and why things work the way they do. You, on the other hand, will never make progress *unless* you understand.

The question for you to ask yourself at this point is – how serious am I about wanting to take control of my finances? If you are serious, then you will have to find the answers to all the questions in this chapter. Either go away now, find them, and come back and do the questions again. Or make a list of the information you need and take your time in getting the answers together.

If you *are* determined to take control of your money, don't worry about how slow a start you have made – just don't give up.

B The spending analysis – a record of your day to day expenditure

In order to know what is happening to the money you spend day by day, you need to keep an accurate record of *every* penny you spend, ideally for three weeks, preferably for four weeks but at least for two. You will then 'read' the information to find out not only how much you spend but what patterns you have, and where you cannot face telling yourself the truth.

People often get very angry when reviewing their figures

because they know it is going to make them have to face their lack of control over their actual spending. Recording figures and reviewing feelings is like talking to yourself. If you have promised to be honest with yourself, that may mean no more games – and that's scary.

For this activity you need a small cash book. It needs to be small, but sturdy enough to be carried everywhere for six or eight weeks without falling apart, because you will also need it for your cost-of-living analysis in C below. But not so small that you won't be able to read your own writing.

Lay out three columns in the following way:

Col 1	Col 2	Col 3
the date	*what you spend your money on*	*the amount you spend*
	e.g. the pub, lunch, newspapers [Comment if you want to]	

Take this book with you everywhere you go and do the following:

(i) Enter expenditure immediately

Enter in your book every penny that you spend each day, for at least two weeks – and that really does mean *every* penny. Record your spending at the time you do it, or as soon thereafter as you can. This is *vital*.

(ii) Omit regular bills

Do not include your regular standing orders or bills. Nor should you enter half-yearly or annual payments if they happen to occur in the weeks during which you are keeping the record.

(iii) Comment on your progress

If you wish, make comments in the book as you go along, e.g. 'An ice-cream often relieves temper', 'I *needed* three beers', 'I wanted to lie about this.'

(iv) Total your monies, daily and weekly

At the end of each day total the monies for that day. Enter no more than two days on each page. At the end of each week do a seven-day total.

(v) Test yourself

When you've totalled up, test yourself. Close the book and ask yourself what the totals for the various days were. Now do you remember what you have just added up for the whole week? We have very clever ways of mentally blocking out uncomfortable information. Practice not just adding up the figures but also taking in the total.

Review your records and your reactions

Look back at your spending analysis book, read your figures and the notes you made.

If you missed recording for a day, ask yourself why. The answer could be, 'I was terribly busy and I just didn't have time . . . it wasn't possible.' Is that really true?

Look at the pages yet again. Can you tell anything from your handwriting? Do several days look the same because you wrote them all at once? Looking back and remembering – not judging – can you see where you faked an entry, for instance, recording lunch as £5 when in fact it was £15, or leaving out the third taxi that you took on Tuesday?

Opposite are sample pages from two books and notes on how to read the signs.

In answering questions about your spending analysis, have you found yourself getting defensive? Think about what is bothering you.

Don't go any further with the analysis at this stage but do hold on to the book. You need it for the last activity.

C The Cost-of-living analysis – an investigation into your overall spending pattern

In order to complete the final stage of gaining a complete picture of your financial situation and how you feel about it, you need to keep a record of your spending for another four weeks. This time it *must be for four weeks*. Do it in exactly the same way as in the spending analysis in B, above, with the following additions:

(i) Add the weeks together

Total the amount of your spending each week, carry the weekly

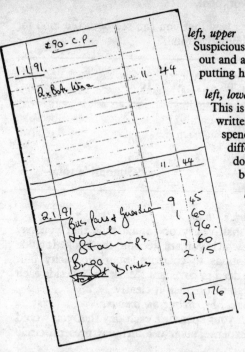

left, upper
Suspicious. Nothing else spent yet was out and about. Probably only putting half the spending down.

left, lower
This is perfect. Obviously written at the time of spending – handwriting is different and apparently done quickly – as would be the case.

below
All of this is suspicious. Handwriting all the same – means all done at one time and therefore grossly inaccurate.

£90 - C.P.

1.1.91.   11 34
2 x Bot. Wine

                11 44

2.1.91   Bus fares & Guardian   9 45
         Lunch   1 60
                                    96.
         Stamps   7 60
         Bingo   2 15
         Food & Drinks

                                21 76

23.1.91
    Lunch   1   60
    Breakfast   1   60
    Seller.   15   00

                  17   20

24.1.91
    Candy   90
    Breakfast   1   25
    Lunch   1   95
    Julie   10
    Dinner   £10   00

                  24   10

25.1.91
    Bus fare   10   00
    Lunch   3   45
    Movies   10   00

                 23   45

26.1.91
    Clothes   14   97
    Groceries   7   61
    Petrol   5   00

                 27   58

total forward in such a way that you can see both the total for each week and the cumulative total.

February	Spent	Total
Week 1	£70	
Week 2	£50	£120
Week 3	£136	£256
Week 4	£39	**£295 month's total**

(ii) Enter bills and mark with an X
Enter any quarterly, half-yearly or annual bills that you pay during the weeks for which you are keeping the book. Include for instance, subscriptions to charities, your electricity bill, television licence or a deed of covenant. Mark an X beside each amount so that you can distinguish it clearly.

(iii) Note unusual expenses by circling the amount
If there is anything in your spending each day that you would consider an unusual expense, such as a birthday present, circle the amount.

Review your records and your reactions

For how many days did you fail to keep a record this time? What were the reasons and were they genuine? If they were, that's fine, e.g. 'I was on holidays for two days', 'I had to go away for the weekend' – anything of that kind was unplanned or otherwise not part of your everyday pattern of life. If there were days when you did not record your spending, make sure you record your spending on additional days so that you have an entire calendar month's records to review.

Look at the bills against which you have written X and total them for the month. Then check if there are more of these types of bills due within the next one or two months. Calculate the total for the bills you have recorded and for the next one or two months and note that total separately.

Then glance at the items which you have circled as 'unusual outgoings'. A holiday, for example, is a legitimate 'unusual' expenditure to circle. But have you yet noticed the 'usual unusual'? These are the odd entries you have indicated as one-offs. Yes, that one, and that one, and that one – in fact, there's one every week. Flowers for your mother, that birthday present, the friend visiting from abroad with whom you went out for a meal. It's all spending, and regular spending, not genuinely unusual. If you often give birthday presents to friends, then the expenditure becomes regular – it's just the recipient who changes. Note the amounts.

Can you see other patterns in the book? For instance, how often you pop in and out to buy things? Or what you regularly buy when under particular pressure: is it food for you, or a bottle of wine? Is it a coffee here, a coffee there? Or just 'bits' – from any shop whose door is open? Is it clothes – that cheap T-shirt, that belt? Is it books?

Summary

Now that you have looked at the results of the financial analysis, the spending analysis and the cost of living analysis, what are your reactions?

Is it a disappointment? What are you actually disappointed about? Can you do anything to change things?

Or is it a shock? And is that because you now realize that what you had been planning for will probably take you much longer to achieve than you had anticipated? Are you prepared to wait that long – and if not, are you able to settle for less, or for something different?

This process is all about choices, not obstacles.

The work on the first two of the 5 Steps has given you the basic information about your goals, your financial situation and your reactions to it. The next three steps help you to look at what, in light of that information, your choices might be, and how to make the most of them in order to live for today and plan for tomorrow – realistically.

STEP 3
CONSIDER THE *REAL* OPTIONS

By now you will have all the basic information you need in order to see what your options are. In order to arrive at options that are realistic for you, you need to:

- list all the possible courses of action
- calculate roughly what each option will cost in terms of money, time and energy
- drop those ideas which no longer appeal to you and/or which are no longer realistic
- draw up your final list of achievable options

List all possible courses of action

List all the courses of action which your work on Steps 1 and 2 have thrown up. At this stage it is important to jot down any ideas for changes and developments in your life which especially appeal to you or which you feel are necessary, such as clearing debts if you have discovered that you are in debt. Try some 'brainstorming' – put down everything that comes to mind, *without making any comments or editing your thoughts*.

When you have listed everything that comes to mind, go back and review the list. Cross off any ideas which you already know are not worth pursuing – and leave those which, though slightly different from your habitual choices, are still worth considering.

* *clear debts*
* *save more in building society*
* *cut down days working*
* *become self-employed*
* *do further study*
* *buy new car*

Calculate roughly what each option will cost you, in terms of money, time and energy

Take your list and make the following notes beside each suggestion:

- rough figures to show how much it would cost to finance each option;
- a guesstimate of the time it would take you to see each course of action through, or give some alternatives, e.g. two years to save the deposit for a house if you gave up holidays abroad both years; four years if you continued to go skiing in France in the winter and to a beach in Spain in the summer; and three years if you cut down on one holiday each year.

- the pros and cons of any other factors that you need to take into account.

For instance,

> *Do a degree course:*
> £   (i) *part-time: fees for 6 years*
>   *expenses for fares, books*
>
>   (ii) *full-time: fees for 2 years*
>   *living expenses for 2 years*
>   *expenses for books, fares, etc.*
>
> *Time* (i) *part-time: 2 evenings a week,*
>   *20 hours study per week, (includes 16 hours at home)*
>   *3 hours tutorial per month,*
>   *1 week residential per year*
>   (ii) *full-time: 2 years*
>
> *Pros* *increased job opportunities*
>   *part-time: can maintain income*
>   *full-time: greater satisfaction from studies*
>
> *Cons* *part-time: can't concentrate at night*
>   *full-time: I'd most likely finish up in debt*

Drop those ideas which no longer appeal to you and/ or which are no longer realistic

Consider the information you have just noted and your reactions to it. Go through and cross out any ideas which, at this point in time, you cannot honestly see yourself undertaking.

Ask yourself about each of them:

- Is this still one of my goals? If it's not, cross it out straightaway.
  If it still is, go on to ask:
- Am I going to have to turn my life upside down to achieve it?
- If so, is this realistic?
- If it's not realistic, can you think of other ways of reaching the same goal?

If you can, add them to your notes. If you can't, and the matter is still important to you, make a note to come back to this idea when you next review your goals and finances.

Draw up your final list of achievable options

Make a fresh list of the options which remain.

STEP 4
MAKE CHOICES– LIVE FOR TODAY
AND PLAN FOR TOMORROW

Now that you have a list of possible courses of action, you need to decide where you want to start to make the changes that will bring you closer to your goals. In order to decide which of the ideas you wish to implement first, you need to:

- divide your list into short/medium/long term aims
- do more detailed costings
- rank your choices in order of priority
- draw up an action plan

Divide your list into short/medium/long term aims

If you are not clear which is short/medium/long term, ask yourself:

- short term: what do I need to do within the next 1–2 years?
- medium term: what do I want to achieve in the next 5–10 years?
- long term: what goals do I wish to reach in 10+ years?

Place your suggestions under the appropriate heading:

- *short term – take an annual holiday abroad*
- *medium term – move house*
- *long term – have some money to help the children when they are 18+*

Every medium and longer term goal is made up of a series of short-term steps. You will be able to sort these out when you make an action plan (see page 162).

Do more detailed costings

For each list, cost the options in more detail than you did in Step 3 above, for money, time and pros and cons.

Rank your choices in order of priority

Look at the costs which you have calculated and ask yourself again: is there any option that is no longer realistic in terms of money and/or time? If so, cross it off.

Next ask yourself: which of these options do I feel like undertaking first? Those for which you have most enthusiasm or most concern are the ones you are most likely to achieve, e.g. you may want to do further training, or you may know that you can't make any real progress on anything else until you have cleared your debts.

Number the options in the order in which you plan to do them.

Test your decisions by checking that they will really allow you to live for today while planning for tomorrow. Only you will know whether your choices meet this criterion – or whether they are unrealistic. To say 'I can manage on two meals a day or on £5 pocket-money a week or with four hours sleep for six months', is unrealistic and self-defeating. That is to say, they are not really choices at all and you are already subverting your stated aim of taking control of your financial life.

Draw up an action plan

Your action plan needs to include both:

- a plan for clearing the decks of any unfinished financial business, and
- plans for moving forward on your choices.

Any action plan needs to detail

- what you need to do
- a deadline and timetable for each of the different tasks or activities which are necessary in reaching your goal
- the financial cost of that overall goal
- any other factors which you need to take into account.

Clearing the decks

Look at your notes from *Step 2: Know Your Facts*. Did you discover any unfinished financial business to which you need to attend before you feel confident about moving towards your new goals? If so, make an action plan for clearing up that business.

Here is an action plan for a teacher who wants to do a further training course but who, at present, is spending more than he earns:

* *cut down on going out and save that money – year 1 £10 per week*
* *clear all debts except bank loan (total £1030) – year 2*
* *start saving that money, plus any salary increase, towards course fees – year 3*
* *decide on day or evening studies – year 3*

Moving forward

Make action plans for your short/medium/long term goals, using the checklist given above to make sure that you have not left anything out.

Aim	*Change from teaching primary level to secondary level*
Need	*Further training*
Deadline	*5 years, i.e.*
	2 years to clear debts
	3 years to train (unless I can find a special programme)
	Year 5: qualify and start applying for other jobs

[This process could be speeded up if holidays were curtailed but this individual felt that, with the pressure of teaching, clearing his debts, and training, he needed his holidays as treats to keep him going.]

The aim is to live for today and plan for tomorrow. Check back that your action plan will allow you to do both.

STEP 5
DO IT – AND REVIEW IT

Finally, what's left is to get on with it – and review your progress. Remember to:

• take one step at a time
• give yourself some credit
• build in regular reviews

Take one step at a time – and remember that steps may not always be forward

Your first step is to see whether you have enough money left to implement your choices after you have covered your basic living expenses. If you haven't got enough left over, where are you prepared to economize? If your answer at this stage is 'nowhere', then you either have to go back and modify your goals and choices, or you will have to work twice as hard to earn the extra money you need.

Perhaps your main goal was to cut down work to only four days a week. In that case, do you want to keep the same level of earnings or are you saying that you will accept a cut in salary? If you want to keep the same level of earnings, what do you need to do to achieve this, and is it possible?

If you would rather take a cut in salary, make a budget and see on how little you can live. Live like that for three months, then reconsider whether you really mean it or not. Put aside the money you have saved and at the end of three months, whether you decide to go ahead or not, give yourself a treat. You deserve it.

At this point beware of backsliding. Do you find yourself wondering whether you really need to go through all this to make what you want of life? Doesn't it all seem a bit heavy and time-consuming? Didn't you manage perfectly well enough before?

Think back to how you have managed until now. You'll probably find that you have managed quite well but many of us (and this may include you) want to manage better than that. That is the motivation for wanting to take control of our financial lives. If your goals are planned, you are more likely to achieve them – and enjoy yourself in the process.

Give yourself some credit

Recognize and enjoy what you have achieved, however small a step forward you have taken.

You have planned for tomorrow and are working through your plans. But if you don't live for today as well, you may not make it – or make it in good health and good spirits.

Write down an amount of money and time that will allow you to enjoy some 'treats'. For example, you have finished paying off a loan in instalments. Next month, use the amount of that instalment to give yourself a treat, then add part of that sum, or all of it, towards clearing the rest of your debts.

Think about what would count as a treat. It could be going to a concert or buying a new item of clothing. Or taking a week's holiday somewhere special or a weekend away at a fancy hotel. The decision is yours.

You will have to match the 'treats' to your available resources – don't skimp or binge. Perhaps you can afford a massage once a month this year but, if things go according to plan, you can aim at having a monthly massage plus three days at the health farm next year.

Build in regular reviews

Making changes in your life requires 'fine tuning' when things are going smoothly, and emergency measures when you hit a snag. Without taking the time to stop and review changed circumstances and new options, you cannot stay in control of your life and your money.

Schedule regular reviews – and be prepared to take time out for emergency reviews. Book a couple of hours with yourself every six months at least – and every three months or even monthly for as long as you don't feel entirely in control of your finances.

Your reviews might include regular items, such as:

- making a list of your outstanding debts and noting the decrease at the time of each review;
- checking whether your bank account has remained at the level at which you have decided to keep it;
- monitoring your telephone bills.

If circumstances change which affect or may affect your finances, do an immediate financial review, however reluctant you feel.

You should find that working through the 5 Steps will cut through some of your anxieties and give you a clearer view of your situation and what to do about it.

Take yourself through the 5 Steps and make new plans based on the new circumstances. Do monthly reviews of your new plan until you feel that you are again on an even keel.

W2
Working for Someone Else

If you are an employee,

1 Acknowledge where you are – and what you want

What is your current situation at work?

- the work you are doing,
- the company for which you are working and the economic health and prospects in your industry;
- your skills and abilities.

In general, are you satisfied with your situation at present? Do have any plans for the future or any ideas about how you would like to develop your career?

You might want to ask yourself:

- what kind of work you would like to be doing – with your present employer, with another one, full-time, part-time, in business for yourself?
- the developments or setbacks that are happening in your field of work and how these could affect your plans;
- the kind of life which you hope to finance from your salary at each stage in your working life, for instance, the kind of home you would like, how many holidays;
- the additional skills and abilities you would like to have, or would need to develop, for promotion and/or greater income, and any training this would require.

Another way to get a sense of where you would like to be going with your working life is to picture yourself in your mind's eye at the point when you retire. What will you be like? What will you have accomplished? What will you regret not having done or developed or experienced?

Are there any changes which you feel you need to make soon in order to move in the direction of your aims?

2 Know the facts – your figures *and* your feelings

You need to know the facts of your working life for two reasons:

- to make sure that you are getting the best deal at work
- to know whether you are living within your income.

Make sure that you are getting the best deal at work. Ask yourself these questions and if you don't know the answers, find out:

1 What is my official job title?
2 What are my duties?
3 Do numbers 1 and 2 match?
4 Does the company contribute towards. . . .
5 Is my payslip correct?
6 What is offered in addition to my salary, e.g. superannuation/pension, car, share options?
7 Are benefits available which I have not been offered?
8 Am I getting the fair market rate for the work I am doing?
9 Am I progressing at work?

Check your payslip and benefits to make sure you are getting everything to which you are entitled, and that no mistakes are being made. (See the sample payslip opposite.)

Is your salary accurate? Are the deductions of the type and amount which you expect i.e. tax, national insurance, and are the extra deductions those to which you had agreed, i.e. share options, union fees, donations to charities?

To get the answers to some of these questions, you may need to make an appointment to see the personnel officer – or the equivalent in your company. Also ask about any other available benefits. These can range from share options to savings plans, help with mortgages and car purchases, help with fees for further training, private health plans and season ticket loans.

You also need to consider your salary and progress in the company. In the public sector most salaries are tied to regular negotiating procedures. In the private sector, you may have to negotiate your own salary. In whichever sector your job is located, review whether you are in the right job or whether you

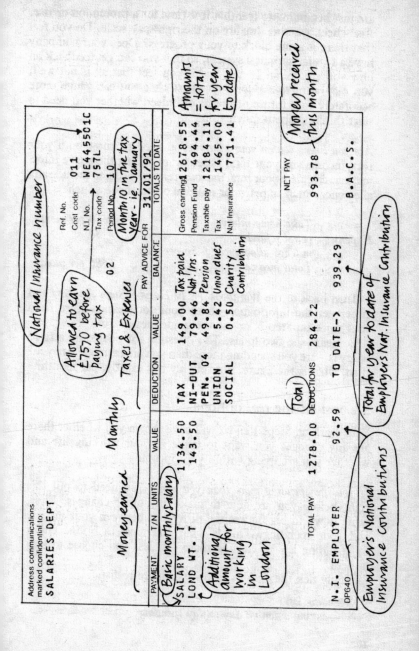

Address communications
marked confidential to:
SALARIES DEPT

National Insurance number

Ref. No.
Cost code   011
N.I. No.   WE445501C
Tax code   757L

Allowed to earn £7570 before paying tax

Period No.   10

Month 10 in the tax Year - ie. January

Money earned   Monthly   Taxes & Expenses   02

PAY ADVICE FOR   31/01/91

TOTALS TO DATE

Amounts = Total for year to date

PAYMENT	T/N	UNITS	VALUE		DEDUCTION	VALUE	BALANCE
SALARY	T		1134.50		TAX	149.00	Tax paid
LOND WT.	T		143.50		NI-OUT	79.46	Nat. Ins.
					PEN. 04	49.84	Pension
					UNION	5.42	Union dues
					SOCIAL	0.50	Charity Contribution

Basic monthly Salary

Additional amount for working in London

	Gross earnings	2678.55
	Pension Fund	494.44
	Taxable pay	12184.11
	Tax	1465.00
	Nat Insurance	751.41

(Total)

TOTAL PAY   1278.00   DEDUCTIONS   284.22   TO DATE →   939.29

N.I. EMPLOYER   92.59

NET PAY   993.78

Money received this month

B.A.C.S.

DP640

Employer's National Insurance Contributions

Total for year to date of Employer's Nat. Insurance Contribution are just beginning to feel that it is time for a promotion or rise. Also check whether you are on the right pay scale. Do you feel that there is some block to your progress? Does your company have a regular appraisal system, so that you can get feedback on how you are doing? If not, and if you feel that all is not well, you may want to ask for a review so that you can gauge more accurately your future prospects or indeed whether you need to start thinking about moving on.

Are you living within your salary? You need to know both your total income and your total expenditure. Using the above information, calculate your total income, remembering to include any allowances such as petrol or mileage or luncheon vouchers.

	Take home salary	£650 per month
Expenses	petrol refund	30
	mileage allowance @ 5p per mile	6
	Total income	£686 per month

Turn back to the *Workbook 1 The Basic 5 Steps Analysis* and either get the information about your total expenditure from your work on Step 2, or use the guidelines to work it out.

Compare the two totals. The question for people on a fixed salary is – are you spending more than you are earning? Are you? If so, what is the figure, not roughly but exactly, per month?

3 Consider the *real* options

Your work on Steps 1 and 2 will have shown you whether there are any changes you want to make in your working life and whether you are living within your income.

If you are spending more than you earn. You need to put this right before you are able to make any other changes. First, write down in big figures the difference between your income and your spending. This is what you have to bridge either by spending less or earning more – unless you choose to stay in debt.

Mentally tick the options below which are realistic.

Spending less
—cutting down on day-to-day spending

—cutting out major expenditures, e.g. a holiday
Earning more
   —changing jobs
   —getting a rise
   —working overtime
   —doing other part-time work

Make notes about the options you have ticked, including:

- how much you could earn/save
- how much time it would involve
- any other factors that need to be taken into account, e.g. the confidence you would need to ask your boss for a rise or what you need to do if you decide to spend less.

If you want to make other changes in your work. List all the options that come immediately to mind, no matter how far-fetched, remembering the direction and aim of your own working life:

- cross out those options which you cannot imagine yourself choosing;
- elaborate on the ones that are left.

4 Make the choices – live for today *and* plan for tomorrow

If you are spending more than you are earning, write down for each realistic option:

- how much you could earn
- how much time it would take
- any other factors, pro or con, about this option
- any preparations you would need to make, such as asking a friend to help you rehearse if you are planning to go for job interviews, or to talk with you before you approach your employer for a rise.

Now put these options in an order of priority. Choose one to start with – but keep the others on your list in case the first one does not work out.

If you want to make other changes at work, remember that you should include in your plan of action anything that you need to do to gain the confidence and skills to follow your plan through.

5 Do it – and review it

Set yourself targets:
If you need to balance your income and expenditure:

- how long will you give yourself to find a way to do this?
- how will you pay off any debt you have accumulated?
- when will you start getting down to tackling any of this?

If you are spending more than you earn, you need to review your situation monthly, otherwise your debts will continue to grow.

Your own plan of action may be affected by other factors, such as the economic climate in which your company and your industry operates or by changes of personnel. Only regular reviewing will help you to adjust quickly to such changes.

You are likely to need the regular support of a friend, colleague or financial professional to see through these changes. Agree regular dates well in advance for review and support.

W3
Thinking about Working for Yourself

If you are considering becoming self-employed,

1 Acknowledge where you are – and what you want

In order to test whether you really want to work for yourself and, if so, how much time and money you will need, list in as much detail as you can:

- the service or product you have to offer
- the market and how you would get access to it
- when you would like to start
- the business skills required and whether you yourself have all of these, and if not, how you would acquire or find them
- the facilities and resources needed.

Then look at your present situation, and think about:

- the work you are doing now, your skills, contacts and lifestyle
- any groundwork you have done already to prepare yourself for working for yourself.

If you are thinking of working with someone else, make sure you think about this, separately and together.

2 Know the facts – your figures *and* your feelings

You need two sets of figures:

- the cost of your goals
- your current cost of living.

Cost your plans. Find out:

- the total costs needed to start up the business and see it through its first year
- the size of the potential market – and where and what it is
- the average fees or prices charged by others in the kind of business you have in mind
- the financial resources on which you could draw, e.g. the equity in your house, a bank loan, a partner who will put money into the business.

Your current cost of living. Go back to the *Basic 5 Steps Analysis, Workbook Chapter 1*. Get the information you have on file and bring it up-to-date. If you have not done the financial analysis, Step 2, do so now.

Write down what you need to earn each month from your own business in order to

- avoid falling into debt
- manage without frills (your definitions, remember!)
- live comfortably

What is your reaction to the information you have gathered?

3 Consider the *real* options

Compare the information from Steps 1 and 2, about your goals/dreams and their cost, both the figures and your reactions.

List the options.

If you are clear that you want to move towards self-employment, list the options for getting there, e.g. if you want to get started two years from now; if five years from now is your target date; if you work for yourself part-time or full-time.

If the work so far has shown you that you are not yet ready to think seriously about working for yourself, your options might be to drop the whole idea or plan what you need to do before you could consider it again, e.g. further training, clearing your debts etc.

4 Make choices – live for today *and* plan for tomorrow

Check your options against what you know about yourself:

- do you at present have the skills and experience which you need in order to do the work you want?
- do you have the confidence to be your own boss?
- in your financial situation and with the resources you have, can you realistically set up a business now; in 2 years; in 5 years?

Choose the option that feels most realistic for you. Make a more detailed plan of what you need to do to implement your choice. Include in the plans the following:

- doing market research
- getting any further training/experience you may need
- financing the venture
- finding premises, if appropriate
- preparing contracts with partners or for employees, if you plan to have these
- contacting sources of help, e.g. special government schemes for setting up your own business, banks which often offer free facilities for the first year to new businesses, an accountant etc.

5 Do it – and review it

While you are getting on with all these preparations, you also need to stop regularly and review what you have done and discovered, so that you can, if necessary, alter your plans.

W4
Being Self-Employed

If you are already self-employed,

1 Acknowledge where you are – and what you want

Remind yourself of the dreams you had for your business when you set it up and the kind of life you were aiming at. If you feel that your own aims might have changed, or that the economic climate in which your business operates is now different, adjust your aims to meet new circumstances.

> *I went into business with four partners. We agreed the percentage of profit which each of us would take. However, during the first year it became apparent that I was the main contributor of the company's income while the others were taking their agreed profit percentage without putting in the agreed amount of work. After several unsuccessful meetings with my partners, I have decided to go it alone – and I feel much happier about this.*

Now take stock of the way things are going right now, and consider:

- how much you are working and whether you are getting time enough for yourself and for your family and/or friends
- your relationship with your business partner and/or employees, if you have either
- the current state of the market in which you are selling your goods or services
- your own energy
- your fees/charges/prices and whether they compare favourably with the going rate
- your business organization: are your accounts up-to-date

and are your clients paying you on time? What are your arrangements for insurances and pensions?

Do you need to make any changes? If so, is there any reason why you have not done so or are reluctant to do so?

If you work with partners or have employees, make sure that you are clear about the goals for the business and about changes that you need to make, either on your own or in consultation with others.

2 Know the facts – your figures *and* your feelings

In order to finance any developments in your business or to make changes, you need to know:

- how much you are earning
- what it is costing you to live
- how you are spending your time.

How much are you earning? Get out your profit and loss accounts for the last year and bring them up to date. (See *The Practical Guide to Book-keeping and Taxation for the Self-Employed.*)

What is it costing you to live? Calculate what your living costs are, using the information from The Basic 5 Steps Analysis, Step 2.

What are you doing with your time? Keep a diary for two weeks, recording what you do with your time – all day, every day, and not just when you are at work. Review the diary. The notes from the Spending Analysis in the Basic 5 Steps Analysis, Step 2, may help you with this. (See pages 176 and 177 for an example.)

3 Consider the *real* options

Compare the information from Steps 1 and 2. Look for any disparity between your goals and the facts about time and money.

Identify options in two areas:

- developments you want to make in your work in the next year, e.g. increase turnover by 15%, expand into a particular market, work with groups as well as with individuals.

- changes you need to make in the way you work in order to sustain your intended developments, e.g. working fewer hours, finding help to write up the accounts, moving the office out of your home.

List your options and, roughly, how much money and time you would have to spend on each.

4th January – Friday TIME DIARY

Time	What done	Comments
8.00– 8.50	Discussions with my partner regarding my planning abilities with the aim of pacing myself.	great step forward
9.00– 9.20	Expected telephone call from client	Consultancy
9.25– 9.50	Telephone call from friend to help her with her interview.	Unpaid Consultancy
9.50– 10.15	Arranging travelling plans and re-arranging diary dates	Administration
10.15– 12.50	Preparing draft for a course. (Fifteen minutes to go back to diary and re-do some scheduling included.)	Paid consultancy Administration
12.50– 1.00	Telephone calls.	Personal
1.10– 1.15	Call regarding Proofs	Business Call.
1.15– 1.20	Apple for lunch	Lunch break!

1.20– 1.55	Draft of report continued.	
1.55– 3.45	Eat, read, and take a nap.	Too long a break
3.45– 4.00	Telephone call regarding Course	Business
4.00– 4.10	Telephone call.	Personal
4.20– 4.45	Break	
4.45– 7.00	Finalising a report, drafting out next project	Paid Consultancy
7.20– 7.45	Telephone call from a colleague	Unpaid Consultancy
7.45	Finished for the day	

4 Make choices – live for today *and* plan for tomorrow

Choose from each list of your options:

- the most important development you want to make in your work during the next year
- the most important change you need to make in the way you work in order to sustain these developments.

Make a detailed plan for each.

5 Do it – and review it

Remember to consult and/or inform any other people who can

help you or who are affected by the changes you are making, e.g. any employees, your bank manager.

Arrange definite times to review whether you are on target, not just with the business developments but with changes in the way you are working. If you are in a partnership, set regular dates for partners' meetings when 'review' is the only agenda item. If you are working on your own, identify someone with whom it is appropriate to talk about your progress. Some of the government schemes for new businesses offer the services of counsellors; or you may prefer to see your financial consultant or your accountant.

Whether the business is flourishing or faltering, give yourself or yourselves regular 'treats' in recognition of the work you are doing.

W5
Creating Financial Security

In order to ensure that you have 'fall back money',

1 Acknowledge where you are – and what you want

Check this list to identify the money which you could make available for contingencies, emergencies and changes:

- bank savings account
- building society account
- savings plan/s
- pension income
- offer of help from someone else

Think about the basic essentials in your life for which you need to make provision in order to feel reasonably secure, e.g. the mortgage payments, school fees, private health insurance, pension contributions, life assurance costs, meeting regular bills.

2 Know the facts – your figures *and* your feelings

In order to give yourself the financial security that you want and can afford, you need to know:

- how much money in total is readily available
- the cost of the basic minimum standard of life you can endure
- how much money you have available at present which you could set aside to provide for future financial security

The total money readily available. Using the above list of money available, value each investment at the current market rate should you need to withdraw or sell in order to support yourself, e.g.

Shares	market value	£4000
Bonds	market value	£3500
PEP	Market value	£2600
Building Society savings available		£15000

Cost your basic minimum standard of living. Using the list of basic essentials which you made, calculate the costs, at the current market rates, of the minimum standard of living you feel you could endure.

Calculate how much money you have at present available to invest in future financial security. Work out how much money you will have left each month after meeting your basic bills and outgoings. Get the information from your *Basic 5 Steps Analysis, Step 2*.

3 Consider the *real* options

Consider how much money you feel you need to put aside to provide for your future financial security.

Make a list of suggestions for the various ways in which you can cover your present living costs while ensuring that you have sufficient funds to buy yourself this security both now and in the future. Make some rough costings.

increase savings from £50 to £100 per month
take out an income protection policy
buy shares instead – it's a risk I'll take

Check through the list and consider which of the suggestions you have made are financially unrealistic, especially if they were to reduce your lifestyle now to below an acceptable minimum.

4 Make choices – live for today *and* plan for tomorrow

Choose the one option which seems to meet best both your present and future needs.

Draw up a detailed plan of action for what you want to achieve. Include in this any questions which you might want to raise with a financial professional on how best to achieve your goal with the money available to you.

5 Do it – and review it

Arrange to see your financial consultant or another financial professional. Amend your plan of action in light of any new information she or he may give you.

When you undertake an annual review of your general circumstances and finances, reconsider at that time:

- whether you can still afford to meet the monthly payments to which you have committed yourself
- whether circumstances have changed and you now need to 'top up' your reserves so as to provide more resources for the future e.g. changes in your health, greater uncertainty about your work

If you have just come through a period of major change which has caused you to draw on your reserves, review the situation to decide what you now need to do and what you can afford to do.

W6
Planning Changes in Your Working Life

If you are considering making changes in the way you earn your living.

1 Acknowledge where you are – and what you want

Get a clear picture of the kind of work and lifestyle at which you are aiming, including:

- when you want to make changes
- how you want to work, e.g. part-time, in a small/large company
- where you want to live
- what skills and resources you would need.

Then look at your present situation. Consider any aspects of your present life that will affect the changes you may be considering:

- your current work satisfaction or dissatisfaction
- the skills and resources you have
- your personal and family circumstances
- your health.

It may also be helpful to review your motives for wanting to change your working life. List them and review them to see whether there are any areas where you are not being entirely honest with yourself, e.g.

- *shorter hours*
- *flexibility*
- *want to spend more time with the children*

2 Know the facts – your figures *and* your feelings

In order to plan for these changes, you need to know:

- how much they will cost
- how much it currently costs you to live
- what your resources are now

How much the changes will cost. At this point, a rough estimate is fine. Depending on the changes, you may need to include:

- the cost to you, both in time and money, to sell your house and buy one in the area in which you want to live
- the cost of any training/studying you want to do: check both full-time and part-time options.

What it costs you to live at present. Do the cost of living analysis in *The Basic 5 Steps Analysis Step 2*, unless you have already done so recently. Once you see how much you are spending at present, mark those areas in which you could cut down on expenditure, at least in the short term, if your plans required you to do so.

Resources on which you might be able to draw to finance the changes. Consider for instance, the equity in your house, savings, help from a potential business partner, or family, loans from the bank etc.

Record the cost of changes, the cost of living and your resources in big letters in three columns, so that you have them to hand while considering your options.

3 Consider the *real* options

Compare the information you have gathered in Steps 1 and 2 and identify as many ways of meeting your goal/s as possible. For example,

my goal is to earn a living as a carpenter
ways I might do this:
* *use my savings to train full-time and get myself started*
* *go to evening classes while doing jobs on the side*

* *wait until I am retired before breaking new ground*
* *work for someone as an apprentice*
* *cash in my pension and take out a loan for training and/or the start-up costs for my business*

Review the list to establish the relevant factors which will ensure that your choice is realistic, e.g. age/time until retirement; current skills; family commitments; ability to deal with debt/financial insecurity/ self-employment; willingness to tighten belt. Cross out those that are not realistic, cost those that are – both for time and money.

4 Make choices – live for today *and* plan for tomorrow

Review your list of options. Ask yourself if you still want to make the change(s) which you had in mind.

If so, which way forward feels most possible and least punishing for you. Consider:

* is this a good time in your and your family's life to move house, if this becomes necessary?
* would you have the discipline to make the intended change(s) e.g. by doing part-time training or a job-share?
* are you willing to get into debt or live frugally in the short term in order to make the change(s) more quickly?

Choose the way you want to proceed – then draw up a full plan of action:

* *Negotiate at work to do a job-share and start private work in the remaining time*
* *Set a stringent budget for three months and see if you can stick to it*

5 Do it – and review it

If the changes you are making require you to tighten your financial belt for a while, build in rewards for yourself to encourage you to keep going. Even if you don't have to cut back financially, pick from your list of 'treats' in *The Basic*

5 Steps Analysis, Step 5 the one you can afford at each stage, as an acknowledgement that managing such change is an achievement in itself.

Identify sources of assistance and support.

Use them.

W7
Dealing with Unexpected Changes in Your Earning Life

If you are faced with sudden changes in your working life, such as the loss of your job,

1 Acknowledge where you are – and what you want

Before you look at your new situation, consider whether you are satisfied with the terms on which you left your job, or whether there is some unfinished business to complete, e.g. the month's pay they kept in hand which has not yet come to you, problems with redundancy payments.

Then look clearly at the new situation in which you find yourself. In particular, check your feelings. Your confidence may have suffered a blow or you may have been living under a great deal of stress in the period before you lost your job. Acknowledge to yourself any fears that have been raised by these changes – and any opportunities.

> *The redundancy pay might let me set up in business for myself, which I've always talked about doing. Need to get some advice about that. The redundancy counsellor the firm mentioned might be worth a try.*
>
> *I don't want to decide anything until after I've taken the family on holiday.*

When you feel you are ready, review your long term goals to see what effect this unexpected change has had on them.

In order to sort yourself out, try at least to set yourself some short-term goals to safeguard your resources.

2 Know the facts – your figures *and* your feelings

If you have just lost your main income or had it cut substantially, you have three tasks before you:

- make sure that you got the best deal for yourself from work
- work out how much you (and your family) need for basic living expenses and what resources you have to finance those in the short term;
- on the basis of the Basic 5 Steps Analysis, review your total situation in order to make decisions for the longer term.

Make sure you got the best deal for yourself when you left the job. Review the terms you have been/are being given for leaving work. Check with your union and/or take legal advice to make sure that you are getting the best deal for yourself.

Work out what you need and what you have. Look at your financial situation to assess:

- your current costs of living
- the cost of the basic essentials you need in order to sustain an acceptable minimum standard of living
- what money you have or could make available
- the time your money will buy for you to sort out the next steps

It will help you use the information from two previous sections in the *Workbook Chapter 1 The Basic 5 Steps Analysis* and *Workbook Chapter 5 Creating Financial Security*, or to work through them if you have not done so recently.

You may also want to investigate whether there are any government benefits for which you are eligible.

As you gather the facts of your financial situation, make a mental note of your reactions to the new realities. Dealing with a drop in – or the disappearance of – an income can be a shock.

3 Consider the *real* options

Put together the information in Steps 1 and 2 and see what courses of action these seem to indicate.

Get a sheet of paper and write down all the possible courses of action that come to mind – no matter how outrageous or impossible some of the suggestions seem.

* *Take a year off – travel or get different qualifications*

* *Invest the redundancy payment to give me a small income so that I can work at something I like doing which is not so well paid*
* *Move to another area*
* *Get a smaller car – or do without one*
* *Take the children out of public school*
* *Set up my own business*
* *Blow the lot on a posh holiday*
* *Pay the bills for the next six months*

Review the list and cross out those suggestions which you know to be unrealistic at this point in time. Make a list of the remaining options and divide them into short/medium/and long-term possibilities. Cost them roughly for time, money, and confidence/energy.

It may be that your first concern is how to pay the bills and maintain the minimum standard of living you want. Having identified in 2 above the expenses you have and the financial resources you could make available, your short-term priority may be to look at the ways in which you will meet your expenses, and for how long.

* *See financial consultant to work out best ways to meet our expenses until I can find work*
* *Savings will cover mortgage and bills for 6 months*
* *Bonds – enough to pay school fees for 1 year but check whether grandparents willing to contribute*
* *Deposit already put down on holidays – check cancellation fee and also discuss with family whether to cut back on something else so that we can still go on holiday*

4 Make choices – live for today *and* plan for tomorrow

Your most urgent step is to choose a course of action for the short term. Choose one or more that feels most immediately important in helping you to manage the unexpected changes with which you have been faced.

Look at your list of medium and long-term options. Do you feel able to act on any of these at present? If so, make choices from those lists. If not, keep the lists for future reference.

Make a detailed plan for any choices that you have made.

5 Do it – and review it

At a time of unexpected change, you will need all the support you can get – but on your terms. Working through these 5 Steps will help you to keep control rather than to feel that things have got beyond you.

Identify where you can get the kind of support you need. This may, for instance, be from a financial consultant, your bank manager, or a redundancy counsellor.

Initially, review your progress weekly – on your own or with someone who will listen to you rather than tell you what is right or wrong. Also, refer regularly to your list of medium and long-term options in order to see whether you are yet in a position to consider those possibilities.

W8
Coming to Terms with Benefits or Inheritance

If any or all of your income comes up from government benefits or inheritance,

1 Acknowledge where you are – and what you want

Having unearned income means that you have to be honest with yourself about the way you manage both the money and your attitudes. For instance,

* *I don't even know how much I got from my grandmother because I pretend that it's not there*
* *The benefits I get are a joke, with three kids. Manage? We barely survive.*

2 Know the facts – your figures *and* your feelings

In order to know whether you are managing your income as effectively as possible, check out in detail:

* what you know about the money
* what you do with it, and
* how you feel about having it.

What you know about the money. Note or find out:

* the total amount
* the amount you receive each month
* any conditions attached to receiving or spending it
* the percentage of your income which it represents
* the tax situation in which it puts you

If you are receiving money from a trust, there are additional questions which you need to answer:

- what is the trust currently worth? How is it made up, i.e. stocks and shares, property, cash, a mixture of all three?
- what is your right of access to the money? Do you get what you want on demand? Can you only have a certain percentage? Is access at the trustees' discretion?
- How much say do you have in the management of the money? i.e. if you don't approve of a certain company in which your money is invested, can you insist that it is removed and invested in something else? What are your rights if you would prefer to see the money earning a fixed rate of interest rather than being invested in the more volatile stocks and shares market? Can you insist on it?
- At what age, if ever, are you given control of the trust? Is there a date when the trustees' responsibilities finish?
- Who handles your tax return information? If the trust has an end date, who is responsible for ensuring that it is closed down in the most tax efficient way possible? If no one has been given responsibility for this, how can you obtain the necessary papers to do this work yourself?
- If the trustees die, who replaces them? Do you have any say in replacing them?

Also ask yourself what you do with your unearned income at present: ignore it and let it accumulate? give it away? top up your earnings with it? live on the interest as your sole income? use the unearned income for special projects, travel, treats?

If you are receiving government benefits, there are additional questions which you need to answer:

- how much can you earn and still receive these benefits?
- are you sure that you are receiving all the benefits to which you, and the rest of your family, are entitled?
- is there a limit to how long you can continue to receive these benefits?
- can you do any government training and still receive the same benefits?
- are you aware of when, if any, changes in benefits are made and when you would start receiving any extras due to you?

Also, ask yourself how you spend this money at present:
- the moment you get your benefits, do you use the monies to pay all outstanding bills?

- do you carefully plan your food menus, or not?
- do you overspend by buying unplanned extras for the children to make up for the lack of money?
- do you put aside any money just for yourself, to keep you going?
- do you save, even if it's pennies? These do add up to pounds eventually.

3 Consider the *real* options

Looking at the information from Steps 1 and 2, is there anything you need to change, about the way you manage the money or your feelings about it? Consider any options that seem realistic to you.

With benefits,

* *check out with the CAB whether I am getting all the benefits to which I am entitled*
* *cut down on cigarettes so I can save half towards a holiday and also give the kids some pocket-money*

With inherited money,

* *managing the money on my own with the help of an adviser*
* *doing my own tax returns so that I am fully informed*

4 Make choices – live for today *and* plan for tomorrow

Has the review so far revealed that you have not really come to terms with having unearned income and/or that you are not taking full responsibility for managing it? If so, decide where you need to start so as to handle things in a more positive way.

If you have mixed feelings about having the money at all, take time to clarify your feelings before making any irrevocable financial decisions.

5 Do it – and review it

In most cases, if you have inherited money you will need to consult trustees or a financial professional, and preferably both, in order to be in control of your unearned income. They will see it as their first responsibility to ensure that your money makes the maximum amount of profit for you. If you have other priorities, such as changing investments to ones that you feel are more ethical, you will need to be clear about this.

If the greater part of your income is from state benefits, you will need a great deal of confidence and persistence in order to deal with the authorities. It can help if you are clear about the facts first – what is due to you, what you need, and how you manage your finances.

Whether your income is from an inheritance or from state benefits, the same ground rules of financial good management still apply. A regular review with one of the financial professionals whom you trust is part of good financial management.

W9

Planning for a Quality Retirement

Use this in conjunction with The Practical Guide to Arranging a Pension.
When you are planning for your retirement,

1 Acknowledge where you are – and what you want

Imagine the kind of life you want to have after you retire and make a list of what you want to be able to do, (assuming you are in good health), and how you would like to be able to manage, or to be cared for, if your health fails.

* *have enough for at least two trips abroad each year and some travel around the British Isles*
* *stay in present home and have enough to maintain it comfortably*
* *full-time nursing help at home if either of us needs it*

List the preparations you have already begun to make to reach those goals, e.g. savings and investments, contributions to a work superannuation scheme and/or to a private pension fund.

2 Know the facts – your figures *and* your feelings

Review the arrangements you have made for your pension/s, remembering that this will provide the major income with which to finance the life you want in retirement.

If you are contributing to a company superannuation scheme, find out:

* how much you are contributing
* whether your company is making a contribution for you and how much that is
* what lump sum, income, and benefits this will give you on retirement

- whether you are entitled to top-up your contributions so as to increase your income on retirement.
  Calculate the total benefits you will receive, then check how this compares with private pension schemes.

If you are contributing to private pension scheme/s, find out:

- how much you are contributing
- whether you are contributing the full amount you are allowed to contribute from your income
- what lump sum and income you will receive on retirement

If you want to retire early, or are undecided about when you want to stop working, ensure that the scheme to which you are contributing will pay out at the time you choose.

Estimate the cost of the standard of living you would like to have when you retire, as identified in Step 1 above e.g. home nursing care if necessary, the maintenance of your house, bills, the amount of travel which you would like to do.

3 Consider the *real* options

Look at the information you have gained from Steps 1 and 2 and list the options that occur to you, without editing them at this stage. Make sure to list not only the financial arrangements you need to make but also other groundwork such as investigating whether you would really like to move to the seaside or country when you retire. This would be a question not only of money but also of inclination and practicability.

The facts of your financial resources will clearly indicate whether you have made sufficient provision for retiring early or whether, in order to do so, you need to start investing heavily now, while you are earning and in good health. Decide how much you can comfortably afford to put away for your pension. For example,

Retire at 55: will need £X and have £Y
Could put away another £100 per month

Review the list. First cross out those options that on reflection, do not attract you sufficiently.

Estimate the cost of the remaining options.

4 Make choices – live for today *and* plan for tomorrow

Decide on the options which will meet two criteria, ie.

- that will move towards a retirement which meets your requirements
- that will allow you to live as nearly as possible the kind of life you want to live.

Make a plan of what you need to do to put the choice/s into practice.

* *increase pension*
* *save in building society and make a lump sum investment in due course*
* *holiday by the seaside for three weeks next winter*

5 Do it – and review it

You need to review your financial arrangements and your other preparations regularly, to check whether:

- your ideas about your retirement have changed,
- you have any further information about the costs of your plans
- your current financial situation affects the contributions you are able to make to the pension scheme of your choice.

W10
Understanding Childhood Messages

In order to understand past influences and to develop your own money style,

1 Acknowledge where you are – and what you want

Look at the messages which you learned from your family about ways of dealing with money. Do you think that they affect the manner in which you deal with money today?

Picture yourself managing money in the way that suits you best. How would you really like to organize your finances, deal with debts, handle money issues in relationships, balance your earning and spending patterns?

Make a mental note of any of the patterns from your childhood which seem positive to you, and of any which seem to be blocking you from dealing with money effectively.

Or have you rejected, or forgotten, the messages which your parents hoped you would adopt and, if so, are the results positive or negative?

2 Know the facts – your figures *and* your feelings

Whenever you encounter a situation involving money which makes you feel uncomfortable, go through this experience in some detail to see how you handled it and why you felt the way you did. Be clear about how much money was involved, and what were the consequences of your actions.

> *Cassie W.: 'At last month's sale I saw a sofa bed that had been marked down from £699 to £349. I didn't have the money, but I've needed a bed for guests for so long that I thought I'd go ahead and buy it with my credit card and pray that something would turn up before the bill arrived.*

> *When the credit card bill did arrive, the total I owed gave me a terrible shock. Of course I only paid the minimum.*
>
> *Then I got really angry with the credit card companies for the amount of interest they charge. On thinking about it, I realized that I was doing what my mother had always done – buying things she couldn't really afford and then blaming someone else for getting into a fix – usually my dad, for not earning enough.'*

3 Consider the *real* options

Looking at the information in Steps 1 and 2, consider the different ways in which you might have handled this kind of situation.

Would you have waited until you could afford to buy something? Or until you were sure that you could pay off the credit card bill?

Or would you have used money which you had earmarked for something else and cleared the credit card bill?

Or cut up the credit card, or asked the credit card company to reduce the credit limit on your card?

Or would you have borrowed the money from the bank?

Try and consider some possible choices of action which are outside your normal pattern of dealing with money.

4 Make choices – live for today *and* plan for tomorrow

Which of the approaches that you have considered in 3 above can you see yourself undertaking most easily and effectively? Is this the way your parents would have handled the situation? If so, and if you feel comfortable with your decision, fine. If not, can you see yourself developing a money style of your own – and can you say how or why the choice you have made is particularly appropriate for your circumstances and inclinations?

Bear in mind that your own money style will be influenced not only by your past habits and experiences, and by your family traditions, but also by your plans and ambitions for the future.

5 Do it – and review it

Keep a check on yourself whenever you see yourself changing an inherited habit – like overspending or blaming someone else for a decision which, on reflection, merely aggravated your current financial situation. Sometimes we can change our spending pattern – only to find ourselves reverting to old habits at the next hurdle. Old habits die hard.

Just keep an eye on yourself. Recognizing your patterns takes you halfway towards making changes which can help you to develop a style of your own.

W11

*Borrowing and Lending – making a contract
between friends or family*

When you are asked to lend or give money to a friend or another
member of your family, or if you are the one who is asking
for money,

1 Acknowledge where you are – and what you want

If you need money, be clear about –

- how much you need and precisely what you need it for
- whom you are going to ask and why
- whether you are asking for a gift or a loan

If you want to give money to someone or have been asked for
money, be clear about –

- whether you are being asked for a gift or a loan
- why you in particular were approached
- whether you want to know what the money is needed for

2 Know the facts – your figures *and* your feelings

Both parties involved in a money transaction need to check the
figures carefully.

If you are asking for money. Make sure the information in your
Basic 5 Steps Analysis, Step 2 is up-to-date. Calculate how much
money you actually need and whether you can afford to pay it
back. Consider also how long this will take you.

If you are thinking of giving/lending money to someone. Find out
exactly how much they want, and whether they are asking for a
gift or a loan. If you are being asked for a loan, how long would
it take them to pay you back? Look at your financial situation
to see how much, if anything, you can afford to give or lend.

Also consider your feelings and your motives. Do you have any sense about the way this transaction might affect your relationship with the other person? Ask yourself – what am I buying?

3 Consider the *real* options

With the information from Steps 1 and 2, look at your options, including the possibility of –

- saying 'no' – to either giving or receiving money
- making it clear that the money to be given or received can be treated as a gift
- agreeing terms that would be acceptable to you if the money is being lent or borrowed.

4 Make choices – live for today *and* plan for tomorrow

Consider all the circumstances and, without having mixed feelings or giving mixed messages, decide which of the options would be clear and unambiguous, both to you and others.

Having confronted your feelings decide whether you are willing to go ahead with the transaction. If so, work out the terms between you and write them down as a contract. If not, then neither offer nor ask.

5 Do it – and review it

You should now be ready to go ahead with the transaction – or not, as the case may be.

Clarify the ground rules between you

- is it a gift or a loan?
- is the money to be repaid and if so, how and by when?
- if the money is to be repaid, is interest to be charged? If so, how much?
- how will you sort things out if there are any problems, either in meeting the repayments or recalling the loan before the agreed term has expired, should this become necessary?

Loan £1,000, at 6% interest = Borrowed £1,060
   Repay monthly at £88.33 starting on the first of next month, for 12 months
   Promised to tell Sandra immediately if I run into any difficulties to discuss reducing or suspending monthly repayments with her.
   She has agreed that if she needs the money before the year is out, she will give me at least two months' notice so I can work out another loan with someone else

If you have asked for money, you may find that the financial terms being offered, or the stress involved in the transaction, cause you anxiety or discomfort. In that case you have the choice of not proceeding with the transaction.

If you are lending money, it is your responsibility to ensure that the terms of the loan are kept and to deal with the situation if they are not. If a payment is missed, it will be healthier to deal with that quickly, rather than to let the situation drag on, with potentially damaging effects on your relationship.

W12
Living Together

If you are living, or planning to live with someone else it may help you to manage your joint financial commitments better if you each work through Steps 1–3 separately first. Then compare your personal information and see which approaches to your day-to-day finances are likely to suit you both.

1 Acknowledge where you are – and what you want

Look honestly at the way things are now in your domestic financial arrangements:

- what you share
- who makes decisions about what
- areas where you are able to work things out easily
- areas where you are in conflict
- if you have children, how you respond to their financial needs and decide on their financial responsibilities
- what lies do you tell to your partner/yourself (and don't assume that this is 'bad': just own up to yourself that that is what you are doing).

How would you describe your and your partner's way of dealing with personal and joint monies?

'I know every penny I spend but she is always surprised at the amount she has spent when her credit card statement arrives.'

'We have a joint account but he has the chequebook and card'.

'I'm never never overdrawn on my personal account but our joint account's always in the red.'

Look at your ideas about the kind of partnership you want in relation to shared money and decisions about spending it:

- how much do you want to share?
- what practical joint arrangements would suit you?
- what will you do if one person is either not earning at all or if you are earning very different amounts?

2 Know the facts – your figures *and* your feelings

It is difficult to work out a healthy way of sharing if you are not clear about certain basic figures:

- how much you each earn and take home
- the bills and other basic expenses, and whether they (i) have to be shared; (ii) need to be discussed because it's not clear whether they are joint expenses or not; (iii) are individual commitments, such as child support, which may affect you or your partner's financial situation.

If you are friends living together. Check that you know all the financial information about the house or flat that you are sharing, and about the contract you have with the landlord (or with each other, if one of you owns the property):

- bills: which are the ones for which you are responsible and what percentage do you each pay?
- whether you made a deposit which is refundable and on what terms?
- how you will readjust the financial arrangements if, in a place which you are renting together, one of you has a partner who moves in to share their room?
- what arrangements have you made if one of you wants to sell a property which you own jointly?

3 Consider the *real* options

Living with someone else means that you not only have to deal with your own money patterns but also with your partner's, and with any new pattern that may develop between you. Look at the information in Steps 1 and 2 and think about the many different ways in which you could work out your joint financial arrangements. Include a wide variety of possible approaches so that you can identify –

- those with which you would be comfortable but which, you imagine, it would be difficult or impossible for your partner to handle
- those you couldn't handle but, you imagine, would be fine for your partner
- ways which would suit you both.

Put a tick beside the options which you feel would best suit you both and an X beside those with which you know that either one or both of you could not live.

4 Make choices – live for today *and* plan for tomorrow

Are there any changes that you know you will need to make in your own money habits in support of your relationship, irrespective of what you decide to do jointly? If so, plan how to implement them.

Are there any changes you can agree jointly? If so, when you plan to implement these changes, remember to be clear about the responsibilities each of you has agreed to take on.

If you find yourselves in conflict about any issues, are you clear about the reasons behind the conflict? Conflicts about money are often about other aspects of your relationship. Do you have a way of resolving your differences?

> 'Every time we talk money, we row, mostly about the telephone bill.
>
> I phone my family in Australia quite often and he thinks he ends up paying more than his share of the phone bill. We used to go on and on about this. Eventually I realized that I wasn't "cheating" our family out of money any more than he was with the amount he spent on cigarettes. We agreed that we each had a right to make some personal choices. That helped to clear the air. But the practical step that made all the difference was when we agreed to change to a telephone system which itemizes all phone calls. Now it is clear which calls are his, which are family business, and which are mine.'

5 Do it – and review it

Personal relationships change and so do financial circumstances. You will need to review your joint finances, and the way you manage them, regularly in order to check whether:

- either of your incomes has changed, so that you might need to adjust your respective contributions to the common pot
- you or your partner's costs and commitments have changed, possibly requiring additional contributions from one or both of you
- either of you is beginning to get into debt, or has already gone into debt owing to shared commitments, such as your mortgage
- if you have children, what adjustments you may need to make to take care of their financial needs and to encourage them to develop a sense of financial responsibility.

The more regularly you can make time to check out how you are managing, the more likely you are to be able to prevent difficulties worsening – either financially or between yourselves.

W13
Splitting Up

The following 5 Steps are concerned particularly with the situation which arises when couples are deciding to separate. Steps 1 and 2 could also be helpful to friends who have been sharing a house or flat and are ending that arrangement.

If you have acknowledged that your partnership is in serious trouble,

1 Acknowledge where you are – and what you want

Remind yourself of the agreements which you made when you started to live together. Did you put anything in writing? If so, retrieve that information. If not, write down what you remember of your informal arrangements – then compare notes.

You may decide that you can only continue to live together if certain changes are made. Or you may already have decided to separate. In either case, look at the situation realistically. Look particularly at those issues between you that seem to involve money.

What could give your partnership a new lease of life? Be specific about the changes you would want your partner to make, and the ones you would be prepared to make yourself.

> 'I am no longer prepared to work all hours in order to pay for her credit card bills. She keeps saying that if only I'd spend more time with her, she wouldn't be so tempted to go out and spend so much. So I'm willing to take her on a holiday this year and only to work every other Saturday, if she will agree to halving her credit card bills.

If you are giving your partnership a second chance, it may be useful to know what steps to take if this does not, after all, work out. Steps 2 – 5 below deal with what to do if you finally decide to separate. But while you are still trying to work things out together, the previous chapter, *W12 Living Together*, suggests steps you might like to think about at this point.

If, however, you have already decided that separation or divorce has to be the next step, decide on the kind of relationship you want with your present partner after you have ceased to live together.

How would you handle financial arrangements during the process of separating and afterwards? Will you continue to have financial ties because one of you will be looking after your children?

Some couples find that being counselled by a neutral outsider can be helpful, so that both parties gain support in handling the personal and the financial aspects of a painful situation. *Resources for Readers* gives information about where to contact the network of marriage guidance counsellors.

2 Know the facts – your figures *and* your feelings

When a partnership has reached the stage of breaking up, you immediately need to get to grips with the facts of your financial situation. The figures are the basis on which you will work out the terms of the separation; your feelings will determine how you go about this.

You need to find and look at –

- bank statements
- building society books
- details of any investments
- information about major items which you or your partner has purchased (this information can often be found in credit card statements)
- notes of any money which you are given, or give, for shared expenses
- the title to the house/flat if you own one
- details of any outstanding loans.

Also keep a day by day record of what it costs you to maintain your present lifestyle, including all the children's needs. This information is essential if you are married or if you have children.

If you are not married and there are no children, you need to get the facts about any financial agreements which you may have made when you began living together. For instance, what is to happen to –

- the balance in your joint account
- the money you each put into the house/flat
- major purchases which you have each made.

You also need to know the facts of your legal situation. You may want to consult a solicitor before you make the decision to separate, in order to know exactly what your position is and what steps you need to take to protect your interests. You need to be clear about this right from the start.

To make the most of consulting a solicitor – and to get the kind of help you want and need – prepare for the meeting by working through the 5 Steps and be clear about the way you want to approach the separation.

It is important to feel that the solicitor whom you have chosen will handle the separation in a way that is comfortable for you. If you do not know a solicitor who handles divorce cases, ask friends for recommendations. And don't be embarrassed to change solicitors if the first one you consult has an approach which does not feel right for you.

3 Consider the *real* options

With the information you have put together about your finances, and about your feelings for the kind of relationship you would want after your separation or divorce, examine the options you have about how you could or should proceed. It may help if you can list every option that comes to mind – even if you feel that you yourself would never consider adopting one or other of these. How you feel, and how you choose to behave, may make some of these options more or less acceptable to you when eventually you have to make decisions – but at this stage, let rip!

* *refusing to take a penny*
* *giving him the children*
* *arsenic*
* *having the children on alternate weeks*
* *going to live with my mother*

Review your list. Go back to Step 1 and consider the sort of relationship you would eventually like to have not only with your present partner and with your children, but also with his or her parents. Delete those options which you would never consider putting into effect, however satisfying it was to write them down.

4 Make choices – live for today *and* plan for tomorrow

Look at your list of options. Neither of you is likely to end up with the same lifestyle which you enjoyed when you were together: there is unlikely to be enough money for that. Choose the option that promises to give you the best possible deal both for today and tomorrow – and, if you care about it, for your former partner as well.

Make a plan of precisely what you need to do to see this separation through, financially, emotionally, and legally.

close all joint accounts and divide the money
agree on who owns what
discuss with the children what we have decided
agree each other's cost of living expenses
try not to let the legal side of it push us into conflict
don't pretend we're the best of friends but try not to drag the children into our conflicts

5 Do it – and review it

You will need to review the situation frequently to be clear about the changes that are going on and their financial consequences.

It is a time for using all the support you can get – your solicitor, a financial consultant, a counsellor if that would be helpful. But review for yourself whether you are moving in the direction in which you want to go – or whether that direction has changed. If you are not clear about that, you may find yourself torn between advice from friends, family and professionals who are inclined to think that they know what is best for you.

W14
Managing on Your Own

If you are the only adult in a household or the only one with responsibility for managing the finances,

1 Acknowledge where you are – and what you want

Look clearly at your present situation:

- how are you managing financially?
- for whom are you financially responsible, yourself only, children, other dependent relatives?
- where, how and when do you feel uncomfortable about making financial decisions – or find that you are avoiding them?
- are there any aspects of your financial life about which you lie to yourself? Be honest!
- where are you managing well? Be honest here, too!
- do you get regular or occasional financial gifts from parents, or child support from an ex-partner?
- have you any back-up – either as regards people or money reserves?
- how do you feel about managing on your own?

2 Know the facts – your figures *and* your feelings

It is essential that you know the facts in your *Basic 5 Steps Analysis* precisely and that you review that analysis as soon as your circumstances change.

Turn to the *Basic 5 Steps Analysis, Workbook Chapter 1, and*:

- * work through Step 2 if you have not already done so
- * review the information if the analysis was done more than 2 months ago.

If you get money from family members or support from an ex-partner, can you count on this as regular income or do you use it for extras? If you consider it as regular income, remember to include the amount when you are calculating your living expenses.

3 Consider the *real* options

Look at the information in Steps 1 and 2. Are there any changes you want to make:

- in the way in which you manage your money?
- in the way you are living, e.g. examine options such as moving to shared accommodation, buying your own place, taking in a lodger now that the children are away from home, spending more on yourself now?

  Use your imagination – list as many suggestions as you can for what you could do to get closer to the kind of life you want for yourself. If meeting Prince or Princess Charming is part of that, don't leave him or her off the list.

4 Make choices – live for today *and* plan for tomorrow

Are there any ways in which your hopes for the future are blocking you from managing your financial life effectively right now, e.g. finding a partner, coming into some money?

Choose a way forward that takes into account that you alone are responsible for taking care of yourself and for your future financial security.

- *take in a lodger who will baby-sit as part of the rent*
- *take in a lodger to help towards the cost of doing a training course so I can get a job when the kids start going to school*
- *find work a couple of evenings a week to get out of the house and to earn some more money*

5 Do it – and review it

If you are on your own, and more particularly if the only reserves you have are the ones you have created and will create in the future, it is essential that you keep a close eye on any changes in your financial circumstances.

You may also find it useful to have a financial consultant or bank manager or accountant whom you trust to give you a second opinion and act as a sounding board.

W 15
Making a Will

(If you have children under the age of majority, also read the special section at the end of the 5 Steps before you complete Steps 4 and 5.)
In order to prepare a Will,

1 Acknowledge where you are – and what you want

If you have made a Will, check when you last reviewed it and whether your circumstances have changed. If so, take yourself through the next 4 steps.

Look at your situation. You need a Will if you have –

- any assets
- children under the age of majority
  You also particularly need one if:
- you live and share your financial life with someone to whom you are not married
- you don't automatically want all your assets to go to your spouse
- you have strong ideas about how you want to be buried

2 Know the facts – your figures *and* your feelings

Whether you choose to use a solicitor, or get a Will form from a stationers and do it yourself, you need to prepare the following information:

Your assets List what belongs to you, starting with your most valuable assets, and work down to those that are of personal value. Here is a checklist that might help:
a house or flat which you own, either outright or on a mortgage

b money and other financial assets: bank accounts, shares, National Savings bonds, superannuation, assurance policies
c large items, e.g. car, computer
d other items at home – jewellery, clothes, paintings, sculptures, clothes, books, records and videos, furniture
e items of little value but important to you: photograph albums, personal letters

After you have listed your assets, you will need to decide what to do with them. Make two lists of the people and causes which are important in your life:
a the family, friends and causes (e.g. charities, political or religious organizations) to which you want to leave something
b the people and causes to which, at this point in time, you do *not* want to leave anything.

3 Consider the *real* options

Compare your assets and the two lists which you have made. Before you make any decisions, it may be helpful to record precisely what you want to do:

- *a house or flat:* Do you want to leave the house to someone? Or do you want everything converted into cash? Remember, if you have an assurance policy which will redeem your mortgage, the property will be worth its total market value. If you do not have such a policy, the house may have to be sold to repay the lender – or other monies will have to be used to repay the lender first.

- *marriages and partnerships:* Do you want your entire assets to go to your partner? If not, how much of what is in the house do you want them to have? Do you want them to have the house, or your share, outright, or do you only want them to live it in for their lifetime? Remember you can only choose this option if you have arranged the mortgage or ownership as 'tenants in common'. If you are joint tenants, as is the usual practice, then your share automatically goes to the other person, whether you are married to that person or not. If you are tenants in common, do remember to allow the other person time to raise the cash to buy your share, if this is what you wish, or to be able to sell the property. Legally he or she is allowed one year to do this

– and remember to take this into account when making your Will.

- *family:* Do you want your children, parents, brothers and sisters to get anything and if so, do you want them all to get the same? Do you have any special items that you want to leave to particular individuals? Have you asked them, so as to make sure that they would actually like to have what you have in mind for them? If the selection seems unequal or open to misunderstanding, would it make sense for you to leave a letter with your Will, or to make a tape recording, to explain your reasons?

- *burial:* Do you feel strongly about this, or are you happy to leave arrangements to your next of kin? Do you want to be cremated? Do you have a plot in a cemetery? How will the funeral be paid for? What kind of service would you like? Do you want a religious service, or would you rather have a secular memorial service? Do you have ideas about what you would like to be included in a service?

4 Make choices – live for today *and* plan for tomorrow

Consider the options you have and divide up your estate in such a way that you can live comfortably with your decision. There are several stages to this process:

Put people in order of priority Take your list of family, friends and causes to which you would like to leave something. Rearrange it it to show to whom you are leaving the most and to whom least.

Decide whether you want the people on this list to receive individually named items, whether you want everything converted into cash and the money divided up, or whether you want to do a bit of both.

Work out the total value of your estate This includes your savings, your pension, any life assurance, your share of the house, your car, valuables, such as paintings and jewellery.

Find out if your estate will be liable to inheritance tax: the Inland Revenue or a financial professional can tell you this.

Choose who gets what Go through your list of assets and decide what you want the person who is most important to you to get, including cash if appropriate. If you want everything converted into cash, note the percentage of your total estate which you would like this person to have, bearing in mind that it is the net estate, not the gross, that you are dividing up, i.e. after inheritance tax has been deducted.

Divide the balance among the others.

Everything to cash:
John P. 50%   *M.J. 10%*   *Charities 40%*

5 Do it – and review it

Make your Will The above preparations will not stand up in a court of law unless you turn them into a legal Will.

If your affairs involve a simple division of your estate, you can buy a Will Form at a stationers. Alternately, consult a solicitor if you do not have the confidence to write the Will yourself. If you decide to see a solicitor, take the notes you have made in 1 and 2 above. If you decide on a Will Form, draft it out first and then fill out the form carefully, with no alterations, and complete it by:
A deciding whom you would choose as executors and asking them if they would be willing to act as such: it is better to have two executors, in case one dies shortly after you. It makes sense to have beneficiaries as executors because they are more likely to ensure that the process is completed quickly. It is worth considering carefully whether you really need to name a solicitor or a Bank as one of your executors; if you do, a slice of your assets will then go on fees;
B getting two witnesses, people who are not benefiting from the Will, to witness your signing and dating of the Will. They do not need to know the contents of the Will.
C taking a photocopy of the Will and telling your two executors where you have put the original and the photocopy, e.g. in your strongbox, on file with your financial consultant, at the Bank. Do not put the original and the photocopy in the same place – and remember that only the original is the legal document. A photocopy has no legal standing.

One place to lodge a Will is at Somerset House, for which you will be charged a fee. Your death certificate is registered with Somerset House. When the registration is made, as is required by law within a certain period following your death, it will automatically show that your Will is lodged there. If you decide to use Somerset House put your Will in a sealed envelope on which you write your name and address, the executors' names and addresses, the witnesses' names and addresses. In addition, you and the witnesses must put your signatures on the outside of the sealed envelope. On your death, Somerset House will then send your Will to the correct person. They are not allowed to open the Will as it is a legal document. If you keep your Will in your home and there is a burglary or a fire, you risk the possibility of dying intestate, i.e. without a Will.

D making sure that you have torn up any previous Will, as this could cause confusion if you have forgotten to tell those concerned that you have made a new one. It can also be upsetting if someone reads the old Will in which they were included whereas your current Will excludes them.

Review it A Will can and should be reviewed regularly. It is important to realize that on marriage any previous Will is immediately invalid, though this is not true when you get divorced. The review ought to be undertaken in three steps:

- review your list of assets and add anything that you have earned, purchased, or accumulated since you made the Will, and change the value or percentage if, for instance, house prices have risen;
- review your two 'people lists': have your feelings changed about anyone on either of these lists – or is there anyone whom you wish to add?
- if there are changes, write a new Will, going through the steps in 3 above, making sure that you destroy the old Will;
- consider whether any guardians and trustees (see below) whom you have appointed for your children are still the right ones now that the children are older. If not, approach other members of your family or friends and make any necessary changes, both in regard to guardians and trustees;
- don't forget to tell your executors where you have put the new Will. If you are lodging it at Somerset House, enclose a letter with the new Will requesting them to destroy the old one. You must also send another fee.

If you have children

If your children have not yet reached their age of majority, which is 18 in the UK, decide upon:

- whom you would like to act as their guardians, and obtain the agreement of your nominees
- whom you would like to act as trustees for any assets which you plan to leave the children, and obtain the agreement of your nominees. It is a good idea to have a guardian as one of the trustees, but it is important to have one or two other trustees as well. Often a guardian, out of sympathy, will tend to spoil a bereaved child; a trustee should be able to take a more balanced view. It is important to have a guardian and a trustee who can trust and get on with each other.

  If the parent of a child under the age of majority dies, the other parent automatically becomes the guardian, provided that the parents are married at the time of death. If they are divorced and have joint custody, the other parent will also automatically become the guardian. Except in these circumstances, the remaining parent has to apply to the courts for custody; otherwise the children, by law, go to the next of kin of the deceased. In all cases, the decision about who will be guardian (assuming that this is not clear in law) is based on the children's best interests as interpreted by the court.

  In the case of single parents, the father's name must be on the birth certificate. If it is not, the father is not recognized under law and has no rights. If a father wishes to be named on the birth certificate as the father of the child, he can go to court at the time of the birth of the child and state his case.

- at what age you would like your children to come into any of the money you are leaving them, e.g. 18 or 25? Leave instructions about this for the trustees.

  If your children are adults, decide how you will apportion your assets among them, and write them a note or make a tape if you think that that will help them to understand your choices and minimize conflicts.

  If you have a child who is handicapped in some way, of whatever age, you may want to make special arrangements for both their care and their financial future. Often a charity which specializes in your child's particular handicap has more experience and information than your solicitor, such as advice on trusts, so that contacting them first can give you more up-to-date information. This may also help to cut down your solicitor's fees.

If is very important to remember that if you are married, your spouse is the automatic guardian of your children – but what if your spouse dies at the same time as you? You must make provision for this possibility in your Will.

If your partner has not left a Will and you die at the same time, then your Will controls the disposition of your joint assets and the care of your children.

W16
Managing after the Death of Your Partner

If the person with whom you share your day-to-day financial life has just died,

1 Acknowledge where you are – and what you want

If the person with whom you share your day-to-day financial life has just died or is terminally ill, you will suddenly have sole responsibility for your finances and for sorting out what she or he is likely to leave. Check with yourself:

- do you know where to find your partner's Will or, indeed, if there is one?
- do you feel that you will manage to sort things out on your own, or will you need some help when your partner's death, or impending death, becomes a reality?

Below are the steps you need to take to deal with your changed situation in a way that buys time for you today until you are ready to plan for tomorrow.

2 Know the facts – your figures *and* your feelings

You need to establish both your immediate financial situation and your overall circumstances.

Check the immediate financial situation Find out where your partner's papers are and get all relevant documents together, which may include:

- their Will
- life assurance policies
- bank account numbers
- savings account numbers

- National Insurance number
- tax reference number and District.

Be clear about the overall financial situation Do the following in detail. If you don't feel able to do so on your own, get someone to help you.

- establish whether you can get access to any monies in bank accounts or savings accounts. Legally speaking, unless the accounts are in joint names you have no right to these monies until probate has been granted. However, bank managers are often sympathetic to the needs of a spouse. If you were not married or do not have a joint account, the response may be less helpful.
- if you have to spend your own money on funeral and other arrangements, ensure that you keep all receipts and records of the amounts spent so that you will be repaid when the estate is finalized.
- if you were dependent in any way on income from the person who has died, talk to your bank manager and arrange an overdraft or loan facility to cover exactly the same weekly needs, not more and not less. Keep records meticulously so that you can be reimbursed from the estate, assuming that the Will provides for this.

3 Consider the *real* options

Looking at the information in Steps 1 and 2, what do you feel you need to do – in the immediate weeks and months following your partner's death? Will you need help? Will you want this help from members of the family (yours or your partner's) or would you feel more confident and reassured if you contacted a financial consultant?

4 Make choices – live for today *and* plan for tomorrow

Buy yourself time You are likely to need some time to get a clear idea about your future plans, short, medium and long term. Your short-term financial objective is to buy yourself as much time and financial security as you need. Don't be pressured into making decisions on the spur of the moment, such as where and how you will live and what you want to do with your money.

If there is a lump sum of money to which you have access (e.g. a joint account), put it in a building society for at least six months, or until you feel ready to deal with your longer term financial objectives. If it is clear that you do not have the resources to buy yourself that much time, how much time can you buy yourself? If you can avoid it, do not take any major financial decisions in the interim. If you are nevertheless forced to do so, make sure that you have a clear grasp of the facts in your *Basic 5 Steps Analysis*, no matter how reluctant you are to deal with that at this time.

5 Do it – and review it

When you are emotionally ready, or when it becomes financially necessary, look again at *The Basic 5 Steps Analysis*. In particular, you will, in the light of new circumstances, need to review the goals which you set yourself and the life you now want to live.

Remember that the goals which you set yourself must be right – and affordable – for you. There can be enormous pressures on you from other family members and even friends about what you should or should not do with your money. At this stage, you may find it helpful to get the assistance of a financial professional to help you to organize and manage your money. By all means get help to see you through this transition, but do not lose control. Responsibility for the next step is yours and yours alone.

W17

Managing Your Own Money

In order to develop a system of financial management that works for you,

1 Acknowledge where you are – and what you want

Go to the place or places where you keep any of your financial records. Look at the way –

- you keep your current cheque books and old counterfoils (the bit that's left when you have used a cheque)
- you deal with bills, when you receive them and when you have paid them
- you keep relevant correspondence and records, e.g. in separate files, in a shoe box or drawer, or not at all.

How would you describe your style of organizing your present financial system?

- meticulous – in files, and a place for everything
- haphazard – the necessary information is there – somewhere
- chaotic – it's not even clear to you that the necessary information exists.

Be clear about who has responsibility for handling your domestic finances:

- you manage on your own
- you and your partner divide responsibilities
- it is primarily your responsibility and your partner doesn't have much idea about the situation
- it is primarily your partner's responsibility and you are not clear about your financial situation at any point.

Finally, review your management for the past six months to see when – or whether – you have made the time to take care of your financial business.

2 Know the facts – your figures *and* your feelings

In order to develop a system that works for you, you need to take into account information that has to be kept in some sort of order, and the way in which you organize yourself. And you have to find the time to do all this.

The basic information needed for a system of managing your finances has to include a *basic filing system kept up to date*. This has to include files for:

- *mortgages*
  'mortgage information' a copy of your original mortgage application, the offer of the mortgage from the building society, the survey report, the house insurance application form, your leasehold agreement if any, etc.
  'mortgage correspondence' – all letters to and from the mortgage company, your solicitor, and anybody else who had dealings with you or on your behalf regarding your mortgage.
- insurance and assurance
  'insurance correspondence' about your house/flat and contents, copies of all correspondence
  'assurance correspondence' – correspondence about your pension endowment policies
  'policy documents' – ensure that you have copies of all your insurance and assurance policies.
- *banking*
  'bank statements' – keep bank statements in order after checking them thoroughly for their accuracy. Do not assume that banks are perfect and never make mistakes
  'bank correspondence' – keep copies of all letters you write to your bank, and their replies.
- *credit cards*
  'credit card statements' – make a note on each statement when, and how much, you paid
  'credit card correspondence'.
- *the Inland Revenue*
  you must be able to put your hands on copies of your

tax returns, and your P60, and pay slips for the current year. *Always* make copies of your tax return.

Do remember that once you have your P60, and once you have checked that it is correct, then you no longer need to keep your payslips for that year, unless you want a record of superannuation contributions.

- *if you are self-employed* you need to have files for dealings with your accountant, such as correspondence, Profit and Loss Accounts.
- *other* – using this method, add any other files that you think will help you to keep control. Do not make the mistake of opening a miscellaneous file as this will just become a dumping ground.

Keep a copy of all letters you send when dealing with your affairs, for example, chasing the Gas Board about an incorrect bill.

A system for managing bills You can deal with your regular bills in a variety of ways. Some, such as your water rates, gas, tv licence, electricity, telephone, local taxes, car insurance, car tax and service charge bills can be paid yearly, half-yearly, or monthly. If you have enough money to pay a yearly bill when it becomes due, and if you prefer to do that, fine. But if you do not have that much money at any one time, or if you have a tendency to go into debt, it is essential to work out a regular, monthly system for paying bills.

Find the time Systems won't work unless you find the time to make them work. You need:

- each week – time to keep an eye on your spending
- each month – time to answer all letters, chase outstanding business, pay bills
- every six months – time to review how your system of financial management is working, and to make any changes you feel are necessary.

If, somehow or other, you never seem to have the time to get your finances properly under control, keep a diary for a month. Turn to the *Workbook Chapter 4 Being Self-Employed* to find suggestions on how to do this.

3 Consider the *real* options

Looking at the information from 1 and 2 above – decide what you ought to change in four key areas –

- organizing a filing system
- having a system for paying bills
- making time to manage your system
- sharing financial tasks with someone else.

If you work for yourself, one of your options may be to get a bookkeeper or an accountant. If your personal finances are particularly complex, you may want to consider employing an accountant to complete your tax return.

4 Make choices – live for today *and* plan for tomorrow

Know what you need to do and how to approach your financial system. Make a plan to show how you intend to get your affairs into better order.

> '*I intend to get my files in sufficiently good order so that I won't feel embarrassed about handing them over to a bookkeeper. I will ask my friends if they can recommend someone who'd like to take on a small but regular bookkeeping job. And I'll book half-yearly appointments with my financial consultant because I found out last year that she is booked months ahead of time.*

Be sure to give yourself time for regularly working at your plan of action.

5 Do it – and review it

This way of organizing yourself is a trial and error system. After a few months you will find that you can revise the system and either add more files or get rid of some unnecessary ones. If you are sharing these responsibilities with someone else, you also need to check whether the way you are sharing this work is comfortable to both of you.

If you find that you don't have time to maintain your system properly, look at the reasons. Did you fail to stick to the time which you said you would set aside for this? Or did you just let things drift?

Use it! The 5 steps Workbook

Decide definitely that you are going to do things better for the next few months – and always review your progress. The longer you leave things, the longer it will take you to deal with them eventually. You can be sure of one thing – your bills, your tax return, your credit card debts won't go away.

W18
Avoiding Debt

If you are about to get into debt,

1 Acknowledge where you are – and what you want

If you suspect that your finances are getting out of control, check first whether you are actually getting into debt. Here are some of the danger signs:

- a small bank overdraft which you never had before – and it's going up every month
- the credit card bills are close to your limit and you can no longer clear them at the end of each month
- you have borrowed money from family or friends and, though you intended paying it back, you haven't been able to do so
- friends or family are putting pressure on you about your spending.

2 Know the facts – your figures *and* your feelings

If you know or suspect that you are beginning to get into debt, check the figures to find out precisely what your situation is and how you got there:

- get out your previous bank statements and find the month when your bank balance started to go into the red.
- look at your cheque book counterfoils and credit card statements. What have you been spending your money on?
- make a note of any loans that you have taken out and not paid off – when you borrowed the money, how much,

how much you have paid off, what remains, and when the balance remaining is due to be paid off.

Look back at this information. Are there any patterns in your spending? Is there any reason why things have begun to slide? Such as an old car that is beginning to cost you a lot in repair bills, some spending splurges when your relationship was going through a bad patch, a lot of eating out because, with pressure at work, you didn't feel like cooking.

3 Consider the *real* options

Look at the information in Steps 1 and 2. Consider the kinds of options you have:

- what you can do to clear the debts you have already accumulated
- what you can do so that you don't repeat the pattern that has caused the situation which you are now trying to remedy.

4 Make choices – live for today *and* plan for tomorrow

Decide: what you are going to do about clearing your debts and what you are going to do about the pattern that got you into debt in the first place.

Make a plan for clearing your debts which leaves you with a realistic amount of money each week – and a bit extra. It is better to give yourself longer to pay off the debts and still have enough left over to do or buy something special.

Look at the circumstances which have got you into debt. What do you feel you can do to change these? If, for example, there are pressures at work which seem likely to continue for the foreseeable future, buying ready prepared food (which is not cheap) may nevertheless be more economical than continuing to run up restaurant bills. But double check your resolutions. If you've decided, 'I'll cook a big pot of stew on Sunday and it will last me all week', or 'I'll just discipline myself to do some cooking', are you sure these are realistic choices? Your choices need to be both financially sound and practically sound for them to succeed.

5 Do it – and review it

If you are going to catch your debts before they grow any bigger, you need to review your situation at the end of each month, making any necessary adjustments to your plans for clearing the debts and for preventing a repeat performance.

If you are beginning to get in arrears with your mortgage payments or are failing to make payments towards clearing your overdraft, the sooner you discuss the situation with the mortgage lender or the bank manager, the more helpful you are likely to find them.

W19
Dealing with Debt

If you know that you are in debt,

1 Acknowledge where you are – and what you want

Face the situation in which you find yourself. Decide whether you really want to clear the debts or not. It may help you to look at the financial, personal and legal consequences if you continue at the same level of indebtedness, or if your debts grow.

Remind yourself of the goals you have for your life and ask if their achievement is being hindered by your debts.

2 Know the facts – your figures *and* your feelings

Write down all *the details of your debts:*

- the names of those to whom you are in debt
- what the loans were actually for
- how much you still owe on each loan
- what the interest rates are
- how much you have got to repay each month,
- what the outstanding balances are
- whether, if you cleared any of the loans early, you would be able to reduce your repayments, i.e. are there any interest reductions?

Make a note of everybody to whom you owe money – friends, parents, the corner shop. Ask yourself whether there are certain debts which you don't really have to pay back. We often know that we don't really intend to pay back that loan from our parents – and, anyway, they half expect us not to. If you are not intending to repay a loan, then don't add it to your debts. It isn't one.

If you have personal debts, write down the details, such as

'John loaned me £2000 to buy a car and on the sale of my flat, I'm to pay it off, plus 7% interest per year.'

When listing your debts, don't make life harder for yourself by writing down the gross amount borrowed for every kind of debt. If you do that, the total can shock you into believing that your debt problem has gone beyond retrieval. Remember that some debts, like those you owe to certain credit card companies, can be paid monthly.

Break your list down into two columns, for monthly repayments and for lump sums. Separate out those of your creditors who are accepting – or would accept – monthly amounts in repayment, from those to whom lump sums are due. (See the example given in 4 below).

Make three different lists of your living expenses. The first is for **fixed bills** and should include all your outgoings, aside from debts: your rent or mortgage payments, local taxes, gas, electricity and water.

The second list is for **variable bills** and should include phone bills and the cost of travel to and from work.

The last list should be made up your **'lifestyle choices'**, such as going out, extra-curricular spending (e.g. swimming lessons, going to the gym), what you eat and the clothes you buy.

If you have children, list their activities (e.g. piano lessons, private school fees, Scouts), how often they go and how much it costs.

People with little money often spend more on their children. You may find that this is an area in which you will have to cut down.

Remember to include your other expenditure, including food, holidays, your social life, gifts, drinks, tobacco. Whether we eat is a matter of life and death. What we eat is a choice not primarily based on our income but rather on our lifestyle. Drink and tobacco are also choices. Unless you have an addiction to either of these, you have a choice about this expenditure.

Now calculate what you are left with. Are you left with anything at all after subtracting your debt repayments and your living expenses from your income?

Here is an example of what Andrew W. faced when he did these calculations:

Debts	total due	payments	time left
Access	*£ 900*	*£ 40 per month*	*27 m approx*
Carpet loan	*£1200*	*£ 20 per month*	*60 months*
Bank loan	*£4000*	*£144 per month*	*28 months*
Mother	*£ 300*	*whenever*	
Hoover	*£ 40*	*£ 10 per month*	*4 months*
Peter Jones	*£ 300*	*£ 20 per month*	*15 months*
Jim	*£ 100*	*as soon as possible*	

Total: £234 per month

Living expenses:

Rent	*£150 per month*
local Taxes	*£ 40 per month*
Gas	*£ 50 per month*
Electricity	*£ 10 per month*
phone	*£ 50 per month*
Children's extras	*£ 90 per month*

Total £390 per month

Total monthly payments including living expenses and debt repayments come to £624 per month. After deducting this from a total monthly income of £710 (including child benefit of £86 per month) Andrew W. was left with £86 each month, or roughly £21 per week to spend.

3 Consider the *real* options

You have three general options: to spend less, to remain in debt, to earn more.

Taking into account all the information from Steps 1 and 2 above, consider the following factors:

Do you want to clear your debts? First of all, do you feel like clearing your debts? If not, can you live with the consequences, which may simply mean continuing to carry a large overdraft or, more seriously, facing legal action?

If you do want to get out of debt, consider:

Negotiating changes in repayments. Monthly repayments can be negotiated for many quarterly and annual bills. This is important when you are trying to get a grip on your debts because there are then no unexpected shocks every three months or so. Don't try and put aside cash to pay these debts. You may not be able to resist the temptation to use this for some other purpose.

In order to make the change to monthly payments, you need to write to the companies concerned and ask them to make the necessary arrangement. They will confirm the monthly amount you need to pay.

Your repayment psychology. The repayment plans you make depend not only on what you owe but also on being realistic about your ability to make and keep up your repayments.

For instance, at this point in time you might feel that you would really prefer to clear your credit card debts – right now, all at once – because you know how high the interest charges are. True, any credit card debt costs you a lot in interest if you do not pay it off in full each month. But with the debts you have got, you are not in any position to pay off a lump sum. Instead, you may be looking at a 2 or 3 year plan which will systematically reduce your debts. And in these circumstances, it does not always make sense to repay the debts on which you have to pay the highest interest.

You may not necessarily want to use what capital you may have to pay off the biggest debt first; rather, use your capital to pay off half a dozen smaller ones. Psychologically speaking, you may feel happier with fewer debts, even though one of them is a big one. You have to balance the question of interest charges on your various debts with the psychological cost of having too many debts all at once.

Sketch out several plans on ways in which you might repay your debts. It may help you to get a clearer idea if you make rough plans for each of three options:

- to cut down on expenditure and make do with the amount of money you have left each month after paying your debts and basic living expenses, both fixed and variable
- to stay in debt
- to earn more, so that you will have more to spend while still clearing your debts.

4 Make choices – live for today *and* plan for tomorrow

Look first at the rough plan you have made for making do with the amount of money that you have left after paying your debts and living expenses. Do you feel that this amount is sufficient to cover your spending?

If not, are you willing to continue in debt? If, on the other hand, you are not willing to continue in debt, then look at your plan for earning more money.

You have two choices to control and monitor your spending:

- traditional budgeting
- an alternative way of dealing with your finances, which gives more flexibility – and more rewards

In *traditional budgeting*, you take the amount of money you have left and set against this certain expenses such as £30 a week for food.

An alternative system gives you more flexibility – and more rewards. This is what you do –
1 Cost what you regularly have to pay each month, e.g. food, gas, rent, electricity, debt repayments, any other regular bills
2 Subtract this total from all your income including child benefit, extra jobs, anything else that brings in money
3 What remains is all that you have left to spend for the month. That's it. It won't stretch.
4 Divide this remaining money between debts and treats. As you clear each debt, put aside part of what you were paying monthly to clear that debt towards clearing another debt, and part towards treats. 70%–30%, debt to treat, is a reasonable share out.
5 Do not worry about how long it is all going to take. Just keep your eyes on clearing one debt at a time – and mark it off your list. Watch that list get smaller.

5 Do it – and review it

You need to check the progress of your debt clearance plan every month for as long as it takes to complete it. Because clearing debts also requires you to change your living and spending patterns, it can be difficult to sustain this entirely on your own. At least every six months – and more often if necessary – review the situation with someone whom you trust.

This may be the debt counsellor at the Citizens' Advice Bureau, a financial consultant, or your bank manager.

If, because of your past debts, you have credit judgements against you, these stay registered on an unofficial credit rating 'blacklist'. When you have cleared the debt, you will need to approach the agencies which store information on people's credit references and pay a nominal fee to ensure that you are removed from that list. The details of the main agencies which keep these records are in the *Resources for Readers* section at the end of the book. If your name remains on such a list, your future borrowing transactions, such as getting a new credit card or arranging a mortgage, are likely to be jeopardized.

W20
Getting Professional Assistance

If you need, or already use, the help of one of the professionals who deals with financial matters,

1 Acknowledge where you are – and what you want

Make a note of anyone, outside your family, who helps you with your finances, and what they do for you.

Do you need any other help for which you have so far put off making appropriate arrangements?

2 Know the facts – your figures *and* your feelings

There are two stages to using a financial professional:

- finding one/s you trust
- preparing for a meeting and using their assistance.

Finding someone you trust. Using any adviser may help you but it does not remove responsibility from you. It is essential, therefore, that you should find someone whom you can trust to be competent with your figures and sensitive to your feelings.

The following checklist will help you when you meet a financial adviser for the first time:

- Ask them to explain something you already understand and see if they explain it in a way that makes sense to you.
- Ask an awkward question and see how they react. For instance, if it is a bank manager, ask him or her precisely how they work out the charges on your account, whether they have any discretion, and if so, how they use it.
- Check with yourself: can you honestly say that you are

being understood? Or do you feel that the point which you are trying to make is being missed, or that all the answers sound like prerecorded messages rather than considered responses to your particular questions?

- Ask what is being expected of you, e.g. are you expected to produce meticulous accounting records for your accountant or will it be sufficient for you simply to hand over to her or him all your receipts and invoices?
- Ask precisely what they will be doing on your behalf, e.g. will your financial consultant simply look at the monies you have available and suggest a suitable investment or will she or he also collate for you a selection of documentation that will help you to make an informed decision, e.g. about a pension scheme?

Preparing for and using the assistance of a financial professional. Here are the steps that you need to take in order to prepare for, and use, any financial professional:

- gather together all your financial information, such as recent bank statements, details of loans, payslips
- write down a list of questions that you wish to ask and the information you want
- if the answers you get don't seem to match your questions, keep discussing the matter until you are clear about things
- listen
- write down accurately all the relevant information which you are given.

It is a common mistake to make an appointment with a financial professional and to feel rushed. Consequently, you may not be writing down correctly, or completely, the answers to your questions, or you may think that you can recall the answers when you get home.

- answer accurately any questions that you are asked.
- check out with your adviser any conclusions or decisions that you have noted down, in order to make quite sure that you both agree.

3 Consider the *real* options

When you meet someone for the first time, your judgement of them will be coloured by whether you like and trust them. If something in your meeting did not feel quite right to you, look for the reasons and what you might do about them, such as

* *'He's my husband's cousin so I don't feel I can speak freely . . .'*
* *'I don't think he knows his stuff . . .'*
* *'She never once looked at me . . .'*
* *'I realized half way through that I wasn't at all sure what I wanted and nor was she.'*

4 Make choices – live for today *and* plan for tomorrow

Staying with a financial professional just because you are embarrassed to end the relationship will add stress to your life – and possibly jeopardize the plans with which you had expected to be helped.

Using a professional without adequately preparing yourself is a waste of time for both of you. A professional cannot advise you if you are not clear about what you want.

5 Do it – and review it

As your needs change, so may your need for particular advisers. The bank manager who advised you on your current and savings accounts may not necessarily be the only, or even the best, person to help you with the financial affairs of your small business, or with the money you have just inherited.

When you review your money management, in Chapter 13, *Maintaining Your Progress*, also review the advice you are getting, so as to make sure that it continues to be the best you can get.

W21
Maintaining Your Progress

In order to keep yourself moving in the direction of a better financial life,

1 Acknowledge where you are – and what you want

Check to see whether there has been a change in any of your circumstances since you last reviewed your financial situation. The sorts of questions you could ask yourself might include –

- are things alright at work – or not?
- domestically, has your family grown (another child?)? Have you moved in with someone, got married, or has your partnership split up?
- have you made any plans for the future? Perhaps a holiday, or a new house?
- Are you in danger of losing control of your finances and getting into debt? Or are you already there?

The amount of time which you need to set aside to review your finances will depend on whether there are any or many changes in your circumstances and/or in your goals.

2 Know the facts – both your figures *and* your feelings

What have you been doing since your last review? Is your bank balance at the level at which you decided to keep it? Have you saved the amount you intended to save? Do you want to change or sell your investments or buy new ones? Has your salary increased? Do you need to increase your pension contributions? Have you lost your job or faced some other downturn in financial circumstances? Have you made any new plans? Or revised those you had already made? Can you identify areas in which you have made progress and areas where you have failed to do so? What are the financial implications?

Where do you see yourself going in the next three to six months? Identify plans you have for the next three to six months and cost these.

* *Go on a skiing holiday, £750 for two weeks, including some new ski clothing and spending money*
* *Finish paying back rent – owe £420 and could pay that back at £20 per week.*

What is your current financial situation? Look at your bills, to see if any remain unpaid; any loans and whether your repayments are on target and consider your patterns of spending. Check whether there is any decrease or increase in any areas of earning or spending and why this has happened.

3 Consider the *real* options

With the information from 1 and 2 above, identify whether you need or want to make adjustments to your goals and/or to your financial arrangements.

Be honest with yourself about targets which you set yourself but failed to achieve. Do you still want to meet those targets, e.g. saving for a car? Or have your priorities changed? Drop or amend anything that is no longer realistic.

4 Make choices – live for today *and* plan for tomorrow

Don't be too hard on yourself – but also don't run away from the reality of what is going on. Look at what lies ahead of you for the next three or so months and set new financial targets, if necessary.

5 Do it – and review it

Review the review! You may find that you do not have the discipline to take time for undertaking this check on your own. If that is clear, then make an appointment – now – for three months ahead, with your financial consultant, accountant, partner – or even a trusted friend.

Refer to it!

What's What –
and How To

What's What – and How To

Introduction

One problem with financial planning is that what you need to know is often couched in language you do not understand. You do not need to talk 'their' language but it will help you to take responsibility for your decisions if you know what the financial professionals are talking about.

The Practical Guides aim to present six major financial transactions in a way that will give you the two ingredients you need – an understanding of the issues and a grasp of the financial facts.

The Glossary translates some of the most common terms used in financial language into plain English.

Finally, *Resources for Readers* lists some of the available agencies and publications which can help you with your money management.

The information in *What's What – and How To* comes with a

Financial Health Warning
Double Check All Information You Are Given

The information presented here is an overview. It is intended to introduce you to the basics of financial transactions. The information is based on the laws of the United Kingdom and does not include the particular rules of different religions or the laws of other countries.

The financial facts presented in the following pages are accurate at the time of going to press. The problem is that the law and/or the ground rules set by financial institutions can change quickly. What's right today can be wrong tomorrow. It is always your responsibility to check whether information is up to date. Never assume that it is.

Double checking information is difficult. Most of us settle for building up a network of professionals and periodicals which we find trustworthy. That is fine. Just remember – the ultimate responsibility is yours.

The Practical Guide to Bookkeeping and Taxation for the Self-Employed

If you are working for yourself, you have to 'keep books' – an account of what you are earning and spending. There are two major reasons for this: you *may* want to know whether or not you are making any money – and you *must* submit a profit and loss account to the Inland Revenue (IR) at the end of each trading year so that they will be able to assess your taxes.

In this guide, the following stages of bookkeeping and taxation for the self-employed are covered:

1 Establishing self-employed status, called Schedule D
2 Deciding who keeps the books and when
3 Keeping books

- choosing the right books
- using the books correctly
- knowing what to claim
- recording petty cash
- keeping VAT records

4 Keeping records of IR business
5 Making your yearly tax return

- what Inland Revenue requires
- preparing books for your accountant
- preparing your own books for the IR

6 Dealing with losses.

1 Establishing self-employed status

The Inland Revenue must be notified within one year of the beginning of self-employment that you are earning non-taxed income. If you delay or fail to inform them of your status and earnings, they can fine you and charge interest on any tax overdue to them.

To register with the IR, simply telephone any Inland Revenue Office and give them your address. Then write to that office stating that you wish to register yourself as a self-employed person. You will receive a form which needs to be correctly completed, signed and returned. At the same time you should inform your local DSS office and ask for the relevant form to be sent to you to start paying your self-employed National Insurance stamp. Your liability is to pay a stamp for any one week in which you have done any work whatsoever for your business. The simplest method of paying this stamp is to request a direct debiting mandate form, so that the money is transferred out of your bank account regularly. Do this if you know you will be working full-time as a self-employed person. Otherwise, buy stamps from your Post Office in the weeks for which you need them.

In order to be taxed as self-employed, you have to meet one fundamental requirement in the eyes of the Inland Revenue – that in your area of work you are not in, what is termed, a Master/Servant relationship, but that you are your own boss or Master. In the main, this means that you must have more than one person supplying you with contracts to work for them. The Inland Revenue is trying very hard *at the present time* to incorporate as many people as possible, who have traditionally been self-employed, into the PAYE system. Factors such as not being paid for holidays or being able to set your own hours, do not guarantee that you are seen to be self-employed. If you believe that you are self-employed and this is challenged by the IR, be prepared to argue your case. You will need factual information to back up your contention, such as evidence of having several different contracts or having to provide your own equipment.

2 Deciding who keeps the books and when

There are two stages to keeping the books: weekly accounts of earnings and expenditures; and annual accounts for the Inland Revenue.

You have three options about how you undertake both the weekly bookkeeping and the annual accounting:

- to do the weekly bookkeeping yourself and pay an accountant to prepare your books for the IR
- to pay a bookkeeper to keep your books and an accountant to prepare them for the IR;
- to do both yourself.

Which of these you choose depends on how much you earn and how comfortable and competent you are at keeping the books. Although the fees you pay a bookkeeper and/or accountant can be deducted from your taxes, only you can work out whether you are earning enough to justify this expenditure or whether doing the accounts yourself, at a time when you could be earning good money, is a form of false economy.

It makes sense for most people who work for themselves to keep their own weekly books and records, even if these are then given to an accountant at the end of the year. Keeping your own books *greatly* reduces the cost of the accountant's time and therefore the final bill.

3 Keeping books

Keeping the books really means keeping two books, an analysis book for income and expenditure and a petty cash book.

Choosing the right analysis book. You need one Cathedral Analysis type book in order to keep correct accounts. These books will have two numbers in their title such as, Cathedral Analysis 2/10. This means two columns to enter earnings under two definite headings, such as 'training' and 'group work', and 10 columns to enter different types of spending, such as 'travel', 'office bills', 'books and journals'.

Using the book correctly. You record two different things in this book: income on the left and expenditure on the right. The information needed on each side is:

Income
- the date you received payment
- the name of the person who, or company which, paid you

Refer to it! What's what – and How to

- the amount you received.

You need to keep invoices and/or payment slips to tally with these entries.

Expenditure
- the date of each payment
- the name of the person/company receiving payment (e.g. London Transport, not tube fare)
- the number which you have given to the receipt
- the total which you paid out
- the breakdown of that total under the subheadings for the various categories of expenses (see below).

You need to keep receipts to tally with at least 70% of these entries. It can help your accounting or your accountant

MONEY IN

Date Received	Name	No	Amount	
19 May	Stourbridge	1	869	40
30 "	Ensor Assn	2	179	89

MONEY OUT

Date	Name	Receipt No	Total		Car	Travel
9 May	PO	1	13	90		
5	M. Mouse Mercantile	2	12	12		
9	A & J Partners	3	3	16		
12	Boots	4	4	74		
30	LJ	5	2	30		2.30
13	"	6	1	30		1.30

if you number these receipts and put the matching numbers in a column in the book.

It is advisable to enter your income and expenditures in your book at least once a week; if you don't you are sure to have forgotten items. Remember, every pound that is not entered and receipted is a gift to the Inland Revenue through sheer forgetfulness.

At the end of every month, simply total up the figures and start the next month on a new page. Always make your entries in pencil; this allows errors to be corrected later.

Knowing what to claim. A self-employed person can claim for all items and services relevant to the work they do. Different items can be claimed depending on the type of business you run. The Inland Revenue or an accountant can give you a list of the headings under which you can claim expenses. As an example, the claims list below is for a financial or management consultant:

Heading	Types of entries
Travel	tube, bus, taxi, air fare where applicable
Car	petrol, parking meters, car parks, MOT, tax, insurance, servicing and repair bills, running costs, oil (claiming

MAY 1990

ationary	Bills	Books & Journals	Training & Research	Petty Cash	Printing & Postage	Misc.	Notes
					13.90		
2.12							
3.16							
				4.74			

	relevant percentage for professional use)
Stationery	pens, pencils, paper, ink, paper-clips, staplers, scissors, box cards, desk set
Printing and postage	self-explanatory
Papers/journals	newspapers, books, relevant magazines, professional journals
Equipment	briefcase (1 per year if relevant), calculator, desk (for home use), chairs, telephones, answerphone, computer equipmen filing cabinets, storage units, etc.
Research/fees	courses, union fees, professional body subscriptions
Use of home as office	a proportion of gas, electricity, telephone bills, contents insurance and buildings insurance and any maintenance that you do to the house that is specific to that part of the house which you use as an office (any proportion of regular maintenance for the upkeep of your home relevant to that room or rooms); You are not entitled to include any part of the Community Charge as a bill.
Petty cash/ bank charges/ bank interest charged	see discussion in *petty cash* below
Miscellaneous	anything that does not fit in to any of the other columns, with a simple explanation in the final column in your book.

Other costs you would enter for your final accounts would be depreciation of equipment, which means the amount that you can claim on items as they get older; this would include your car as well as furniture. The amount is worked out on an exact percentage basis and changes with various government budgets.

Keeping petty cash records. Petty cash is a sum of money you draw out per week for such items as tea, coffee, calls from public telephones, parking meters. You should keep a separate record of this money in a small petty cash notebook and the receipts (if any) to go with this amount.

Enter the amount of petty cash you draw out weekly in your big analysis book. Then keep a record in the petty cash notebook of how you spent the money. Enter each item penny by penny. Obviously it is not possible to obtain receipts for some of the small items, such as calls from public telephones and parking meters. It is therefore vital that these entries are made by date and sum in your petty cash book. Make sure the entries are in the petty cash book correspond with your appointments/work diary. If your diary shows that you saw clients all day in your office, but your petty cash book shows parking meter amounts for which you have no receipts on the same day, there is a mismatch and the claim will be disallowed by the Inland Revenue. The IR will charge you interest on monies which are collected late in this way, and they also are entitled to fine you on top of that, the amount of which is now unlimited. Errors of this kind are likely to make the Inland Revenue suspicious of your other accounting records.

Keeping VAT records. If you are registered for VAT (Valued Added Tax) you must keep accurate records and receipts. To complete your VAT returns you need all your invoices and receipts with a VAT number on them. The simplest method to use is a 3/3 Cathedral Analysis book as shown below:

Date	Payer	Gross incl. VAT	VAT	Net ex-VAT	Date	Payer	Gross incl. VAT	VAT	Net ex-VAT

The Customs and Excise department inspects people's records, usually within the first couple of years and randomly thereafter. If you keep your records as shown above this is a very simple procedure for which you need to set aside some time each week. This should only take about 15–30 minutes depending on the volume of your business.

4 Keeping records of Inland Revenue business

Keep copies of *everything* you send to the Inland Revenue, including forms that you have filled in and signed. Never leave requests from the IR unanswered for more than a month, as this will lead to your files getting refiled in the IR offices and will put you further behind in the queue.

It is better to be up-to-date rather than run the risk of having two or three years' tax returns piling up. The IR is entitled to have all monies due to it paid immediately, so the more cooperative you are, the more helpful its staff will be. It is worth remembering that the IR is usually not the ogre that it is made out to be. Its staff have two jobs: to collect taxes *and* to assist the taxpayer.

5 Making your annual profit and loss return

At the end of your tax year, you are required to submit to the Inland Revenue the figures for the profit or loss you have made during the preceding year. The exact date will be the one that has been agreed with the Inland Revenue when you registered as self-employed and is the same each year. It can be a year from the start of your business. Many people find it easier to choose the same date as the Inland Revenue's tax year, i.e. 6 April – 5 April.

If you are using an accountant, you simply send the Cathedral Analysis book off to him or her together with all relevant receipts and invoices, bank paying-in books, and statements and cheque books. If you have a pension plan, you need also to send the PPCC (the Personal Pension Contribution Certificate) as well as your Certificate of Interest Paid from the building society in connection with your mortgage, if you have one. The building society will provide it each year if requested to do so.

If you are not using an accountant, then you will need to draw up a simple Profit and Loss sheet yourself (see below). The figures for the Profit and Loss sheet are taken from the totals in your Cathedral Analysis Book. You send the Profit and Loss sheet directly to your Inland Revenue Office.

The IR have the right to ask to see the analysis book together with all receipts to ensure that you have submitted accurate accounts. Occasionally, the IR will try to argue costs, e.g. the percentage claimed for phone bills and petrol. Be prepared to argue the point – unless you have put in an amount which you cannot defend, such as claiming 100% of the phone bill as a business expense when you work from home. Compromise can usually be reached.

Look at the example of a Profit and Loss sheet. The final figure of £6150 is called the *net taxable profit*. This is also the figure that is referred to, for a self-employed person, as the *net relevant earnings*. This figure is important as it is used when calculating how much pension contributions you are allowed to make or, by a lender, when deciding whether or not to lend money to you, for whatever purpose, and in particular for mortgage purposes. The IR then automatically deducts from this figure the following:

1 your individual tax allowance
2 pension contribution, if applicable
3 mortgage interest relief, if applicable

The figure that is left is subject to tax.

Profit and Loss Account
example

Gross earnings		£12,000
Less expenses		
Travel	£ 200	
Car	1300	
Stationery*	100	
Printing/postage	100	
Equipment	3000	
Use of home**	500	
Miscellaneous***	650	
Expenses		£5850
net taxable profit		£6150

*   Includes papers and journals
** Bills
*** Petty cash, research and fees

6 Losses

If you have made a loss, carry it forward to next year and deduct it from whatever profits you make – or add it instead to your loss if that is your position.

Summary

Keeping your own books is a simple and very effective way of not only saving accountants' bills and tax but also of keeping yourself up-to-date with the true profitability of your earnings.

Tax returns on the other hand just need a deep breath and 30 minutes time to be completed. Ensure before you start that you have all relevant information. Once you have done your first one you will know how easy it is.

The Practical Guide to
Arranging Life Cover

The point of having life assurance is either to take care of others after your death or to give yourself a lump sum for your own use when the policy expires. It is the first purpose that is discussed in this guide, when your life is assured for a sum which will be paid to your estate on your death or, if you wish, to individual/s or organization/s named to receive this benefit on your death. Further details about life policies which you can take out to provide yourself with a lump sum are mentioned in *The Practical Guide to Saving and Investing*.

Life assurance is *not* for everybody. In fact, it is not for *you* at all, even though you are the person who is *assured* and you are the one who generally pays the premiums. Life assurance is for the benefit of those whom you leave behind after your death. The benefit can be for whomsoever or whatsoever you choose: your family, charities, certain friends, or to cover the costs of your funeral.

Life assurance is also called *life insurance*. These terms mean the same thing. Assurance is the correct term for protection taken out on a person; insurance means protection taken out for an object such as a house or a car. The payments which are made are known as premiums.

This guide shows the two steps necessary to take to choose the life cover that is most appropriate for you:

1 Consider your circumstances
- Why do you want life cover – and how much?
- What have you already got?
- How much money have you got to spend?

2 Examine the kinds of life assurance contracts
There are basically two kinds of contracts:
- protection-only contracts (described below)

- protection with investment contracts (described in *The Practical Guide to Saving and Investing*)

1 Consider your circumstances

Which type of life assurance – if any – is for you depends on your needs and circumstances. Before you consider the various kinds of life assurance cover, ask yourself the following questions. The answers will point you towards the most appropriate policy.

Why do you want it? If it is to cover your partner and/or children in the event of your death, how do you want to leave things: with the mortgage paid off? With enough additional funds to cover the children's education? With enough money for them to be very comfortably off? Or to be able to maintain the lifestyle they have had with you?

If the cover is for friends or for a favourite organization such as a charity, do you wish to leave them a token amount of money or is it for a specified item?

Is the cover simply so that you can leave enough money for your burial?

Cost your answers. How much is the mortgage that would have to be paid off? What is the sum that would be needed to cover the children's education, or to leave the family very comfortably off? By doing these costings, you will know how much cover you will need. Then you can look at how much you can afford at the present time – and work out where to make adjustments if what you want and what you can afford do not match.

What have you already got? Do you already have life cover under any existing arrangement? Sometimes when you take out insurance, such as when you buy a washing machine on credit or take out a pension scheme, there is a provision to provide a lump sum of money in the event of your death. If so, how much is it?

How much money have you got to spend? Remember, the best product/contract/policy for a good return in the future will also cost more now. You may feel that you cannot afford the full amount now. When looking at what you can afford, remember that if you make the commitment to life assurance, it becomes part of your basic bills. It is not a luxury.

2 Considering the kinds of life assurance contracts

There are basically two kinds of life assurance: that which offers protection only, i.e. money paid out if you die during the time the policy is in force; and that which is an investment as well as a protection. Investment and protection policies can be cashed in after a fixed period of time, referred to as 'the term'.

The protection-only contracts are described below:

- level term assurance
- convertible term assurance
- increasing term assurance
- decreasing term assurance

The protection with investment contracts are described in *The Practical Guide to Saving and Investing*, and cover:

- endowment
- whole of life assurance
- with profits
- unit-linked

Which policy is most suitable will depend on your circumstances; the most monetarily suitable is not necessarily the one that is overall most suitable for you. Use the chart below as a rough guide to the kind of contract which will best suit you.

What for	Which contract
Mortgage repayment	protection-only or investment with protection
leaving a lump sum on death	protection-only or investment with protection
future spending	investment with protection

Protection-only contracts pay out money only if your death occurs during the period during which you have contracted to pay premiums. There is no cash-in and no surrender value *at any point*. If you are still alive at the end of the set period, you get nothing. These policies fall under three headings:

Level term assurance. A set amount of life assurance is guaranteed for which you pay a fixed premium during a fixed term, e.g. £20,000 sum assured for 20 years would cover the life which is assured for the sum of £20,000 during a 20-year period. At the end of that period the contract would cease, with no cash value nor any guaranteed option to take out a new policy.

Convertible term assurance. This is basically the same as level term assurance above, with the addition of the option to *convert* the policy to a more permanent form of life assurance or a different type of policy such as an endowment policy at a given date. It is therefore slightly more expensive than level term assurance as the company is *guaranteeing* the person whose life is assured the option of continuing the same amount of life cover, regardless of their state of health. For example, a convertible term policy, with a sum assured of £20,000 over a period, or 'term', of 20 years would, on expiry, offer the policyholder the opportunity to take out a new policy (usually a whole of life policy described in *The Practical Guide to Saving and Investing*) with a sum assured of up to £20,000 irrespective of their present state of health. A convertible term policy cannot be cashed in.

Increasing term assurance. This is simply a form of level or convertible term assurance under which the premium and the sum assured increase annually at a set rate or in line with the RPI (retail prices index).

Decreasing term assurance. This is the cheapest form of life assurance policy. The sum assured, that is the amount paid on death, decreases during the period of the policy, meaning that a claim made towards the end of the policy term will pay significantly less than the original sum assured. Once again, there is no cash-in value at any stage of the policy. This type of life assurance was designed to accompany capital repayment mortgages, where the capital owed to the building society which holds the mortgage gradually reduces during the term of the loan. *Decreasing term assurance* should ensure that if you die before your mortgage is fully redeemed, the outstanding balance on your mortgage is paid off through the life assurance policy. A decreasing term assurance policy should therefore always cover the amount outstanding on the mortgage in the event of the death of the mortgage holder during the period of the policy. This would leave those who inherit your house with a mortgage-free house on your death. Due to the high fluctuating mortgage rates, it is advisable to check on a regular basis, at least every 2–3 years, that the sum assured is the same as (or higher than) the outstanding mortgage.

Summary

Review your decision on an annual basis, or if there is a significant change in your circumstances. You can always increase the sum for which you are assuring yourself – and there is likely to be provision to decrease the payments, and the benefits, if you hit harder times.

The Practical Guide to
Setting Up a Mortgage

A mortgage is the means by which you borrow money for the specific purpose of purchasing a property. This property can be your home, a second house such as a holiday cottage, a property for renting or a property to be used for business purposes. The lender of money for mortgages is usually a building society or bank.

The principle for obtaining a mortgage is basically the same for any kind of property – the lender decides whether you can afford the property and whether the amount being asked for the property is reasonable. *It is not your decision; it is the lender's decision.*

The general steps for obtaining a mortgage are the same for any kind of property, but this guide focuses on arranging the mortgage for an individual home.

Steps in getting and keeping a mortgage

1 Find what size of mortgage you can afford
2 Select the kind of mortgage you want
3 Claim the available tax relief
4 Deal immediately with any problems in repayment.

1 Find what size of mortgage you can afford.

The first step is not to look at a property or properties but to work out whether you would be able to live on what is left of your income after paying for a mortgage and all its attendant costs.

This is what you do. Ring any mortgage lender and ask them two questions: what they would be prepared to lend to you and what would be the current repayment of that mortgage per month. They will want to know how much you are earning and, if you are buying with somebody else, their income as well. From that information they will be able to answer both questions. Do not concern yourself at this stage with finding out about the different types of mortgages that are on offer.

The next step is to see whether you could manage to pay this amount. From the monthly figure you have been quoted, subtract the amount of rent you are currently paying. Add to that balance a figure to represent what you will pay for buildings and contents insurance on your property, and an amount of money to cover maintenance or a service charge.

This is the equation:

Mortgage amount you would have to repay monthly at current rates	£600
− Amount you currently pay in rent	−250
Sub-total: Difference between mortgage and renting	350
+ figures for building and contents insurances	+20
+ upkeep money for maintenance/service charge	+30
Total amount you need to save each month	**£400**

At your bank or building society open a savings account that pays interest and have that final amount of money transferred by standing order from your current bank account each month. A standing order ensures that money is transferred automatically each from your banking current account into your savings account. This method of saving has three uses: it will tell you whether you can live on what is left in your current account; you are saving money to which you still have instant access; and at the end of the day you will either have money towards the deposit on the purchase of a house or an extra sum in your pocket.

How do you judge whether you can live on what's left in your current account? It is up to you to decide that. If you decide you cannot survive – in your terms – by saving the figure you originally calculated, then reduce the standing order by the extra amount you need each month so as to allow you to live at the standard you have decided you must have. The new standing order now tells you how much you feel you can afford to pay for a mortgage.

At this point, go back to the lender and ask them how much of a mortgage that monthly amount will give you at current rates of mortgage interest.

You now need to do two more calculations –

Amount of mortgage	£45,000	
+amount of deposit you have saved	£5,000	
Sub-total:		*£50,000*
Less		
+ Legal fees	+£1200	
+ First month's mortgage	+£500	
+ sum of money you want to include for decorating, repairs, etc., if applicable	+£500	
	£2,700	
Total cost of property you can afford		*£47,300*

Very few people get a mortgage to cover 100% of the price of a property. Instead, you will need to put down a cash deposit which is usually 5% of the purchase price. If you do not have this available you run the risk of nobody being prepared to lend any monies to you. The more you can put down as a deposit, the more deals, in mortgage terms, will be available to you – for instance a lower interest rate for a given period.

When you are doing the calculations about the price of property you can afford, do bear in mind that interest rates can go up as well as down, and allow yourself some leeway in case they go up in the future. It is advisable never to take out the absolute maximum that you can afford as this gives you no room to manoeuvre, for instance for unexpected repairs as well as rises in interest rates.

If you know or suspect that at some time in the near future there will be significant changes in your circumstances, take these into account when calculating the maximum price of property you can afford – and leave yourself some leeway. If two of you are buying together, do either of you expect to reduce your earning capacity for whatever reason? Is your job secure or is your industry going through a bad time? If you are a couple who are planning to have children, will you have to manage on a single salary?

2 Select the kind of mortgage you want

In order to select the right type, you need to ask yourself several questions and then match your answers to the mortgage which comes closest to meeting your particular circumstances.

(i) To how much can you afford to commit yourself each month for 25 years, this being the usual length of time for a mortgage? You have already calculated the answer to this in stage 1.

(ii) Do you want to receive a tax-free lump sum at the end of the term of mortgage? If so, look at the endowment and pension mortgages.

(iii) Can you incorporate the mortgage with your pension requirements? If so, look at a pension mortgage.

(iv) Do you expect to be qualified in your profession within the next five years, thereby dramatically increasing your salary, or are you expecting your earning capacity to increase significantly during the next five years? In both of these instances, is money tight right now? If so, the deferred or low start mortgage options may suit you. Either of these options also require you to choose which type of mortgage you would like, i.e. repayment, endowment, pension, or any combination of the three – if the lender allows this.

(v) Are you self-employed?

The amount that the lender is prepared to advance you is usually based upon the net relevant profit that you declare to the Inland Revenue. Most lenders will want your last three years' profit and loss accounts and will take the average of those three years as their base figure for working out what they are prepared to lend you. The lower your taxable income, the lower your mortgage. Occasionally, the lender may be prepared to accept a letter from your accountant instead of accounts. The letter would need to confirm that, based on the potential earning evidence she or he has seen, their personal opinion is that you can afford to repay the mortgage you have selected. Another option is the *high equity mortgage* described below.

The mortgage which is the cheapest now is not necessarily the best for you; nor is the most expensive necessarily the best type of mortgage to have. The answer lies with your circumstances.

There are three basic types of mortgage and two variations:
- a repayment mortgage
- an endowment/pension mortgage

variations
- a deferred or low start mortgage
- fixed rate mortgage
- high equity mortgage

A repayment mortgage. With this mortgage you pay back both interest and capital – capital being the amount of money you have borrowed, and interest being the money the lender is charging you for borrowing the capital. By the time you reach the end of the mortgage term, and providing all payments have been kept up-to-date, there will be nothing further to pay to the lender and you own the property completely. Most lenders will insist that you take out a life assurance contract to go with the mortgage, to cover their investment, in the event of your death, so that they will not be forced to sell the house to recoup their monies. (See *The Practical Guide to Arranging Life Cover*.)

It is important that you realize you are not obliged to take the life assurance policy from the lender or on the lender's recommendation.

An endowment/pension mortgage. With this type of mortgage, you repay interest only for the term of the mortgage; you never repay the capital. At the end of the life of the mortgage, your endowment and/or pension is cashed in to provide you with the monies to pay off the mortgage plus leaving you with either a tax-free lump sum and/or a pension. With both of these contracts, if you die during the term of the mortgage, there is life assurance to pay off the mortgage. If you move properties, you simply move the policy or policies to be assigned to the next mortgage. If the next mortgage is larger then take out another policy to cover the additional amount.

There are two elements to an endowment or pension mortgage: the interest that is repaid to the lender, and the cost of the policy which you take out on your life. This will either cover the lender's investment in the event of your death or, at the end of the term, repay the mortgage plus give you a lump sum.

Variations. With any of the above types of mortgage further options can be offered to you by the lender. The main ones are:

A deferred or low start mortgage. These mortgages need to be investigated thoroughly and compared with your financial circumstances before you make any decision. In the first years of the mortgage they have the advantage that you will be making lower repayments to the lender than the other two types of mortgages mentioned above. The cost to you, however, is that either the monthly repayments increase on an annual basis and/or the saving you have made each year is added to the original amount of money you borrowed, so that at the end of the agreed deferred or low start period, you have a significantly larger mortgage to repay at normal rates.

This effectively means you have less equity in your property. In a market where properties are not increasing in value or increasing very slightly, you run the risk of using up most of your equity by choosing this mortgage option.

Equity is the difference between what you would have to repay to the lender if you sold your house and any balance or surplus which would be your own. 'Equity' is another word for profit.

Fixed interest mortgage. A fixed interest mortgage is one where the lender offers you the option of having the interest rate stay the same, i.e. fixed, for a set period of time. It is of advantage in times when interest rates are uncertain. Its disadvantage is that interest rates could drop below the rate at which you have fixed your mortgage. Bear in mind most fixed rates are for a 2–3 year period, and at the start of a mortgage are going to be at least 1% lower than the current interest rate. Therefore, if the rate drops during the term, you need to take account of the fact that you have already enjoyed a lower rate up to that time.

High equity mortgage. The other option is the *high equity mortgage or self-certification mortgage*. It is open to everybody but is of particular interest to any self-employed person who may not be able to provide the necessary profit and loss accounts, for example in their first year of trading. This kind of mortgage is most appropriate in cases where the loan which you are seeking is less than 70% of the lender's valuation of the property. The lender only requires you to confirm yourself, that is with no attached paperwork in the form of payslips or profit and loss accounts, your current earnings. This is called *self-certification*.

For example,

Asking price of house:	*£185,000*
Lender's valuation:	*£140,000*
High Equity mortgage at 70% of valuation:	*£98,600*
Deposit:	*£86,400*

3 Claim the tax relief on the mortgage

If the mortgage you have taken out is for your main residence, you will be entitled to tax relief on the interest you pay for part of the loan. This amount is determined by the government and can be changed by the annual Budget. At the present time you receive tax relief based on the basic rate of tax which you pay. For most people, the MIRAS system applies. MIRAS, i.e. Mortgage Interest Relief At Source, is a system whereby the lender deducts the basic rate of tax from the interest which you pay on the amount of your loan which qualifies for tax relief. You don't have to do anything except check that these deductions are being made.

Above the allowable amount there is no other tax relief on a mortgage. The allowable amount of tax relief is applicable to the house, not to a particular person, and can be shared between individuals. But there is only one allowable amount to be shared between you, whether you are married or not.

4 Deal immediately with any problems in repayment

It is worth bearing in mind that life does not always run smoothly and that many circumstances can affect your ability to keep up your repayments. If you know that you are having, or are about to have, difficulties in meeting your repayments in full, contact the lender immediately. Inform him or her of the problems – and of suggested solutions, if you have any. It is usual practice to try to assist you in ways which ensure that you do *not* lose your home. If there are ways in which you can be helped, say by extending the mortgage or changing it to a cheaper mortgage, lenders will usually try and help.

It is in nobody's interest for your home to be repossessed by the lender and, possibly, to be sold at a price lower than that for which you bought it, with all that this costs the lender. Lenders are more likely to take this action if you have fallen behind with your repayments without first discussing your difficulties with them, or if you have simply walked out of your property.

Do not think that by handing over the keys to your house you are abdicating your responsibilities for repayment: you are not. Even if you simply walk out and leave the keys, the interest on the mortgage will continue to build up and be added to *your* debt and the lenders can then sell the house for whatever amount they wish. You will find that they will sell it for just enough to cover their outstanding loan, there will be nothing left for you – and you will have obtained a bad mortgage record which can seriously hinder you in future attempts to obtain a mortgage with *any* lender.

This is a circumstance in which quick honesty can only pay dividends.

Summary

When setting up a mortgage, make sure that you do not over-stretch yourself in relation to your current earnings. You will then be on safer ground if interest rates rise, or your income drops, dramatically.

Also, do not under-mortgage yourself, in other words set up too small a mortgage. Using up most or all of your available spare monies in order to have a low mortgage, leaves you with less back-up, in money terms, either for your lifestyle or for emergencies.

The Practical Guide to
Arranging a Pension

If you don't want to be poor when you retire – whether you plan to retire at 50 or 80 – you need to start contributing to a pension scheme so as to have made contributions for 25 to 30 years before you retire. For each year that you delay, you will have to pay more to reach the same goal. *But it is never too late to start.*

Your goal for the years of your retirement should be to have an income that corresponds as nearly as possible to your final salary. This means that you should aim at maintaining your level of income and ensuring that this stays in line with the index which determines the cost of living, that is the Retail Price Index – rather than take a drop in your income on retirement, as many people have come to expect. The most common way to do this is through a pension. Whereas a superannuation scheme, which is a company pension scheme, provides you with only a percentage of your final salary, there are now ways of topping this up, and these are explained further below.

This guide will answer the following questions:

1 What is a pension? What is a pension policy?
2 What are the different schemes?
3 What are the tax advantages?
4 Where do you go to get the best pension?
5 When can you get your pension?
6 When you are finally retiring, what are the criteria for selecting a pension?

1 WHAT IS A PENSION? WHAT IS A PENSION POLICY? WHAT IS A PENSION FUND?

A *pension* is the income you arrange for yourself for your retirement as a result of contributions made to one or more pension policies while you were working.

A *pension policy* is the same as a *pension scheme*. It is a long-term savings plan which, because it has particular tax advantages, is the best way of providing an income for your retirement. You get immediate tax advantages when you contribute to a pension policy, in the form of tax relief on your contributions, and you can take a tax-free lump sum when you are finally ready to take your pension from the pension fund in which you have invested your money.

A *pension fund* is the mechanism by which monies that are intended to provide pensions are invested in the open market. A pension fund has a special tax status called 'exempt'. That means that, unlike other investment funds, pension funds do not have to pay certain taxes to the government. This is the reason why your money grows more if it is invested in a pension fund than in an ordinary investment such as a savings plan.

When you contribute to a personal pension plan, you are building up a fund of money which you can then use to buy pension benefits on your retirement. The money will not come into your hands on retirement as cash, unless you opt for part of it, which you are allowed to take as a lump sum, to be paid to you tax-free in cash. Instead, on retirement you are able to buy pension benefits. If you are part of a company scheme, or superannuation scheme, the company scheme will be doing the same for you.

If you have contributed to a personal pension plan you will, when you finally decide to take your pension, get a statement from the pension company with which you have been investing your money telling you how much your pension fund is worth. In most cases you then have the right to contact other pension companies and request them to give you information as to how much pension they will provide for you with that sum of money.

2 WHAT ARE THE DIFFERENT SCHEMES?

There are a variety of ways in which you can contribute towards a pension. The following will be discussed below:

Pension schemes from the State
  • The basic state pension

- SERPS: The state earnings-related pension

Pension schemes for employees
- Company pension schemes
- A combination of company and personal pension schemes
- Free-standing voluntary contributions (FSAVCs) and Additional voluntary contributions (AVCs)

Pension schemes for employees and the self-employed
- Personal pension schemes

Pension schemes for the self-employed

PENSION SCHEMES FROM THE STATE

The present state pension scheme is based on the amount of National Insurance contributions you have made during your working life. The state decides when you can take your state pension. At present, the age is 60 for a woman and 65 for a man.

The Basic State Pension

The 'old age pension' is now called the basic pension and is available to everyone whether employed or self-employed provided they have paid the necessary national insurance stamps during their working lives.

People who have never paid a national insurance contribution are the losers. Non-earning women can only get some or all of the state pension if they are, or have been, married because their pension is based upon their husband's contributions. If you have never had a husband who has paid national insurance contributions (NICs) you are not entitled to a state pension and will have to apply for benefits.

Women who are divorced are entitled to a state pension based on the NICs made by their husbands during the period of their marriage, providing that they have not remarried. They can then apply for income support to make up the difference in income. If they have remarried, the amount of pension they get is based on their new husband's contributions.

There are allowances and sometimes national insurance contribution protection for women and men who are unable to work regularly because they stay at home to look after someone. This is called Home Responsibilities Protection (HRP).

The State Earnings-Related Pension (SERPS)

The state earnings-related pension (SERPS) was introduced in April 1978 as an addition to the basic pension. *It is available only to employed people, not to those who are self-employed.* The reason for this is that a self-employed person pays considerably less National Insurance than an employed person.

The intention was to provide an additional pension related to earnings during the person's working life. This pension is inflation-proof, which means that it automatically increases in line with the RPI. The state scheme, SERPS, has an upper and lower limit on what you can contribute each year, regardless of what you earn. The reason for this is that over the upper limit you as the employee do not make any NI contributions (the employer does) and under the lower limit, you do not pay the extra 2% relating to SERPS in NI contributions. You can get the current rate by phoning a Tax Office or DSS office.

People who are or were in pension schemes organized by the company that employs them need to check whether their company contracted out of the SERPS scheme or not. If the company has opted out, you will have been paying a lower NI contribution. Most company pension/superannuation schemes will have contracted out of SERPS. If your company contracted out of SERPS, then the amount represented by SERPS is already included in the pension you will be getting from the company at retirement. You will still get the basic pension, i.e. the old age pension.

The self-employed are only entitled to the basic pension, not to SERPS. Actors are the only exception at the present time: They do not pay the self-employed stamp. Instead, the full national insurance contribution is deducted from their fees before they are paid. They are, therefore, entitled to take out a SERPS pension plan based on their national insurance contributions in a way similar to that of an employed person.

PENSION SCHEMES FOR EMPLOYEES

Company pension schemes

Company pension schemes are also called superannuation schemes. What this means is that the company you work for has set up a pension scheme for the benefit of its employees. The company either decides that it wishes to run the scheme and appoints itself as Trustee, or contracts this work to somebody else.

The company decides how much you will contribute and whether the company itself will or will not contribute. It will also have decided on the benefits which employees are going to receive, such as whether or not there will be any death-in-service benefit, widow's or widower's pension, children's pension, what percentage of your final salary will be paid as a pension, and the age at which they will pay the pension to you. It is usually called a 1/80th or 1/60th final salary scheme.

If there is a superannuation scheme at your place of work, you have the choice of whether you join it or not, or contribute to a personal pension scheme. Your aim is to get the scheme that will best suit you. Before making a choice, take the following steps:

- Find out what your contribution to the pension/ superannuation scheme at work will be and what the penalties would be for withdrawing from the scheme if you leave the job
- Look at what benefits the scheme offers you
- Work out what you would expect to receive as a pension from your company scheme when you retire.

The way to calculate this is not to speculate about the future but use the following formula to work out what you would get if you retired today. This will then give you a figure with which you can compare what is on offer from other pension schemes.

Current salary divided by the type of final salary %, i.e. 1/60 or 1/80
× *the number of years you have worked for the company*

= **Total**: *the pension you would get if you retired today*

For example, a man of 65 on £12,500 and with a 1/80 scheme, who has worked for the company for 30 years: £12,500.80 ÷ £156.25 × 30 = £4667.50.

This is the pension he will get.

Do not worry about either inflation or higher earnings. Of course you may be earning more when you retire, but then you will also be contributing more. The important thing for making comparisons between pension schemes is to compare like with like as of today.

- Get a direct comparison with a pension company or companies and see what these will give you.

Remember to get them to quote you figures based on the same contributions and retirement age as you calculated above.

- Compare the different schemes and choose the one that is right for you.

Look at the figures for your superannuation scheme and for any personal pension plans you are investigating. Compare them directly – and remember some of the differences.

A company superannuation scheme usually gives you benefits which a personal pension schemes does not, such as a widow's/widower's pension and death-in-service, a lump sum that goes to your estate if you die before you retire. Think about whether these are relevant to you. In a superannuation scheme, the pension you get includes SERPs. A personal pension scheme does not include SERPs. However, providing you have notified the DSS on the correct form that you wish your SERPs to be added to your personal pension scheme, you will receive these monies in addition to your personal pension.

Superannuation schemes at work also take into account the possibility of early retirement and enhanced service. This means that if you retire earlier than the stated age of 60 or 65, you will get what you have contributed to date plus a few extra years. Don't get hooked into thinking that you are getting something for nothing before you check your figures.

You need to take responsibility for working all this out for yesterday. Do not expect either your employer or your union to give you unbiased help. Of course consult them, but remember that the only person who can guarantee to have your best interests at heart is you.

A combination of company and personal pension schemes

There are only two instances in which an employed person can have both a company scheme and a personal pension scheme: if your company pension scheme only provides benefits if you die while you are still working for them – 'death-in-service benefits' – or if you are not contributing the maximum of 15% of your salary which the government at present allows towards pension schemes. In the latter case, you can take out a free-standing voluntary contribution (FSAVC), which is explained below.

If you cannot afford pension contributions, either to a superannuation scheme or a personal pension scheme, to ensure that you get this extra pension you *must* notify the DSS that you would like them to pay your SERPs into a personal pension scheme on your behalf.

Free-standing voluntary contributions (FSAVCs) and additional voluntary contributions (AVCs)

FSAVCs and AVCs are pensions which are available for people who are in company pension/superannuation schemes and who wish to increase their pension. A free-standing scheme, FSAVC, simply means that you can pay into your own personal pension plan. An AVC means that you pay via your company scheme.

The maximum anyone who is working can contribute towards a pension is 15% of their gross – before tax – annual earnings. Earnings in this case include bonuses, commissions and overtime. For example,

Salary	*£10,000*
15% legal maximum pension contribution	*= £ 1500*
– 4% being contributed to company	
scheme	*= £ 400*
Maximum AVCs allowed	*= £1100*

Contributions are normally paid either monthly or annually. Within the 15% limit you can also make contributions in lump sums to both the above schemes.

PENSION SCHEMES FOR THE SELF-EMPLOYED AS WELL AS FOR EMPLOYEES

Personal pension schemes

In order to be eligible for a personal plan that is one that you arrange for yourself, you must either be self-employed or if employed, not a member of a company pension scheme.

In order to arrange a personal pension that is right for you, take the following steps:

- Look at how much you have left at the end of the month after paying your bills and decide how much you want to put into a pension. There is a maximum percentage allowed, and this is set by the government.
- Get details from several pension schemes and decide which one makes most sense for you.
- Pay at least the minimum amount you can afford, and on a monthly basis.
- Review this amount annually.

The less you pay the smaller the pension on your retirement. But do not allow your accountant or financial adviser or bank manager to frighten you into paying the maximum amount. It is easy to work out a sensible figure by looking at how much you have left at the end of the month, and deciding how much of that to put away. It is wiser to pay a monthly sum rather than hoping that there will be enough left out of your profits at the end of the year to pay one lump sum. You can, of course, pay a lump sum instead of, or in addition to, your monthly payments provided you are within the limits of contributions that are allowable according to your age and net relevant earnings.

Pensions can always be reduced, after an initial period of time, to the minimum level which is set by the particular company. This varies from pension company to pension company and means that if you start on a good year but then hit a bad one – or two – you can reduce your payments. Check what minimum payment would be required at the time when you are obtaining quotations.

An important feature of personal pension plans is an *open market option*. This means that on retirement you do not have to use your accumulated fund to purchase pension benefits from the company with which you have been investing but can shop around, as already discussed. This option allows you to obtain exactly the type of pension benefits you require. For example, you may want a pension that is linked to the cost of living index rather than one which pays a fixed sum; you may want a pension which increases 10% per annum, or one which provides for spouse's or dependents' benefits in the event of your death. An *open market option* is therefore very important to anyone taking out a personal pension plan as it is this option which will enable you to secure the most suitable pension on retirement.

You can also 'buy back' years during which you did not contribute fully to a pension scheme. To work out how much you can 'buy back', subtract the percentage that you have contributed each year for the last six years to your pension from the percentage you were allowed to contribute each year. You can 'buy back' the difference in a single lump sum, covering either one year at a time or the whole six years added together, and get tax relief on your contributions.

For example, if 6 years ago the allowable contribution was 17¹/2% and you only contributed 1% of your net relevant earnings, you can now buy back some or all of the 16¹/2% in a lump sum.

PENSION SCHEMES FOR THE SELF-EMPLOYED

The self-employed are eligible for the basic state pension but not for SERPS as they do not pay the same level of national insurance contribution. The only way to get an adequate pension if you work for yourself, therefore, is to contribute towards a personal pension scheme. It is also possible to purchase life assurance as part of your pension: this option is discussed in *The Practical Guide to Saving and Investing*. The maximum percentage of net relevant income which can be used to purchase life assurance under a pension contract is 5% of the allowable contribution towards a pension.

3 WHAT ARE THE TAX ADVANTAGES FOR PENSIONS?

Your pension, when you receive it, including your basic state pension, is regarded as income. Therefore you will pay income tax in the normal way on these monies.

There are three tax advantages for pension plans:

- tax relief on contributions at your highest rate of tax
- investment in tax exempt funds
- a tax-free lump sum on retirement.

Tax relief on your contributions. If you are a PAYE (Pay As You Earn) employee, basic rate tax relief on your pension contributions is deducted before you pay the premium. For example, if your gross contribution is £40 per month, the basic rate of tax is deducted from this and you only pay the net amount (after basic rate tax that is £30). The balance is being paid by the Inland Revenue. This example is based on someone paying a tax rate of 25%.

Any higher rate tax relief is claimed by sending the personal pension contribution certificate (PPCC), which you have to request from your pension company, direct to your Inland Revenue office with a request that they alter your Notice of Coding. The net result will be that you have a higher Tax Code/Notice of Coding which in turn gives you more tax relief and you therefore receive more money in your pay packet.

In order to get this tax benefit if you are self-employed, you have to pay your total – gross – pension contributions, and then claim back the tax relief. You do this by sending a personal pension contribution certificate (PPCC) when you present your accounts at the end of the tax year. You send this to your accountant (if you are using one) or directly to the Inland Revenue with your profit and loss account. See sample PPCC on page 280.

Investment in tax exempt funds. Current legislation provides for pension funds to be exempt from all UK taxes. This means that money invested in pension funds, or *exempt funds*, can appreciate/grow more than money invested in life funds, which are liable to tax.

A tax-free lump sum on retirement. When you reach retirement and wish to take your pension, up to 25% of the money which has accumulated, called in pension terms your 'pension fund', can be taken as a lump sum free from tax. The balance then has to be used to purchase the pension benefits you require. Your pension is taxable.

These days it is necessary to have your pension index-linked. The income from your pension then goes up in line with the RPI. If you do not do this, the purchasing power of your pension will

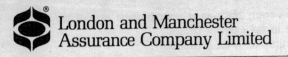
LONDON AND MANCHESTER (TRUSTEES) LIMITED   BLUEPRINT PENSION SCHEME

PERSONAL PENSION CONTRIBUTION CERTIFICATE (PPCC)
SELF-EMPLOYED: REGULAR CONTRIBUTIONS

The Inland Revenue, Superannuation Funds Office has approved the Scheme mentioned above as a Personal Pension Scheme for the purposes of Chapter IV, Part XIV, Income and Corporation Taxes Act 1988 under the reference SF87/080/1A.

A. **SCHEME ADMINISTRATOR**

London and Manchester (Trustees) Limited
Winslade Park
Exeter EX5 1DS

B. **MEMBER**

Name:
Policy Number:
Address:

Date of Birth: 10/09/1960
Selected Retirement Date 10/09/2015
National Insurance Number

C. **CONTRIBUTIONS (REGULAR)**

1.   The member paid h   first contribution to the Scheme on 01/10/1989

2.   This contribution was of the following amount or amounts:
        a. Pension   £200.00
        b. Life Assurance   £

3.   Periodic contributions, which can be varied, will be paid by the member at MONTHLY intervals.

4.   The amount of each contribution will be:
        a. Pension   £200.00
        b. Life Assurance   £

5.   The member may make additional single contributions to the Scheme.

6.   The member is due to pay his last contribution to the Scheme on the following date.
        a. Pension   01/08/2015
        b. Life Assurance

NOTES

1.   This certificate is not a guarantee that contributions will qualify for tax relief. It is issued for the purpose of production to the Inland Revenue and is of no value for any other purpose.

decrease year by year as the cost of goods rises – and you will get poorer and poorer.

4 WHERE TO GO TO GET THE BEST PENSION

There is no such thing as 'the best' pension. The reason for this is is that the figures produced by the various pension companies produce vary from day to day and even with the particular time of the day!

But there is a 'best place' to go to get a pension. The place to get your pension is from a financial adviser whom you know and trust. This could be your bank, an individual company, or a financial consultant. The individual company from which you will get your pension is not as important as having an adviser whom you can question about the policy both now and in the future. It is important that you take responsibility for questioning them until you are clear that you understand the costs and benefits of the pension policy.

5 WHEN CAN YOU TAKE YOUR PENSION?

Legislation determines when personal pension benefits can be taken. Currently this is any time between the ages of 50 and 75. You choose when.

Benefits taken from a personal pension plan are in addition to those obtained under the state schemes. The age under the state basic pension scheme and for SERPS, is 60 for women and 65 for men. If you are in a company superannuation scheme or indeed have been in one and have left money there when you moved to another company, you will receive these benefits at the age stated by the Trustees of that scheme. In effect, this may mean that you are receiving several different pensions at several different stages in your life. *All of them combined are liable to income tax*.

Receiving a pension does not prohibit you from earning monies as well. Any additional earnings are added to the total pension monies you receive, and the total is liable to income tax.

6 WHAT ARE THE CRITERIA FOR FINALLY RECEIVING YOUR PENSION?

When you finally decide to receive your pension, remember that the one which is best for you is the one that best suits your particular circumstances. Before asking for quotations, it may help to check your answers to the basic questions about what you want from a pension:

1 Do you want all your money to come to you as a pension?

2 Do you want to take a proportion as a tax-free lump sum and the balance as a pension?

3 Do you want it index-linked, which means that it rises with the rate of inflation as reflected in the RPI?

4 Do you want to state the percentage by which you want the pension to increase each year, i.e. 5%, 8%?

5 Do you want any other benefits added, such as a widow/widower's pension, in the event of your death, or a lump sum?

When obtaining different quotations from companies which offer pensions, ensure that you are asking the same questions and that the answers they give to you correspond to your question. Only by doing this can you compare the benefits being offered by different companies.

Summary

It is essential to make the best possible pension provision. This gives you the options of semi-retiring, retiring early and, most important of all, maintaining your standard of living when you no longer earn an income.

The Practical Guide to
Saving and Investing

Saving money is the core of a good financial attitude. Saving money in banks and building societies allows you to build up a pool of money on which you will be able to draw as and when you need it – for security and for emergencies. The amount you save is not the main point: pennies grow into larger sums just as much as pounds do.

Investing money is a riskier way of building up your money, with the probability of greater profit and the possibility of loss. The four basic levels of saving or investing are described below. All the institutions behind these savings and investment schemes make money in the same way: they take your savings and invest the money that you place with them in order to make profits both for themselves and for you. The greater the risk, the greater the potential profit – or loss. In the four basic levels described below, the risk is least in no. 1 and greatest in no. 4.

Levels of saving to investing
> *Savings*
> 1 Building societies, banks, post offices
> *Investing*
> 2 Savings plans, via life assurance companies
> 3 Bonds, unit trusts, PEPs
> 4 Stocks and shares

1 Building societies, banks, post offices

Why save this way? You can save small amounts or large amounts in any of these institutions and there is very little risk. These institutions are so fundamental to the UK and Ireland that they cannot be allowed to go broke. You get a low return on savings made with any of these institutions because you are paying for the stability and the facilities. The lower return is primarily because banks, building societies and the Post Office provide facilities for you in every high street and most shopping areas, and it is your money that pays for the fact that all these branches are so accessible. With basic savings accounts in any one of these institutions, you can also withdraw money most easily.

What are the terms? In regular accounts with building societies, banks and the Post Office, interest is paid in almost any way you choose – monthly, yearly, half-yearly – at the current interest rate and according to the terms of the particular account. The interest rate can change at any time. Some accounts offering higher than basic interest rates are also available; these will often require you to deposit large amounts of money for a set period. Some of these higher interest paying accounts have penalties if you withdraw your money without giving the required amount of notice. For example, if the term is 3 months notice, and you withdraw your money sooner than this, you lose 3 months interest.

If you are a taxpayer, the basic rate of tax is deducted from your interest 'at source', which means before the interest is paid to you. Building societies show two figures for their accounts: the higher one is the gross or total interest, and the lower one is what you will actually receive after the tax has been deducted. However, if your income is such that you do not even pay basic income tax you can, under recent legislation, opt for having your interest paid to you at the gross amount that is without deduction of basic rate tax. See samples on opposite page

Taxpayers who are assessed at the higher tax rate will have to pay a further 15% tax on their interest to the Inland Revenue. If you are a non-taxpayer, whether you are one month old or one hundred years old, do make sure that you have an account that pays your interest gross. In other words, that only one figure is shown with no tax deducted. To ensure that this happens, you need to complete a form provided by the bank or building society.

In recent years people have been spending more and saving less. The Government is offering a new incentive to start people saving again. It is called TESSA, or the Tax Exempt Special Savings Account. After a set period of time, the interest is added to a TESSA account tax-free for any investor. There is a maximum limit to the amount which can be invested in this

THE LONDON SHARE ACCOUNT

R A T E S

EFFECTIVE FROM MARCH 1st 1990

12.25%NET

Rates may vary:
Current monthly rate 11.61% net = 12.25% CAR
CAR — Compounded Annual Rate when
interest added to account monthly.
Gross Equivalent (CAR) = 16.33% to
tax payers at a basic rate of 25%.

Available exclusively by post from
Cheltenham & Gloucester Building Society

The London Share Account
C&G (...ondon Share Account)
...O. BOX 161
...ter GL4 7UY

3/90

INTEREST RATES

*Investment	Gross †	Net †
£25,000+	14.05%	10.53%
£10,000-24,999	13.75%	10.31%
£2,000-9,999	13.10%	9.82%

If your minimum balance falls below £2,000 the interest rate
will be 8.00% Gross, 6.00% Net.

way. Leaflets are available at banks or building societies giving you more detailed information.

What is the risk? Because all of these institutions are seen as fundamental to the stability of society in the United Kingdom and Ireland, the risks of losing your money are slight and there is protection if something goes wrong.

Banks If a bank goes bust, the law says that you can get back 75% of the first £20,000 you have in one or more accounts, whether that is a joint account or in your name alone. All the money in all your accounts with the bank that has gone bust would be added together and you are guaranteed up to £15,000 of the first £20,000 total. After that there is no guarantee. In practice, the banks cannot afford to allow customers to lose faith in the banking system.

Building societies The same rules apply to building societies as to banks, except that you get back 90% of the first £20,000. Like banks, building societies rally round if one of their number is in trouble. They try to ensure that investors get back most of their money, whatever the amount – and, if possible, all of it.

In order to protect your savings fully, it will make sense, if you have more than £20,000, to spread it around in several different bank and building society accounts.

The Post Office The Post Office is backed by the Government and the likelihood of the government going into liquidation is so remote that the risk factor is negligible. Remember, they are the ones who print the money!

2 Savings plans, via life assurance companies

Why invest in this way? Savings plans arranged via life assurance companies are a way of building up money for the medium (10–20 years) to longer (20+ years) term. 10 years is the minimum length of most plans. These plans are only appropriate if you are looking for a return on your monies with or without life assurance cover, called 'investment with protection contracts'. If you only want life assurance, turn to *The Practical Guide to Arranging Life Cover*.

Although commonly called 'savings plans', they are actually 'investment plans'.

There are four kinds of investment contracts:

- endowment
- whole of life assurance
- with profits
- unit-linked

Investment with protection contracts commonly provide the policyholder with a level of life assurance cover during the term of the policy but they also provide for a lump sum to be paid to the policy holder when the policy matures. The older you are when starting these contracts, the more expensive they are *or* the less life assurance cover you will get. These contracts come under the headings of endowment or whole-of-life assurances and can be either with-profits or unit-linked, as described below. Whether you choose a with-profits policy or a unit-linked policy depends on your personal choice with regards to a guaranteed return.

If you do not require life assurance, then you are looking at either a whole of life contract with no life cover or a unit-linked savings plan. You make your choice depending on your circumstances. Are you looking for a tax-free lump sum at the end of a specific period of time? Do you wish to have the ability to withdraw the money, though not necessarily all of it, during the period of the contract? Do you wish to have the option of continuing the plan beyond the period for which you originally contracted? Do you need the money for a specific purpose, such as inheritance tax on your death? When you can answer these questions, then you will be able to choose the kind of contract most suited to your purposes.

What are the terms? If you take out a savings plan via a life assurance company, you commit yourself to a minimum period of payments. This is usually 10 years but it can be longer and usually goes up in units of 5 years. Savings plans which run for a 5-year period are usually for people who are investing a larger amount of money for a specific purpose, such as a car, a tax bill, school fees, a repayment of a debt. The difference between them and the longer term plans is that these are not tax-free. The profits are added to your income.

The terms of the four different kinds of contracts are described below:

Endowment: An endowment is a form of life assurance policy which covers the life assured for a set amount during a set period of time. At the end of this agreed period of time, when the policy is said to have 'matured', it pays a tax-free lump sum to the policyholder. While there is no legal limit on the age to which an endowment policy can continue, most companies will have a maximum age at which you can begin such a contract and an age at which the policy finishes. It is always possible to stop payments earlier, i.e. 'surrender the policy', and claim any sum due to you at that point, but you will not get as good a return on your monies as if you had left the policy to run for the full term. Companies charge early surrender penalties and deduct these from the monies before paying you the balance. There is usually a minimum time limit before you can surrender a policy and get monies back; if you surrender the policy earlier than this, you lose everything you put in.

Whole of life assurance This form of policy can run for the whole of your life and is available whatever the policyholder's age. Also, a whole of life policy is available for an indefinite period, which in these terms means until death. It is therefore the type of assurance usually recommended to older clients, or to people who specifically want to provide for costs incurred on their death, such as funeral expenses or inheritance tax. However, whole of life assurance policies do acquire a surrender value in the same way as endowments. This means that at some point which the company specifies, you can choose to stop making payments and cash in the policy for its value at that time. Some companies will let you write these policies with no life assurance provision, so that all of your payments are being used for investment, rather than part of it being used to provide cover in case of your death. Technically you can buy whole-of-life assurance at any age but it is dependent on the rules of the individual life assurance company and of the individual applicant meeting that company's medical requirements.

With profits A with-profits policy – which can be on either endowment or whole of life policies – has a *guaranteed* sum assured which is payable either on death or when the policy matures. However, during the period of the policy, it also gains 'profits' or 'bonuses' declared by the company and based on how well the fund to which your policy is linked has performed. Bonuses are usually added annually; once they are added to a policy, they cannot be taken away. These are called *reversionary* bonuses. On maturity, or on reaching the end of the period of time for which you had contracted to pay, a with-profits policy will also include a *terminal* bonus, which usually significantly increases the cash value of the policy. However, this terminal bonus is only obtained if the policy is run right to its maturity date. If you have a with-profits policy, you should never be tempted to cash in the policy early, particularly towards the end of its term, or you will lose the terminal bonus.

Unit-linked A unit-linked policy guarantees a sum in the event of the policyholder's death but it does not guarantee how much you will receive at the end of the term of the policy. Your money buys units within a large fund each time you pay your money. The number of units you have equates to what your policy is worth.

Unit prices can fall as well as rise. During the period of time you are paying into the policy, a drop in unit prices is beneficial because it means that the company can purchase more units with your premium when prices are low and then, it must be hoped, sell them at higher prices when the policy matures. Unit-linked policies generally offer greater flexibility than with-profit policies. You don't need to wait until the end of the contracted period to get a terminal bonus that makes the with-profit policies worthwhile; your profit depends on what your units are worth at any given time. But units do not always go up – and that is the risk that you take.

Summary With the law as it is at present, the profits on any of these qualifying savings plans become exempt from taxation for both the basic rate and higher rate tax payers after $7^1/2$ years. Some plans do not come under this law and the profits are therefore liable to tax.

What is the risk? If the company goes broke, the investor is covered by the PHPA, the Policy Holders Protection Act 1975. There is a cartel of life assurance companies which operates an arrangement whereby one or more of the companies in the cartel will take over and continue the policies for all the investors of the failed company. In general, full compensation is at present paid on investments up to £30,000 and 90% on a further £20,000, making a maximum pay-out of £48,000.

3 Bonds, unit trusts, PEPs (personal equity plans)

Why invest in this way? Bonds, unit trusts and personal equity plans are ways of saving for people who want to put away a lump sum of money rather than a regular amount. They are also for people who are prepared to leave this sum of money invested for a longer period of time, i.e. 5+ years, than with building societies, banks and the Post Office. These forms of investment are affected by the stock markets and one must therefore be prepared to allow time for your monies to make a profit. The markets go down as easily as they go up!

What are the terms? The terms are different for bonds, unit trusts and PEPS, but with all of these you can withdraw your money at any time. Whether or not there are surrender penalties for taking your money out before the end of the period for which you have committed yourself is dependent on the terms of the company with which you have invested. With most companies, and certainly with all unit trusts and PEPs, there is a surrender charge, known as the 'bid and offer price'. 'Bid' is the higher price at which you buy; 'offer' is the lower price at which you sell: these are figures set by the company. The usual difference is 5%, which represents the charge you pay to the company on sale of your bonds, unit trusts and PEPs.

The particular terms for investing are:

Bonds are liable to higher rate income tax only for people who are already higher rate taxpayers or who, with the addition of profits from the sale of the bonds, become higher rate taxpayers. In order to work out whether you owe tax on such an investment, add the profit you take on the bonds in any one year to the rest of your income. Providing the total of profit plus income does not bring you into the higher rate tax bracket, there is no tax to be paid. If the total does bring you into the higher rate tax bracket, then you will have to pay the difference between basic rate tax and higher rate tax, but only on the amount that has brought you into the higher tax bracket.

In order to check out where you are in these tax categories, use *The Practical Guide to Taxes and Tax Returns*.

Bond prices

London & Manchester Group
Winslade Pk, Exeter EX5 1DS   0392 282246

	Cap	Acc	+/−	Rel N/C
Investment Trust Fd (z)	439.6	624.2	+1.4	718.8
Property Fd (z)	182.3	252.9	+0.2	287.9
Fixed Interest Fd (z)	167.3	231.0	−0.4	254.9
Equity Fd (z)	259.5	361.2	−0.1	393.6
International Fd (z)	188.6	260.6	+0.9	283.2
American Fd (z)	112.0	137.4	+1.2	147.5
Japan Fd (z)	158.2	194.3	−0.6	208.6
European Fd (z)	111.4	134.6	+0.6	142.9
Gtd Deposit Fd (z)	164.8	225.8		245.3
Flexible (z)	290.3	403.7	+0.3	454.4
Unitised with Profits(z)	104.4	109.5	+0.1	
Moneymaker Fd (z)		326.8	+0.1	
Capital Growth Fd (z)		1122.1	+0.5	
Exempt Inv Tst Fd (z)	848.0	1276.6	+12.3	
Exempt Inv Nom Shs (z)		1200.5	+11.4	1343.9
Exempt Ppty Fd (z)	314.7	475.0	+0.4	
Exempt Ppty Nom Shs(z)		446.1	+0.4	498.6
Exempt Fixed Int Fd (z)	150.7	226.5	−0.3	
Exempt Equity Fd (z)	278.5	418.5	+0.1	
Exempt Gtd Dep Fd (z)	155.5	233.2	+0.1	
Exempt Flex Fd (z)	467.8	704.4	+0.7	
Expt Unitsd with Prfts(z)	108.3	114.2		
Exempt Flex Nom Shs(z)		662.2		739.7
Balanced (z)	223.2	278.6	+0.3	
Exempt Intl	77.5	94.2	+0.4	

Price before deduction of 5%

Unit Trust prices

		Offer	Bid			
UK Growth	5	67.25	67.25	70.79	−0.03	3.50
Do (Accum)	5	74.19	74.19	78.10	−0.03	3.50
Worldwide Gwth	5	207.30	207.30	218.30	−2.00	1.39
Do (Accum)	5	300.40	300.40	316.30	−3.10	1.39

London & Manchester Tst Mgmt (1000)H
Winslade Park, Exeter EX5 1DS   0392 282673

American	6	37.54	37.81	40.57	−0.29	1.6
General	6	61.32	61.73	66.23	−0.27	4.0
Income	6	48.74	49.51	53.12	−0.06	4.0
International	6	39.68	40.09	43.02	−0.12	6.6
Japan	6	39.18	39.65	42.54	−0.09	1.2
Tst of Inv Trusts	6	39.62	40.37	43.32	−0.14	0.0	2.6

Unit trusts are liable to capital gains tax (CGT), if your profits exceed your annual profit allowance. Below that amount, the profit is tax-free. This means that you are allowed to take a specified amount of profit in any one tax year, i.e. between 6 April and 5 April, before you pay any CGT. You will pay tax at your own highest rate on the remaining profit you have taken. This really does mean on the money you *take*, not the money you *make*, that is not the money your investment makes for you while still invested. It makes sense for you to look at your investments on an annual basis and decide whether or not you ought to be taking your annual CGT allowance and putting it into something else, so that you are using the tax advantages that are currently available to you.

Personal equity plan (PEP) is another incentive created by the Government to encourage people to invest monies. There is a maximum amount of money that you can invest in this particular way in any one tax year. This can change from year to year. You can have a PEP via a life assurance company, called a unit trust PEP, but the maximum you can currently put away through them is lower than if you invest via a full PEP. You can invest in both types of plan to use your full allowance and spread the risk.

The profits on PEPs are free of any taxation.

What is the risk? The degree of risk increases depending on which type of these investments you have. Bonds are the least volatile; unit trusts and PEPs are the most risky. This is because unit trust funds and PEP funds invest directly in the stock market, which is the riskiest form of investing, while bond funds invest into the unit trust funds, thereby splitting the risk.

The risk means that you take the chance of getting a better return on your lump sum investment than on money you have in a building society or bank – or a less good return if the market has a bad patch.

4 Stocks and shares

Why invest in this way? Stocks and shares are different ways of describing the same thing: the percentages you buy in an individual company, which means that you own a small piece of that company.

There are two monetary reasons for investing in this most risky of sectors: very little money is needed to buy shares initially and there is the potential of making a larger profit on your money than you would expect to get in any of the other forms of investment mentioned above. These investments appeal especially to the entrepreneurial spirit – the desire to make money quickly and the willingness to take the risk.

What are the terms? By buying stocks and shares you are investing your money in a particular company and your fortune grows or falls with the fortunes of that company. Stocks and shares may pay dividends, though not always. The dividend, which is the profits that the company's directors have decided to give to the shareholders, is liable to income tax. When you receive your dividend basic rate tax will already have been deducted. This deduction is called a tax credit. The liability to higher rate tax is calculated in the same way as described for Bonds above. Dividends are normally paid half-yearly. Some people find it very useful to have this regular income from dividends, even though it is not a stable income because the dividend fluctuates according to the profits of the company. On selling your shares, you are liable to CGT on any profit you make from the sale. Your profit is calculated as the price at which you sell minus the price at which you bought your shares. The earliest valuation date is March 1982; anything bought before then will use a March 1982 valuation on sale. A dividend certificate is shown on the opposite page.

British

TELECOM

British Telecommunications plc
Ordinary Shares

security code

0—140—843

Tax voucher

11th February 1991

The attached warrant is in payment of the interim dividend for the year ending 31st March 1991 at the rate of 5.25p per share on the Ordinary Shares registered in your name on 10th January 1991. I certify that advance corporation tax of an amount equal to that shown below as tax credit will be accounted for to the Collector of Taxes.

M Argent,
Group Director and Secretary

A. N. Body
13 Nowhere Road
LONDON W9

04304 / 153

holding	tax credit	dividend payable
400	£7.00	£21.00

Registrar:—
Lloyds Bank Plc
Registrar's Department
Goring-by-Sea
Worthing. West Sussex
BN12 6DA

reference
450/
05722179

0
12

No. of Receipt	Transfer no.	Broker's reference	Date of registration	Number of Shares
8905272	7C7/1C0/106 C175876		3rd November, 1989	–100–

DEPOSITARY RECEIPT

Euro Disneyland S.C.A.

(a société en commandite par actions established in and under the laws of the Republic of France with registered no. PARIS B341.908.945)

This is to certify that on the above date

COCS272   S0116647

    A. N. Body
    13 Nowhere Road
    London W9

is/are registered, under the Deposit Agreement referred to overleaf, as the Holder in respect of

ONE HUNDRED ★★★★

shares of FF 10 each fully paid in the capital of Euro Disneyland S.C.A. (the "Company") subject to the notes set out below and to the *statuts* of the Company and the terms of the Deposit Agreement.

B. Ward, Chief Registrar, for and on behalf of
National Westminster Bank PLC as Registration Agent.

Notes:
— *The registration of the holding which is the subject of this depositary receipt is conditional upon (a) not later than 20th November, 1989 (i) all the Shares in the Company issued, and to be issued in connection with the offers of the Shares in France and other members states of the European Community having been issued and admitted to the Cote Officielle of the Bourse, and (ii) admission of such Shares to the Official List of The Stock Exchange becoming effective, and (b) the International Subscription Agreement dated 5th October, 1989 between the Company, S.G.Warburg Securities and others having become unconditional and not having been terminated in accordance with its terms when conditions (a)(i) and (ii) are satisfied.*
— *No transfer of any portion of the holding which is the subject of this depositary receipt will be registered until this depositary receipt has been lodged at the transfer office of the Registration Agent: National Westminster Bank PLC, P.O. Box 82, Caxton House, Redcliffe Way, Bristol, BS99 7NH.*
— *Any transfer to be registered in the Register maintained by the Registration Agent under the Deposit Agreement may be effected by using the appropriate form prescribed by the Stock Transfer Act 1963 as amended. Any transferee who, by an agent or otherwise, tenders a transfer for such registration agrees to become a party to the Deposit Agreement. Any person who tenders such a transfer warrants his authority to do so as and/or on behalf of the transferee(s) named in it.*
— *As a party to the Deposit Agreement, each Holder irrevocably (a) waives any right to his holding to the extent that it shall have been paid or made available to the Registration Agent or other distribution or right in respect of the Shares which are the subject of his holding, to instruct the Company or the Transfer Agent to arrange for the transfer to him or to any other person of under the Deposit Agreement, (b) waives any right or claim directly to instruct the Company or the Transfer Agent to arrange for the transfer to him or to any other person of some or all of the Shares which are the subject of his holding, (c) agrees that his right to call for any such transfer must be exercised exclusively through the Registration Agent as described in "Withdrawal" overleaf), and (d) agrees not to pledge any such Shares under French law without first arranging for them to be held outside the Deposit Agreement.*
— *Your attention is drawn to the summary of certain provisions of the Deposit Agreement overleaf.*

© 1989 Disney

CE 428 A

What is the risk? This is the most risky/volatile of all savings and investments as all of the money invested in the shares of a particular company is linked to the fortunes of that company. If you make a loss on the shares when you sell, obviously there is no tax to pay. Only buy stocks and shares if you are prepared to lose your money. If a company goes bankrupt there is no guarantee that your shares will be worth anything at all.

Because the risk is greatest if you are investing in one particular company, many people choose to spread the risk by having shares in an assortment of companies, such as 100 Abbey National Shares, 400 British Gas shares, 300 British Telecom shares. This is what is called having a portfolio of shares – no matter how small in quantity. A share certificate is shown on the opposite page.

Reporting profits to the Inland Revenue

The Inland Revenue will require records of your income from some savings and investments. It can save much time and searching if you keep records each time you are notified of an interest or dividend payment.

Summary

Whichever of these methods you choose is up to you. You need to consider carefully how much money you have to save or invest and what level of risk you are willing to take. Remember that having no savings at all is the greatest risk.

The Practical Guide to
Taxes and Tax Returns

Taxes are collected by the Inland Revenue so as to enable the government to run the country. There is no choice as to whether or not to pay them. If they are due then you must pay what you owe. You are breaking the law if you do not.

There are numerous types of taxes: this guide describes the three main direct taxes for individuals:

1 income tax
2 capital gains tax (CGT), and
3 inheritance tax (once called 'death duties')
and then looks at
4 preparing your tax return.

The information on which these taxes are assessed is gathered through an income tax return, which is an official statement of all your income, deductions and exemptions. You are required to file a return from the age of 18 until you die, provided the Inland Revenue has sent you a form. The IR only do this on a random basis so don't expect to receive one – but if you do, you must complete and return it. The categories of information the Inland Revenue require from you are listed at the end of the guide, followed by an explanation of what the Inland Revenue does with the information.

1 Income tax

Income tax is due on all earnings which are considered to be income. 'Income' includes: your salary, whether you are employed or self-employed; building society interest; any profit on investments, such as stocks and shares, unit trusts and bonds; pensions, and income coming from another country.

Every individual, no matter how young or old, is allowed to earn a certain amount of money each year without paying any tax. The amount varies from year to year and it is usually increased in the annual budget announced in March by the government of the day.

**Inland Revenue
Tax Return 1990-91**

Income, Class 4 National Insurance contributions
and Capital Gains for year ended 5 April 1990
Allowances for year ending 5 April 1991

Reference

Date of issue

You are required to complete pages 2-8 of this form, sign the Declaration on page 8 and send it back to me within 30 days. It will help if you also give the information requested below.

Please read the introduction to the enclosed notes which are there to help you before you start to fill in the form.
This is particularly important, if you are a married man, because of the introduction of Independent Taxation.
Independent Taxation is a new way of taxing husbands and wives which started on 6 April 1990. This return asks for details of income for the year to 5 April 1990 so a married man must still declare his wife's income, even if she has got a tax return of her own. It is important to show in the sections marked ☆ whether the entry relates to you or your wife.
If you are a married man you cannot claim reliefs due to your wife – she should claim herself.
Please ask me if you need any further help or information. If you find that there is insufficient room in any section, attach a separate sheet.

Age and Pensions information these details will help me to work out your tax correctly

If you or your wife were born before
6 April 1931 please give date(s) of birth: ▶ Self   Wife

If you receive a pension, please give the following
details –
Type of pension

Say whether it is paid weekly, 4 weekly,
monthly or quarterly

Amount(s)
you receive
£

If you are likely to start receiving a pension before 6 April 1991, please
give the following details –
Starting date   Type of pension

Say whether it is payable weekly, 4 weekly,
monthly or quarterly

Amount(s) you
will receive
£

11 (1990)

1

2 Capital gains tax (CGT)

You do not have to be rich to be liable for this tax. This tax is levied on the sale of assets and the profits, if any, which you make on that disposal, such as a house that is not your main residence, paintings, artwork, collections (whether these be stamps or antiques or Dinky toys), stocks and shares. This tax is not as expensive as you may think.

Capital gains tax is paid on properties other than your main residence and on investments which you dispose of in a tax year, that is from 6 April of one year to 5 April of the next year. An individual is allowed to take a certain amount of profit without becoming liable to CGT each year. This figure is set by the government. The total profit is calculated as the difference between the original purchase price and the price at which you have sold an item, or in the case of stocks and shares, their value as at March 1982 as against the sale price. Capital gains tax is assessed at the highest rate of income tax which you are paying.

shares value at 1982 or when purchased, if later	sale price after commission	less CGT allowance
£3000	£6500	£5500

= £1000 profit to be taxed at highest rate of income being paid by seller at that time.

3 Inheritance tax (death duties)

This is the tax that is paid on your death on the total value of your estate after subtracting an exemption figure. Your estate includes the value of everything you own, from your clothes to your home and everything in between.

You will occasionally hear talk about 'how to avoid paying inheritance tax.' Unless you are prepared to give away some of your assets now, you can't. If you die and you are domiciled in the UK, everything you own – everywhere in the world – is liable to UK inheritance tax. If you are currently living abroad but keep a home and/or investments in the UK with the intention of returning at a later date, then the UK is your domicile.

The only exception to paying inheritance tax is between a husband and wife: they can transfer everything to each other with no tax to be paid whatsoever. There is no way of avoiding inheritance tax otherwise, but, through financial planning, you can make provision for it to be paid rather than leaving that responsibility to those who benefit from your estate. You do this by paying for life assurance which is written in Trust for someone other than your spouse. 'In Trust' means that on your death the sum assured is *not* part of your estate and is used to pay the inheritance tax. Or you can reduce it by using the 'Survivorship Clause' – get further details from your financial adviser. You are allowed to make gifts in your lifetime and there are limits and rules concerning this. Your IR office will give you the necessary details.

value of Estate	less exemption	taxable amount at current rate 40%
£160,000	£140,000	£20,000
= £8000 total inheritance tax which has to be paid		

4 Preparing your income tax return

The purpose of a tax return form is to give the Inland Revenue the information they need to ensure that you are paying the correct amount of tax on your income, whatever the source of that income. It also allows them to give you your Notice of Coding for the next year, on which tax payments will be based, or to update your current coding.

The information you provide on the income tax return is compared by the Inland Revenue, if applicable, with two other forms: P60 and P11D. Form P60 is the slip of paper which each employer you have had during the previous tax year automatically sends to you, the IR, and the DSS, confirming the total monies paid to you, and the total tax and National Insurance contributions paid by you. Form P11D informs the IR about any benefits you have received.

The tax return is a multi-purpose form with roughly 95 boxes. This is what makes it such a daunting looking form, but in fact you may only need to fill in 7 or so boxes. The process of filling in the form can be made easier if you collect the information you will need before you sit down to tackle the form.

A The name and address of all employers for which you have worked for as a PAYE employee in the previous tax year.

B The total of what you earned with each of the employers listed in 1 above.

C A note of any benefits that you received from each employer, such as a car, petrol allowance, telephone allowance, permanent health insurance, medical insurance, tips.

D The name/s of your building societies and the total amount of interest you have been paid on each account.

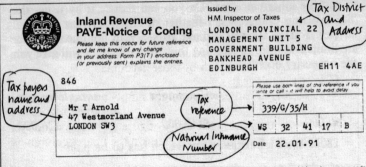

Inland Revenue
PAYE-Notice of Coding

Please keep this notice for future reference and let me know of any change in your address. Form P3(T) enclosed (or previously sent) explains the entries.

Issued by
H.M. Inspector of Taxes

LONDON PROVINCIAL 22
MANAGEMENT UNIT 5
GOVERNMENT BUILDING
BANKHEAD AVENUE
EDINBURGH   EH11 4AE

Tax District and Address

846

Tax payers name and address

Mr T Arnold
47 Westmorland Avenue
LONDON SW3

Tax reference

National Insurance Number

Please use both lines of this reference if you write or call - it will help to avoid delay

339/G/35/H

WS 32 41 17 B

Date 22.01.91

This notice cancels any previous notice of coding for the year shown below. It shows the allowances which make up your code.
Your employer or paying officer will use this code to deduct or refund the right amount of tax under PAYE during the year shown below.
Please check this notice. If you think it is wrong please return it to me and give your reasons. If we cannot agree you have the right of appeal.
Please let me know at once about any change in your personal circumstances which may alter your allowances and coding.
By law you are required to tell me of any income that is not fully taxed, even if you are not sent a Tax Return.

See Note	Allowances	£	See Note	Less Deductions	£
11	EXPENSES	30	25	BENEFITS (CAR)	2200
12	RET ANNUITY RELIEF	3045	29	UNPAID TAX £140.00	350
15	PERSONAL PENSION	756			
17	PERSONAL ALLOWANCE	3005			
17	MARRIED ALLOWANCE	1720			
				Less total deductions	2550
	Total allowances	8556		Allowances set against pay etc. £	6006

Your code for the year to 5 April 1992 is **600T**

Please see Part A overleaf

Can earn £6006 before paying tax

P2 (T)

This person gets:

17 Married and individual allowance
12 & 15 Has 2 pensions and is getting higher rate tax relief
11 Pays expenses such as Union subscription

This person gets and pays:

25 A car and therefore is taxed on benefit
29 Has some tax due since last year
which is being collected in 1991/92 Tax Year

E The name/s of your bank accounts and the total amount of interest you have been paid on each account.

F The name of any account from which you have not had basic rate tax deducted and the amount of interest you have earned from each of those accounts.

G If self-employed:

- your trading name, which might simply be your own name and address
- your net relevant profit or loss figure (if you have not yet done your accounts, simply write in the figures column on the form, 'accounts to follow')
- your Year End date, the date to which you make up your profit and loss accounts.

H A list of any shares, i.e. the company's name, together with the total amount of dividend paid by each company to you and tax credit held back by that company and then paid to the IR. If you have shares in more than 5 different companies, simply write the information required on a separate sheet of paper and in the relevant column on the form write, 'see schedule of dividends attached'.

I Anything that could qualify for capital gains tax (CGT), i.e. anything that you have sold in the previous tax year.

J All mortgage information, i.e. the name of the company, the date the mortgage started, the mortgage number, whether it comes under MIRAS or not.

K Information on any dependents for whom you are claiming allowances: their full name, date of birth and whether or not you are receiving maintenance on their behalf, with all its details.

Dependents include: any children whom you are supporting, within certain parameters; any relative whom you are supporting, in some cases whether they live with you or not. The Inland Revenue will give you details of when children and relatives qualify as dependents.

L Pension information, i.e. the name and address of the scheme, if it is a personal pension your policy number, the gross amount you have paid in the relevant tax year and if you know what you expect to pay next year.

M If you are receiving a pension, from whatever source, the name and address of the source and the total amount of

A & B & C

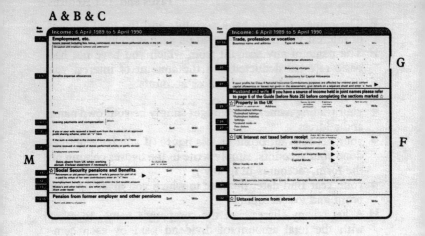

Income: 6 April 1989 to 5 April 1990

Employment, etc.

Income received including pay, bonus, commission, etc from duties performed wholly in the UK

Occupation and employers name and address

| | Self | Wife |

Benefits expense allowances | Self | Wife

Tips | Details

Leaving payments and compensation | Details

If you or your wife received a taxed sum from the trustees of an approved profit sharing scheme, enter an 'x' here

If the sum is included in the income shown above, enter an 'x' here

Income received in respect of duties performed wholly or partly abroad | Self | Wife

Employment continued

Dates absent from UK when working abroad. Enclose statement if necessary

☆ **Social Security pensions and Benefits** | Self | Wife

Retirement or old person's pension. If wife's pension for part of it is paid by virtue of her own contributions enter an 'x' here

Unemployment benefit or income support enter the full taxable amount

Widow's and other benefits say what type (from order book)

Pension from former employer and other pensions | Self | Wife

Name and address of payers

M

Income: 6 April 1989 to 5 April 1990

Trade, profession or vocation

Business name and address   Type of trade, etc.   Self   Wife

Enterprise allowance

Balancing charges

Deductions for Capital Allowance

If your profits for Class 4 National Insurance Contributions purposes are affected by interest paid, certain capital allowances or losses not given in the assessment, give details on a separate sheet and enter 'x' here

Husband and wife If you have a source of income held in joint names please refer to page 6 of the Guide (before Note 25) before completing the sections marked ☆

☆ **Property in the UK**   Address | Self | Wife
*Unfurnished lettings
*Furnished lettings
*Furnished holiday lettings
*Ground rents etc
*Feu duties
*Land

☆ **UK interest not taxed before receipt** | Self | Wife

National Savings   NSB Ordinary account ▶
NSB Investment account ▶
Deposit or Income Bonds ▶
Capital Bonds ▶

Other banks in the UK

Other UK sources including War Loan, British Savings Bonds and loans to private individuals

☆ **Untaxed income from abroad** | Self | Wife

G

F

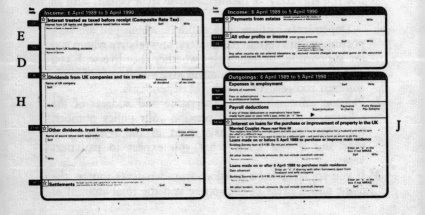

Income: 6 April 1989 to 5 April 1990

☆ **Interest treated as taxed before receipt (Composite Rate Tax)**
Interest from UK banks and deposit takers taxed before receipt | Self | Wife

Name of bank or deposit taker

Interest from UK building societies | Self | Wife
Name of Society

☆ **Dividends from UK companies and tax credits**   Amount of dividend   Amount of tax credit
Name of UK company
Self

Wife

Other dividends, trust income, etc, already taxed   Gross amount of income
Name of source (show each separately)
Self

Wife

☆ **Settlements** | Self | Wife

E

D

H

Income: 6 April 1989 to 5 April 1990

☆ **Payments from estates** | Self | Wife

☆ **All other profits or income** enter gross amounts
Maintenance, alimony, or aliment received | Self | Wife

Any other income not entered elsewhere eg accrued income charges and taxable gains on life assurance policies, and excess life assurance relief

Outgoings: 6 April 1989 to 5 April 1990

Expenses in employment | Self | Wife
Details of expenses

Fees or subscriptions to professional bodies

Payroll deductions   Superannuation   Payments to charity   Profits Related Pay Scheme
If any of these deductions or exemptions have been made from your or your wife's pay, enter an 'x' here ▶

☆ **Interest on loans for the purchase or improvement of property in the UK**
Married Couples Please read Note 58

Loans made on or before 5 April 1988 to purchase or improve main residence
Building Society loan at 5.4.90. Do not pay amount   Enter an 'x' in the box if not MIRAS
Self   Wife
All other lenders Include amounts. Do not include overdraft interest

Loans made on or after 6 April 1988 to purchase main residence
Date advanced   Enter an 'x' if sharing with other borrowers apart from husband and wife occupiers
Building Society loan at 5.4.90. Do not pay amount   Enter an 'x' in the box if not MIRAS
Self   Wife
All other lenders Include amounts. Do not include overdraft interest

J

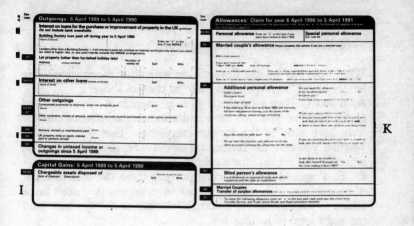

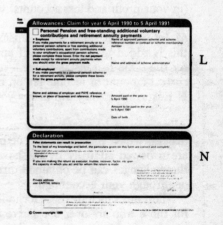

Samples of Income Tax forms
Letters related to explanations on pp 229, 301, 304

pension received and the total amount of tax deducted from each source.

N Your national insurance number.

What does the Inland Revenue do with this information? The letters below correspond to those in the list above:

A, B and **C** They crosscheck your answers in A, B, and C and check whether what you have said matches the information they have been sent by the various employers. This will tell them whether you owe any further tax or not – or, in some instances, whether you are due for a refund or not.

D, E, F and **H** This information tells them the total amount of monies you have made on your investments that need to be added to your income to ascertain whether or not you have paid the right level of income tax.

J, K and **L** The answers here will show whether or not you have received the correct allowances and, based on the information you have given, whether or not you have paid the correct amount of income tax. They then bill you for tax underpaid or send you a cheque if tax was overpaid.

I Whether or not CGT is due will be determined by your answer to this question.

G This alerts them to the fact that you are self-employed and that therefore there are earnings which are recorded elsewhere (in your profit and loss accounts) which will be due for taxation under a separate system.

M Information about your pension income is found here and this is added to **A, B** and **C** if applicable and **D, E, F** and **H** for the same reasons as above – to ensure that you paying the correct amount of income tax on all your income.

N Ensures that they can marry you up with the DSS records.

Allowances and benefits: There are a number of allowances and benefits which you can deduct before your tax is assessed. These are reviewed annually by the government and information on these changes can be obtained direct from the Inland Revenue or through your accountant.

Allowances include those for individuals, married couples and for those who are over 65. There are also allowances for single parents, for those with disabilities, and for people caring for children.

There is tax relief on mortgages, which is described more

fully in *The Practical Guide to Setting Up a Mortgage*. Pension contributions are deducted from the amount on which you have to pay taxes, as described in *The Practical Guide to Arranging a Pension*. Some benefits from employers are allowed, and there is added tax relief for people over 60 for private medical insurance.

The government has recently changed the law on taxes on savings and investments.

Up-to-date information on any allowances and benefits for which you are eligible can be obtained in leaflets from the Inland Revenue, from your accountant, and from various other sources such as Citizens Advice Bureaux. Like most things to do with your finances, it is your responsibility to find out the correct information and then to make any claim to which you may be entitled.

Married couples filing returns Your tax information is personal between you and the IR. Married couples are now taxed separately, and neither has to inform the other of the details which they are obliged to give to the IR.

Deadline for filing tax returns There will be a date by which the form must be returned. If you ignore this, the IR have the right to give you a nil Notice of Coding. This would mean that you will be paying more tax which it will take a long time to reclaim. If this happens to you, remember it was your fault, not theirs.

Summary

The Inland Revenue have taken on the reputation of a national monster. In fact, people who have made enquiries have generally found the IR to be very helpful. They are the only ones, in the final analysis, who can give you certain kinds of advice and information. You can make an appointment to see them if you wish, rather than trying to explain what you want to know on the phone.

Remember that the sooner you deal with your taxes and returns the less trouble it will be in terms of both money and worry.

Glossary

The financial world has its own professional jargon and initials. In order to take control of your own finances and use the advice of the professionals, you need to understand the basics of this language. Below are listed some of the terms most commonly used in matters of individual finance.

AVCs (Additional Voluntary Contributions) The government at present allows members of company pension schemes to pay the difference between what they are currently contributing and what is the legal maximum, i.e. 15% of your gross salary. This difference can either be put either into your existing company scheme or into a separate personal pension. These contributions are called AVCs. See *The Practical Guide to Arranging a Pension* for further details.

Age of majority The age at which a person is allowed to vote and is no longer the legal responsibility of the parent. In the United Kingdom this age is 18.

APR (Annual Percentage Rate) This reflects the true cost of money borrowed. For example if you took a three year loan and were quoted an interest rate per annum, there would be a different APR rate which would be higher, as the annual interest rate does not take account of the interest you are paying on the interest.

e.g. Monthly Net Interest = 11.61% = 12.25% Compound Annual Rate

Appreciation or **Depreciation** In terms of assets, this means the difference between what the asset was worth when you bought it and what it is worth now. If the value has increased, it has *appreciated*. If it has decreased, it has *depreciated*.

The appreciation on a house bought at £30,000 and valued now at £100,000 is £70,000. The depreciation on a house bought at £150,000 and valued now at £125,000 is £25,000.

Assets Anything which you own that is worth money if you were to sell it is deemed an asset. If you said, 'I'm desperate for cash', you would then ask, 'What can I sell?' An asset is the answer to that question. Your house is an asset but only the amount that is left after you have paid off the mortgage (that amount is also called **Equity**). Your clothes would also be called an asset, although a very small one in normal circumstances.

Bank accounts Their main purpose is to enable money to move freely without actually carrying around the cash. *Bank deposit accounts* are also a place to put your money in order to increase its value through savings. *Bank current accounts* in some cases will also increase the value of money through paying **Interest**.

Bank base rate The interest rate that the bank declares it will use as a starting point for charging you money for its services. An overdraft is usually charged at the base rate + 5%. The bank base rate is also the starting point for paying you a lower rate on deposit accounts.

> *interest on an overdraft*
> *base rate 12$\frac{1}{2}$%*
> *extra interest 5%*
>
> *= interest charged 17$\frac{1}{2}$%*

Bookkeeping A basic method to record what you earn and/or what you spend. The purpose of it can be personal, to assist you with budgeting, or for tax return purposes to assist the Inland Revenue to work out what you owe them if you have any income that is not **P.A.Y.E.** (See The *Practical Guide to Bookkeeping and Taxation for the Self-Employed* for further details). A **bookkeeper** is someone who keeps financial records for others professionally.

Bankers draft A grown-up postal order. Both are like cash and guarantee the receiver (or payee) the amount stated on it. The bankers draft is for reasonably large amounts of money; the postal order for smaller amounts. A cheque requires time for clearance before it is worth the cash written on it; a bankers draft or a postal order can be exchanged for cash immediately as the cash for them has already been paid.

Glossary

Building society account A place to put your money in order to increase its value through accumulating interest on the amount of money you deposit. Although building societies now have accounts with chequebooks, their primary function remains savings.

Capital The available cash you have, the money that you can get your hands on. Stocks and shares; building society accounts (even when they require notice of withdrawal); bank accounts; bonds are all capital. Property is not because the cash is tied up.

Capital gains tax The tax that is charged on the profit you make on the sale of certain assets, e.g. a second property, stocks and shares. It is charged at *your* highest rate of income tax. See *The Practical Guide to Taxes and Tax Returns* for further details.

Capital investment The cash you use in order to purchase an asset, e.g. when buying a second home the deposit is your capital investment; the mortgage to cover the rest of the cost is not.

Cashflow The word that is used to describe the amount of money you calculate you need to run your lifestyle or business over a period of time, usually six months to a year.

Collateral The net worth of an asset which a lender will require in certain instances before lending you money, e.g. the bank may be prepared to give you a £1000 overdraft without a collateral but they will only let you have a £10,000 overdraft if you can provide them with collateral, such as a charge against your house or against your deposit account. You risk forfeiting the collateral if you are unable to meet the repayment on the loan.

CCJ (County Court Judgement) A legal debt registered against your address. It means that creditors have gone to court as a last resort when they were not paid and the court has made a CCJ against the address. If you are refused credit and are told that there are CCJs against you, it is worth checking whether the CCJ is actually against you or is shown against your address, in which case it may be a debt incurred by someone who has lived there in the past.

308

If the CCJ is not yours, you can have the records altered to show this.

Credit cards A method used to purchase goods or facilities without necessarily having the available cash to pay for them. Some cards charge monthly interest for this service; others charge an annual fee for having the card and some charge no interest providing you pay the credit card bill monthly when it is sent to you. Also referred to as 'plastic money'.

Death duty As a legal term no longer exists although it is often used to describe **Inheritance tax**.

Death in service The monies that are paid to your estate by the superannuation scheme of your company if you die while you are still working for them.

Depreciation or **Appreciation** In terms of assets, means the difference between what the asset was worth when you bought it and what it is worth now. If the value has increased, it has *appreciated*. If it has decreased, it has *depreciated*.

The appreciation on a house bought at £30,000 and valued now at £100,000 is £70,000. The depreciation on a house bought at £150,000 and valued now at £125,000 is £25,000.

Duty – import A tax levied by the government that has to be paid on specified items brought into the country.

Duty – export There is no such thing.

Earnings The term usually used to describe monies you are paid for work done whether you work for a company or for yourself.

Equity With regard to your home, it is the difference between the total of what you owe on the mortgage and the market value of the house. The market value is what somebody is prepared to pay to buy your home or, if you are remortgaging, the price at which the lender's surveyor values your house – whether you agree with this or not.

Market value of your house: £120,000
– Mortgage of £60,000
Equity = £60,000

Glossary

Executors The person or persons you entrust to carry out the wishes of your Will. They can be a person or a company, i.e. solicitors, banks.

Expenses Monies in agreed categories that you have paid out in the course of your work and for which your company then reimburses you; or monies that you have paid out and are allowed to deduct from your gross income for tax purposes.

Freehold The ground your property is built on. You normally own the freehold of a house which means the rights to the land or 'plot' on which it is built. At the present time, if you own a flat you usually do not have a share in the freehold. This is owned by someone else and you pay them a minimal annual fee, called *ground rent*.

Gross income The total amount of money you are paid, including bonuses, commissions and any other monies on top of your basic salary. **Net income** is the figure with which you are left after deducting all allowable expenses and taxes from your total income.

basic salary	*£14,000*
Annual bonus 5%	*700*
commission 1% on total sales of £30,000	*300*
Total gross income	**£15,000**
less single person's allowance	*3,295*
Total net income	**£11,705**

Gross interest The percentage your money makes before any tax payable is deducted. Deposit accounts quote two different rates, a higher one which is the gross interest and the lower one which is actually paid into your account after the deduction of basic rate tax. A higher rate taxpayer has to pay a further 15% tax on that profit.

Your savings account pays 12.25% net = 16.33% gross

Guardian/s The person/s whom you choose to have legal charge of your children up to **age of majority** if you die or are mentally or physically incapable of caring for them. See *Chapter 9*

Looking at Death and *Workbook Chapter 15 Making a Will* for further discussion and details.

Higher rate taxpayer Someone who pays part of their income tax at the highest rate charged by the Inland Revenue.

HP (Hire purchase) the expression used to describe a loan that a firm or licensed credit broker makes to you, with interest added, when you purchase an item for which you wish to pay over a period of time. It means that the item will eventually cost you more than the listed purchase price.

Interest-free credit is not hire purchase but a way of paying for the purchase of an item over time (usually by monthly instalments) without having to pay interest.

> *cost of goods £1000*
> *interest free credit over 10 months = £100 per month*
> **Total cost of goods £1000**
>
> *vs*
>
> *cost of goods £1000*
> *interest charged @ 24% = £103.33 per month*
> **total cost of goods £1190.16**

Income tax A tax that every individual must pay on their **gross income**, which includes unearned income such as interest paid on building society accounts.

Inflation The difference between what an item cost last year and what it costs this year.

> *cost of goods £100*
> *annual inflation 7.5%*
> **cost of goods following year £107.50**

Interest The amount of money you are charged on monies borrowed; it is also what you are paid when you leave monies in an account such as a building society or bank deposit account. It is calculated as a percentage of the amount borrowed or deposited.

> *lump sum deposited* £1000
> *interest quoted $10^{1}/2$ %* 105
> *Amount in account 1 year later* £1105

Interest-free credit A way of paying for the purchase of an item over time (usually by monthly instalments) without having to pay interest. See **HP** for further details and examples.

Glossary

Inheritance tax The duty on the gross (or total) value of your estate when you die, minus whatever is the current tax allowance. The tax is colloquially called 'death duty'.
e.g. (at 1991 figures)

Total estate worth	*£200,000*
less allowance	*140,000*
Tax due at 40% on	*£60,000*
Total inheritance tax	*£24,000*

Intestate When you die without making a Will.

Invest When you put money into something in the hope of making a profit.

Invoice A bill for goods for which you have not yet paid.

Leasehold The term used to describe the length of time you own a property, usually a flat but also houses where the land (the **Freehold**) is still owned by large estates. The leasehold is expressed in years; when the end of this period is reached, the property reverts to the freeholder and you have no further rights to it. You must either leave or renegotiate to buy more time.

Life insurance/assurance Terms for two different processes that are confused in common usage. 'Insurance' properly means a policy to cover inanimate objects, such as your car or home. 'Assurance' is a policy/contract to pay monies on your death, for which you pay premiums (agreed amounts of money) to a life assurance company for an agreed period of time. The term 'life insurance' is becoming more commonly used for 'life assurance'. See *The Practical Guide to Arranging Life Cover* for further information.

Loan This can be either money or an item that you borrow for a set period.

Loss When your investment is worth less than the original capital you paid for it you have incurred a **loss**. For example, if you bought shares at £3.15 each and they are now worth £1.20 each, your loss is £1.95 per share.

Mortgage This is the amount of money you borrow to purchase a property. You pay interest on the amount you have borrowed for an agreed period of years. The interest you have to pay on the loan can be *variable*, i.e. go up or down, at the lender's discretion, or *fixed*, which means it does not move for a set period of time, or *deferred* which means that you pay a lower amount of interest than the lender's current rate for a set period of time after which the amount which you have not paid will be added to your mortgage, giving you a larger mortgage to be paid.

A *top-up mortgage* is when you increase the amount of money you originally borrowed for the property. A *remortgage* is the term applied when you are changing the lender, whether you wish to increase your mortgage or not.

National Insurance This is the levy made against a certain maximum level of your earnings by the government, whether you are employed or self-employed. The monies collected in this way are used to pay old age pensions and other benefits.

Your *national insurance number* is the number assigned to you by the government by which your taxes and benefits are traced to you.

Net income This is the figure with which you are left after deducting all allowable expenses and taxes from your total income. **Gross income** is the total amount of money you are paid, including bonuses, commissions and any other monies on top of your basic salary. See **Gross Income** for example.

Net interest This is the final figure you receive or pay after deduction of taxes levied on the profits or **gross interest**.

Offshore investments These are monies invested in institutions which are registered outside your country of residence.

Outstanding monies or **debts** These are the monies you have yet to pay on loans of any sort, whether credit cards, mortgages, or personal loans.

PAYE (Pay As You Earn) This is the system of collecting tax from your salary before you receive your monies. This tax only relates to people who are employed.

Pension An income which you receive during your retirement or disability and on which you pay income tax. It is paid to you either by the superannuation scheme or/and by the **life assurance** company to which you have paid monies for a period of time so as to enable them to pay you this income. Anyone who reaches compulsory retirement age and has paid a certain amount of national insurance contributions during their working life is eligible for a *basic pension*, commonly called the 'old age pension'. All of these are liable to income tax.

Personal pension plan is the description used when you save an amount of money via a life assurance company specifically to provide you with a pension.

PEP (Personal Equity Plan) A government incentive to invest money and which has set limits as to how much you can invest. For further details, see *The Practical Guide to Saving and Investing*.

Petty cash This describes small amounts of money paid out for purchases of any sort.

Power of attorney This is when you give someone else the legal right to do what they like with your money and assets, with or without your permission. It is usually confined to specific areas, such as giving your solicitor power of attorney to complete the purchase of a property because you are not going to be available yourself. If a person is mentally incompetent, their relations can get a court to award Power of Attorney to deal with the person's affairs without that person's agreement.

Probate The legal term used to describe the process of clearing a person's Will after their death. The **Granting of Probate** is the term used to say that the Will has finally been legally recognized.

Profit The money you receive over and above the original **capital** which you invested.

Retail price The price paid by the person in the street for goods. The **wholesale price** is the price the person who sells the goods pays for those goods, before adding on extra monies to cover their own costs and profit.

Salary The amount of money which your employer agrees to pay you per annum exclusive of benefits.

Savings plans A way of investing small and regular amounts of money for an agreed period of time in the hopes of making a profit which is higher than saving in a building society or deposit account. For more details, see *The Practical Guide to Saving and Investing*.

SERPS (the state earnings-related pension scheme) This is the method devised by government to allow individuals who have paid **national insurance** levies as employees to receive an extra pension in addition to their basic old age pension. It is related to the amount of **national insurance** they have paid. See *The Practical Guide to Arranging a Pension*.

Stocks and shares These are methods of purchasing a part of a particular company or institution, in the hope of getting a better return, i.e. **profit**, on the original purchase price. Some companies quote stock price; others quote share price. Most people when talking about stocks actually mean Treasury stocks which are shares issued by the government. For more details see *The Practical Guide to Saving and Investing*.

Superannuation (also see **pension**) This is the term given to an institution's pension scheme, also called a company pension scheme. For further details, see *The Practical Guide to Arranging a Pension*.

Tax A levy set by the government on various goods, assets and earnings. See **income tax, capital gains tax, inheritance tax, value-added tax** and *The Practical Guide to Taxes and Tax Returns*.

TESSA (Tax exempt special savings account) A government scheme which allows monies up to a specified maximum to be invested via deposit accounts for five years. The interest will be paid to the account free of any income tax deduction.

Trustees The person or persons you name to oversee the handling of monies you have designated for a special purpose in your Will. This would apply to monies left to an individual who is a minor or to others whom you only wish to receive the interest and not the capital on a sum you have given them. See *Chapter 9 Looking at Death* and *Workbook Chapter 15 Making a Will* for further information.

Turnover The total amount of monies earned per year in a business before deducting costs or expenses.

VAT (value added tax) A levy charged on specified goods or services provided. It is collected by the provider of the goods or services and paid by them to the government via HM Customs and Excise.

```
    cost of goods   £100
  VAT @ 17.5%      17.50
  Total price      £117.50
```

Wholesale This is the price the person who sells the goods pays for those goods, before adding on extra monies to cover their own costs and profit. **Retail price** is the price the person in the street pays for goods.

Will A legal document wherein you state what you want to happen to your assets after your death. A Will can also include personal wishes such as how you wish to be buried. See **Trustees, Executors** and **Guardians**. For further discussion and details, see *Chapter 9 Looking at Death* and *Workbook Chapter 15 Making a Will*.

Resources for Readers

There are numerous organizations and publications which can offer you financial assistance. You will get the best out of any of them if you know what your question or complaint is and, where appropriate, have copies of any relevant documentation.

General advice

The National Association of Citizens Advice Bureaux (CAB) have been pioneers in helping members of the public with debts and other financial advice. There is a local CAB in most areas, staffed by both paid workers and well-trained volunteers. The National Association of CABs is an independent charity, funded by the government. You can phone or visit. Remember that they are overstretched and underfunded, so that it may take you some time to get the help you need. You can help them by bringing with you any correspondence and other information about the problem about which you are seeking their help. Unlike any of the financial bodies, they are not promoting their own interests, so they are often a good place to start if you need help to decide upon next steps.

> *The National Association of Citizens Advice Bureaux,*
> *Myddleton House, 115–123 Pentonville Road, London*
> *N1 9L2. Tel: 071 833 2181.*

The Consumers Association and their publication series, *Which?* deal with a variety of concerns to consumers, including evaluating various financial services. Subscribers to *Which?* are also eligible, for payment of an extra fee, to subscribe to *Which? Personal Services* which advises on consumer issues and will answer questions about consumer rights.

317

Copies of their publications are available for reference in many libraries.

Which? 2 Marylebone Road, London NW1 4DX
Tel: 071 486 5544

Specialist Advice

The way to go about selecting the professional financial help you need has been described more fully in *Chapter 12 Getting Professional Assistance*. Other sources of specialist advice are:

Tax – The Inland Revenue, Public Enquiry Rooms, Room G1, West Wing, Somerset House, London WC2R 1LB or any office will give you information about taxation and can tell you the office which deals with your return. Tel: 071 438 6420/5.

Social security queries – Department of Social Services, Richmond House, 79 Whitehall, London SW1A 2NS, Tel: 071 219 3000.

VAT queries – HM Customs & Excise, New Kings Beam House, 22 Upper Ground, London SE1 9PJ. Tel: 071 620 1313.

Wills – The Will Company Ltd, Grosvenor House, 76 High Street, Sidcup, Kent DA14 6DS. Tel: 081 300 9333. They can also store your Will as well as act on your Executor's behalf with the business of getting Probate granted.

If you want to put your Will on record, the original can be deposited at *The Will Company*, above, or at *Somerset House*, London WC2R 1LB, by sending the properly prepared Will (see *Workbook Chapter 15 Making a Will*) plus a small fee.

Living Wills, Power of Attorney Forms, and Emergency Medical Cards [see Chapter 9 Looking at Death]. If you wish to make a 'Living Will' to indicate to the doctor your wishes in the event of there being no reasonable prospect of your recovery from serious illness, the Voluntary Euthanasia Society provides 'The Advance Declaration' forms, as well as an Emergency Medical Card and a Power of Attorney Form. The Voluntary Euthanasia Society, 13 Prince of Wales Terrace, London W8 5PG.

Regulating bodies

If you have a complaint about the treatment and service you have received in dealing with a financial professional, you may want to approach the appropriate regulating body. Go with copies of all the financial business and correspondence relating to your complaint. Depending on the type of complaint you have, you will need to be persistent in order to get the service you are entitled to expect – but don't go with high expectations.

Fimbra This is the body responsible for independent financial advisers.
   Financial Intermediary Managers and Brokers Regulatory Association, Heartsmere House, Heartsmere Road, London E14 4AB. Tel: 071 538 8860.

Lautro This is the body responsible for companies which deal in life assurance and unit trusts.
Life Assurance and Unit Trust Regulatory Organization Ltd., Centre Point, 103 New Oxford Street, London WC1A 1QH. Tel: 071 379 0444.

SIB The overall City watchdog.
Securities and Investments Board, Gavrelle House, 2–14 Bunhill Row, London EC1Y 8RA. Tel: 071 638 1240.

The Insurance Ombudsman Bureau
31 Southampton Row, London WC1. Tel: 071 242 8613.

The Pensions Ombudsman
151 Great Titchfield Street, London W1.

Publications

Which? (see The Consumers Association above) produces regular consumer publications, including *Which Money?* and a series of leaflets on specialist topics. These publications will be of most use to you if you are clear first about your own needs and the state of your own finances, then use their information to answer your questions.
   Which? is researched by the Association for Consumer Research and published by ACR's subsidiary, Consumer's Association Ltd. ACR is a registered charity.

Resources for Readers

The Ethical Consumer is published by a non-profit making ICOM (Industrial Common Ownership Movement) co-operative. It is the publishing arm of the Ethical Consumer Research Association which exists to research and publish information on companies behind brand names and to promote the ethical use of consumer power. Recent issues have included a guide to ethical investments and an alternative investments directory. Refreshing in that they put before the reader the complexities of making 'ethical' or 'alternative' choices in financial as well as other industries.

The Ethical Consumer, ECRA Publishing Limited, 100 Gretney Walk, Moss Side, Manchester M15 5ND.

Miscellaneous

Credit rating If you have a credit judgement against you and have now cleared the debt, you need to ensure that your name is removed from the 'blacklist' of those who have bad credit references.

Although there are many agencies which keep such information, the three major ones are:

Infolink, CCA Dept. Regency House, Whitworth Street, Manchester M60 1QH;

CCN Systems, Talbot House, Talbot Street, Nottingham NG1 5HF;

Westcot Data, Spectrum House, 1A North Avenue, Clydebank, Glasgow G81 2DR.

For a nominal fee they will show you any information they have on you and, if you provide them with evidence that the debt is cleared, take your name off the list.

Counselling **RELATE** (formerly the Marriage Guidance Council) is a government-funded organization which offers counselling to individuals and couples who are having difficulties, including financial ones, in their relationship. There are RELATE offices in all areas of the country. The length of time you may have to spend on a waiting list will vary. If you cannot find your local office, contact their national headquarters:

RELATE, Herbert Gray College, Little Church Street, Rugby CV21 3AP. Tel: Rugby (0788) 573241.

Index

Index

Index

Index

Index